THROUGH
HER MOTHER'S

SURVIVING MY DAUGHTER'S MURDER

THROUGH HER MOTHER'S EYES
First Edition
Copyright ©2022 Tiffany Starrett
All rights reserved.
Published by The Lighthouse Books, Agape Inc.

ISBN: 978-1-950320-45-5
Library of Congress Control Number:

For information regarding permission, write to:
The Lighthouse Books
13721 East Rice Pl, Aurora
CO 80015.
Visit us at: www.thelighthousebooks.com
Printed in the USA
For more information about Author: www.EverlastingEchoes.com
First Printing Edition, 2022

THROUGH HER MOTHER'S

SURVIVING MY DAUGHTER'S MURDER

TIFFANY STARRETT

PRAISE FOR TIFFANY STARRETT

The title is so perfect and says it all. No one wants to be in the writer's shoes, but yet after reading your book, my feet hurt. You guided me through your eyes and heartache so clearly, while introducing your inner self. You are an incredible mom, and I truly believe Ally is and always be with you. Both you and Andy have done an amazing job!

Noemi Berry
Mother, Retired Law Enforcement

Life is messy, and grief is complicated. No parent should have to grieve the loss of a child, much less a murder. If you have the misfortune of being inducted into a club that nobody wants to be a member of, you may feel alone and like nobody understands what you are going through. In similar circumstances, nobody knows how they would respond, as grief doesn't follow a prescriptive path, and anger and isolation tend to rear their heads in unexpected ways. Tiffany's story about the loss of Ally is raw, unfiltered, and real. As I read this story, Tiffany's writing style gave a voice like I was listening to her tell her story in person (including unexpected moments of wit and forgiveness). Tiffany does a great job expressing insight into her world while surviving a tragedy. If you are experiencing a similar loss or are connected to someone similarly situated, this is a must-read to gain access to some of the possible insights into their mind.

Michelle Boot, MS, RYT 500
Mother, Trauma Yoga Instructor,
Chief Human Resources Officer (CHRO)

Tiffany's journey through the aftermath of the murder of her daughter and path to recovery is nothing less than pure honesty and raw emotion, which gripped and held my attention like no other book I have ever read. I finished the book in one day. To anyone who has lost a child to violence, or is currently employed in law enforcement, Through Her Mother's Eyes is a must-read.

Brian B.
Father, Las Vegas Metropolitan Police

Tiffany's journey has been on a path traveled by few, a path that should be traveled by none. Over the course of her journey, she reveals an intense range of emotions ranging from ambivalence to zen, and everything in between. Her insights into learning how to find acceptance and learning to cope, as a result of such a tragic, irreversible loss, are nothing short of amazingly remarkable.

Bruce Tonilas
Father, Uncle, Professional Services Manager

"Having officiated Ally's funeral was one of the most tragic events to be a part of. Experiencing over 300 family members, young people, members of law enforcement and a TV camera sharing in this atrocity called for a depth of compassion, outrage and a challenge of hope for the future of all of those with this trauma-notch forever etched in their hearts, minds, souls and lives. The tidal wave of impact has such a broad reach! As a Domestic Violence Counselor for over 28 years, I have used Ally's story to help train Probation

Officers, Crisis Responders, Therapists and clients to have a deeper understanding of the cycle of violence. As a Pastor, recognizing that we all have a choice...to become bitter...or to become better! Watching the birth of the Ally Remembered Foundation and witnessing firsthand how Ally's family and friends have chosen to become better...and to make their community better by supporting victims of domestic violence and by choosing to make themselves and the world a safer and better place to live in. As a parent, reading "Through Her Mother's Eyes" becomes a journey through any parent's worst nightmare. I am so proud of Tiffany for helping herself and her world become better through the journey of her pain! This book is a must-read!

Debbie Stafford

MA, CAS, Domestic Violence Counselor

A very heartfelt true story, described moment by moment from the beginning of a horrendous act on a loving daughter all the way to the guilty verdict on the man responsible for her murder. Extremely detailed, a story every mother should read.

Bud Orr

Father, Air Force Veteran

Contents

WELCOME TO MY NEW LIFE

I t still feels surreal to share my story. Even now, there's a pit in my stomach. "I am now the mother of a murdered child." Who says that?

How would you know my story? Did you watch the news? Are you a social-media connoisseur? Or do I look like a regular gal at Starbucks enjoying her favorite nonfat vanilla chai-tea latte? Based on your own experiences, would you judge or even notice me? It's not like I have a stamp on my forehead – my wounds are invisible.

As I grieve for my daughter, Ally, merging back into the real world has been excruciating. Being a wife and a mother didn't change, and our house wasn't going to pay for itself, moving forward was "my justice" for her.

It didn't take long to understand, one skinned, bloodied knee after another, that my everyday routine was only making things worse. It amplified the emptiness I carried inside. Not to mention, it was difficult for anyone to know what I was going through.

The death of a child disrupts the understood cycle of life, and the chaos of murder caused an earth-shattering trauma that even fewer can comprehend. My mask was beginning to crumble, and it was clear that the inevitable had finally happened – I felt like a total failure. I've never needed so many damn Band-Aids in all my life!

Realizing how alone I was on my island, I felt no one was coming to rescue me. How was I going to survive as an outcast in a world I once knew and trusted?

My story often feels like a predictable storyline of a movie, probably because watching films is one of my favorite pastimes. It was now time to make a sequel better than the original. To do that, I needed to admit that my life would never be like it was. I may be a victim of a horrific crime, but instead I chose to become a survivor, the superhero of my own story. I needed to take my first step down the yellow brick road to reveal who was really behind the curtain. This was when my real journey began.

When Ally died, I thought her chance to continue her positive impact on the planet was over, but not anymore. Once I began working to reassemble myself (with the help of counseling, of course), I could see the truth right in front of me. I realized I would not have looked at life through a different lens or learned what I already have if Ally had not gifted those things to me through her death. I love that my baby girl is still looking out for her mama.

This memoir is a mirror, sharing my reflections with you while casting them back to me. I am providing this insight because I don't think Ally's continued contribution to my life lessons is just for me. I say this message with the greatest sincerity: I believe she has brought you and me together today. That's the best gift a mother could ever wish for, isn't it?

CHAPTER 1

Blacker than Black

JULY 2, 2017

My gut said something was wrong – this time was different. Where was Ally? I kept looking at my phone. Why hadn't she texted? It was almost 10:30 in the morning, for crying out loud. I knew there had to be an explanation, but what?

After tracking Ally's iPhone to the Knights Inn motel, I never expected to be greeted by yellow tape and police cars. I was in total, utter shock! Sure, the area of town we were in wasn't the best, and it was an older motel, pretty run down too, but a crime scene? I'd never seen one in person before. The only reference point I had was the movies, which didn't look anything like that.

The parking lot wasn't full of officers working the scene. Instead, I witnessed two officers walking the perimeter looking side to side, and neither took notes; I didn't understand. What were they looking for, anyway? I also noticed another set of officers going in and out of Room 139. Their animated hand movements suggested a code of some sort, but I wasn't sure. Why weren't they writing down anything, either? Where was the lead detective in his fancy suit instructing the officers?

I begged every higher power, "Please don't let Ally be in there!" I was so pissed she didn't come home the night before, and yet, it wasn't the first time. Damn kids, they'll never understand the torture they can put us parents through, do they? Yes, she was a self-absorbed eighteen-year-old, but still, where was the respect? Did she forget our house rules about at least calling if she wasn't coming home?

"Jesus! She'd better be all right so that I can strangle her myself!" I mumbled. My anxiousness turned into sheer panic. I screamed at myself to get out of the car; somehow, I forced my shaking hands to open the door.

Inching toward the yellow tape made me uneasy. I didn't want to disrupt the officers' process, but I needed to see. The closest police officer ordered me to stay behind the barrier. I wanted nothing more than to slap his stupid hand out of my face – I was beyond livid! He didn't care why I was there, and it didn't matter my relation to the person in the room. What an asshole!

I stared him down, muttering, "Let's see you be on the other side of the tape, wondering if that's your kid!" I stepped back but stayed close enough to eavesdrop, hoping I could hear any tiny detail.

With every passing second, I became more desperate. Nothing felt right. Where was Ally? Was she around the corner giving a statement or something?

Looking all over the place, I didn't see an EMT or any curious bystanders. Where were they? It was clear we had arrived minutes after the police did. I noticed Ally's best friend's car in the parking lot. What in the world was Maddie doing at the motel?

My heart dropped as a different officer slowly approached me. Why? My parents, who also drove to the motel, were standing only a few feet away. Why didn't he walk toward them? What about my husband, Andy, or his daughter Kylie? Why was I so special? He did look familiar, although it was difficult to tell because he kept scratching his head. When our eyes met, I *did* know him. He was an officer from Ally's past. He had assisted her with the domestic-

THROUGH HER MOTHER'S EYES

violence case against her ex-boyfriend months earlier. If anyone could tell me what was going on, it would be him! We had a history, after all – wouldn't that mean something?

I stood there, not saying anything. I guess I didn't have to. My look of total desperation was enough. The officer's eyes were blank, and his face was stern. I waited for a greeting. Instead, without hesitation, he announced a dead teenage girl lay in the room behind him. "Oh, my God!" I gasped.

Staring at me with such deep sorrow, he muttered a few words. Some were clearer than others. "I think" and "Ally" were all I could make out.

He turned quickly and walked away before I could find words. No fucking way! He was wrong! He hadn't seen her since she had dyed her hair red and gotten the rose tattoo on her arm. I couldn't catch my breath. Wait! What just happened?

Hearing an officer say Ally's name at a crime scene was the last thing I ever expected to happen to me. I was paralyzed as though time stood still, yet it seemed everyone kept moving. Why would he "think" it's Ally? I tried to process. Why would he choose such an uncertain word? Was that girl so severely mangled that she was unidentifiable, or was he telling me the truth when he shouldn't?

I immediately had an internal debate that I didn't want that girl to be my baby, but I didn't want it to be anyone else's, either. Oh-God-please-no! The double-edged sword split me in two polar opposite directions. If it was someone else's daughter, how could I even celebrate? But if it were my girl, would the others cheer, grateful it wasn't their child?

How could it be that only hours before standing in front of the motel, my family and I had walked Washington Park trying not to be mad at Ally? God – I was so pissed that she didn't let us know she wasn't coming home. I constructed some nasty texts, but I didn't send them. Something told me not to. Instead, I wanted to focus on a beautiful morning with my family. I loved how the five of us hogged the path together like a game of Red Rover. And now – I stood alone on my island, astounded.

Scattered everywhere across the parking lot, none of my family comforted me. Each was in their world, doing what felt right to them. Why was my dad fiddling with an old raggedy bush? Where on Earth was Kylie? Was that my mom sitting in her car? Why did Andy give me a quick hug and head in the other direction on his phone? I didn't blame them, and yet I hated feeling alone. How could they leave me there by myself? Ally was *my* flesh and blood, my *only* biological daughter. What could be more important than hugging her mother?

Gazing at the ground, I scoffed at my family. If the roles had been reversed in any other way, Ally wouldn't have left my side. Would she have been melodramatic? Probably. But at least she would have been there. No matter her age, her need to connect emotionally was obvious. Once she felt understood, she'd follow with the warmest hug, like clockwork. And that's what I needed now – more than anything.

Everything I knew was spinning out of control. Nothing seemed right to me. I paced back and forth, forcing myself not to react. Although I couldn't deny how much I was sweating like a pig. Was it my nerves or Hell oozing through all the cracks of the old parking lot? Did I even put on sunscreen? Shit – a sunburn was all I needed.

My phone rang. It was Andy's sister, Amy. The timing seemed odd for her to call, or was it? I answered calmly, not letting on anything at all. My years of mommy training – keeping it together during a crisis when the kids would get hurt – took over.

She was profusely crying, asking if it were true. Oh, my God! Is that what Andy was doing? Was he already calling his family? What the hell? We didn't even know if it was Ally yet. What an asshole! I couldn't believe it. Annoyed and overwhelmed, I confirmed we were at a crime scene but said we didn't know who it was. I told Amy I would call her back after I knew more. Thank God she was understanding. I didn't know what else to say.

Standing there, I became fixated on "taking out" the massive bodybuilder police guy guarding the door. I'd heard of moms lifting cars to save someone, and I asked myself, *could I?* The consequences didn't matter – I needed to see who was in that goddam room! I

THROUGH HER MOTHER'S EYES

had to know. I knew my thought was ridiculous, but I'd never felt so helpless. All I wanted was to see a glimpse of Ally's pinky toe. That's it. I'd know from seeing that. There was no way what was happening could be real!

I was adamant that I wouldn't do a thing until someone could confirm who was at the scene. Was that unreasonable? How do you even process the possibility it could be her in the room? My questions turned into a debate. If Andy were calling for support, then why shouldn't I? Fine! Two can play this game.

In a hasty moment, I called my best friend of twenty-five years. After spending the last week with me, Petra had returned to Texas the day before, and now, I needed her here with me more than ever! I didn't know what to say. Should I suggest that she should remain calm or sit down? What if Ally was fine? Was I creating unnecessary stress? Would she even believe me? Juggling all the what-ifs made me want to scream.

As the phone rang, I didn't know what I should say. The typical "How's it going?" seemed inappropriate. Petra's greeting was hesitant and full of curiosity because I didn't text her first.

I somehow mumbled the words, "Ally might be dead, and I can't see her."

Who says this? There was total silence on her end. I wanted her to say something, anything. *Please tell me I'm going crazy and that this is some kind of horrible joke!* I listened for any sound, but there was nothing. *Someone please just wake me up and make this all go away.*

After a few seconds, Petra cleared her throat. I could tell she was going into crisis-management mommy mode, having done it a million times myself. Our conversation was frank and to the point.

"Start from the beginning," she said.

I replied, "I am at a motel not far from our house."

"OK," she said.

I replied, "Ally didn't come home last night."

She gave another, "OK."

I replied, "I am standing at a crime scene."

"All right," she answered.

Each word I spoke made my body ache in misery. Was I making any sense? I couldn't even imagine what she must be thinking. But I knew she was collecting data. If two and a half decades doesn't give you some peace of mind that they know you, I'm unsure what does.

"Is anyone wearing a trenchcoat?" Petra asked.

Wait. What? It was the absolute best question. Without controlling it, I laughed out loud. Oh, my God! I must be insane! How could I find humor at a time like this, seriously? What kind of screwed-up person could laugh at a crime scene? Especially when there's a possibility it's your damn kid. It didn't matter, though. It was the exact thing I needed in this nightmare!

Petra continued with short questions, allowing me to answer with ease. I then told her my idea about taking out the officer at the door. She acted like a therapist and talked me through different scenarios. Which, of course, meant not tackling him. But I didn't care. I needed to know if that was Ally.

I asked, "What am I supposed to fucking do?" She then coached that I wouldn't want to disrupt any evidence *if* Ally were in the room. Shit! She was right – a valuable viewpoint I overlooked. Her voice comforted me, and I appreciated that she understood what I needed. I didn't want to hang up; she was my rock.

A loud ruckus caught my attention on the other side of the parking lot, disrupting our conversation. The officers shouted commands and moved orange cones. They waved in two cars, permitting them to park, and a couple of women exited their vehicles. They neither looked like the police nor even detectives, more like librarians. I didn't understand.

Then, one of the women came toward me. Whispering to Petra, I told her I needed to go and that I loved her. All I could feel was animosity building in my body as I stared ahead. Was I wearing a beacon, for Christ's sake? It's not like anyone was by my side; it wasn't a mistake.

With her graceful approach, this gentle stranger introduced herself as an advocate. A what? I'd never heard of such a thing. She explained her role as "family support." I still didn't get it. I needed her help *because…?* She then asked me to meet with the other advocates at the police station. Why should I drive to the station without knowing if it's Ally? She was kidding, right? Or was it her way of telling me that Ally was in the motel room?

As my panic began to rise, I tried to talk myself down. Why was the advocate so polite, like a smooth door-to-door salesperson? She treated me with over-the-top accommodation. Handling me with white kid gloves made it all that much worse. I felt like she was trying to ease whatever blow she was about to deliver. Was my Ally dead? I couldn't think or move, and nothing made sense. She was kind, but it didn't make a difference. I wanted answers! Yet I was too chickenshit to ask them to her face.

With my family finally by my side, they stood there as tense as I was. None of them was questioning the advocate, either. Why? Was I supposed to take charge and demand answers because I am the mother? She repeated her request, now to my entire family, to meet them at the station. My controlled patience exhausted me to the point of agreeing, and like robots, we headed that way.

I STARED AT THE CLOCK TURNING TO NOON. IT WAS THE ONLY THING I comprehended from the terrorizing thoughts that consumed me, playing one right after another. Why didn't Ally come home? Was it true that she was dead? Why didn't she call me for help?

At every stoplight, staring at the surrounding businesses, I saw something that reminded me of Ally. And if I wasn't thinking about her, it was Andy. He drove home to drop off our dog Nikki and would meet us at the station. Let's be real. His driving on a normal day makes your heart thump. I could only imagine how erratic it was especially after what we'd just experienced.

Thankfully, Kylie was sitting next to me in the back seat of my parents' SUV. Drowning in fear, I did something somewhat out of character.

I nervously asked, "Kylie, will you hold my hand?"

Replying through her tears, she said, "Of course."

It was awful; I didn't know whom to direct my anger at — the advocates for asking us to drive there or that, still, no one in my family had really comforted me.

I'd never stood outside a police station before. It was intimidating. I knew once I walked through that door, my life would never be the same. Stepping inside, I expected to be inserted right into the movie and onto the big screen. Yet, around every corner, it didn't look or feel like the movies. No stereotypical officers were eating Chinese food with chopsticks. Nor was there an angry police captain screaming at an out-of-line officer. Yes, I knew movies (and television) weren't real. And no, I didn't hear the swells of music in the background telling me how to feel. But I was so confused. What else was I supposed to do? It was, for sure, another sad moment I didn't expect. I hated feeling betrayed by my beloved movies.

Thinking my family and I would be seated in a conference room of some kind, I had another disappointment. The advocates led us to a small room decorated for children. The pale tone painted on the walls only highlighted all the colorful children's toys and Dr. Seuss books that much more. The audacity of some people! What were they thinking? I knew they were supposed to help and offer us resources, but I wanted to seriously lose my shit.

Suddenly, there was a knock on the door. A casual but professional-looking woman entered the room. Good God, she was tall. Oh, great, another damned advocate. How was I supposed to keep them all straight? Her button-down long-sleeve shirt and slacks meant nothing until I saw her badge. She reminded me of Sandra Bullock, so I'll refer to her as Detective Bullock moving forward.

She went straight to my mother, asking if she knew who she was. What the hell? Her voice was familiar, but I couldn't figure it out. My mom's dazed expression turned into a smile as they hugged while my mom cried.

Next, she turned to me. No way! It was my school friend and soccer teammate whom I'd known for many years. What were the odds that after losing touch once we graduated, this is how destiny would reunite us? How can the world be so small to join us in tragedy and be so vast to allow us to lose touch in the first place? My dad then called out her old nickname, "Bigfoot," and she blushed. Andy and Kylie didn't quite understand the dynamic between us. It didn't matter, though. At least they smiled.

After I settled on the couch, she announced she would be one of the assistant detectives on our case. I could find some measure of trust and comfort in knowing she was part of our support system. I whispered, "Thank you" to whoever was listening. Stopping myself, I wondered why I had a case in the first place.

I asked her to clarify who the teenage girl was and why I was there. She avoided the why but instead explained that the coroner would identify the deceased.

I was about to say, "Is that what we are calling Ally now, 'The Deceased?'" But I didn't, keeping it to myself.

All I could do was envision myself walking into a cold room with a creepy man in a starched white coat. He would then unfold the cotton sheet, revealing who was lying on a cold, sterile table and ask if I could identify the body as Ally. I couldn't believe that television was so deceiving, and I was pissed! By now, there would be a commercial break and thirty minutes left to solve this case.

Being in the police station seemed real, and yet it didn't. From tears to talking yardwork, sitting there felt like a never-ending nightmare. Should I tell my family how pissed I was because they left me alone at the crime scene? It was so confusing. Was it fair to be angry at my family, when coping with this situation was as unknown to me as it was to them?

The room became noticeably uncomfortable. Feeling out of sorts, I didn't know what to do. Suddenly, there was more knocking at our door. *What now? Good news, I hope?* Andy stared at the men who entered like a pissed-off caged tiger waiting to escape and hunt his prey.

Detectives we hadn't previously met escorted Andy and me to separate rooms for interviews. Why? What in the hell did we know? My confusion fed my resentment. There wasn't a two-way mirror on the wall, much to my surprise. Instead, the room was tiny and musty. It reminded me more of a broom closet, of all things.

Sitting directly across from me, they introduced themselves, as if it mattered. Where was the detective who sits on the edge of the table trying to be my best friend? I wanted all the formalities over with and to get right to it. "Can someone just please explain what's going on?" I begged.

Taking me off-guard, they then asked if an advocate could observe. Why? Did she need to speak on behalf of someone? If so, who? It made no sense. But, of course, I agreed.

They fired questions at me without wasting a second like a machine gun.

"Do you know why Ally didn't come home?" asked the detective.

The dialogue in my mind was out of control. Of course I didn't know why Ally didn't come home. Seriously! Would I be sitting here desperate to understand what was happening if I did?

I firmly replied, "No."

"Do you know if Ally is dating anyone?" asked the detective.

Grinding my teeth, I shook my head that I didn't. Their grey, drab suits were very fitting to their personalities. How were these even real people? Their callous tone was offensive and insensitive, failing to provide me with clarity – or any answers.

Were my responses telling them anything they didn't already know? Or were they asking because it was their stupid protocol? For Christ's sake! Why hadn't anyone told me the truth? I became angrier by the second. Dare I mention that the officer I knew said Ally's name to me at the crime scene? Something told me not to. Getting him in trouble didn't seem right. All I wanted from them was a simple head nod confirming (or denying) that the victim was Ally. I tried to be polite and answer their questions, but they weren't throwing me a bone. Can you imagine? I tried to be cooperative, but they denied even a hint to ease my pain. Why wouldn't they tell me anything?

After the longest five minutes, the detectives presented me with the epic twist that almost knocked me off my chair. They asked me to ID a suspect! Wait – did that seem right? Rather interesting that they would ask me before telling me *why* I need to identify someone, don't you think? I did too.

When I flipped over the photo that the detective put in front of me, I almost threw up. Right away, I knew. I knew this person – all too well. But what did it mean? I didn't know how to feel or what to think. Confused, I said the suspect's name, confirming what they already knew again. It was Ally's ex-boyfriend, Arturo!

My head was pounding. Ally hadn't mentioned he was out of jail yet from his domestic violence charges, which had occurred months earlier, and I still thought he had several weeks left to serve. Everything became fuzzy, and I wished things would start making sense.

The advocate then dismissed herself from the room; it seemed somewhat disruptive. It took only a second before I heard the beeping sound of the door down the hall. It was weird, not something I expected. Panic set in. Was she relaying what I said to someone else? Who was it? What kind of game of tattletale was going on here? It seemed like I was overreacting, but my instinct told me otherwise.

I'll never forget sitting there, beating myself up. *I am a mom!* Mothers should be able to handle anything that comes our way. We are strong for a reason – because we give life. But the truth was, being human meant I too was susceptible to feeling pain, and the guilt swallowed me whole.

Every direction I looked, I couldn't wrap my head around what was happening. How is it that Ally and I were just sitting in the kitchen the day before, laughing to the point of tears about farting? Who in the hell could take that from me? She was only a baby! She didn't deserve any of this, regardless of how naïve she was to the world.

I found myself asking the simple question for which I already knew what was coming. I am not sure I've ever felt so foolish. And yet, the answer seemed to hold my salvation somehow. I mustered up the gall to ask if Ally was dead. They'd have to answer if I asked, right? Wouldn't they want to know if it were the other way around? Come on! I tried to make it easier for them. They did this for a living; they had the training.

The detective replied with a cold, stale delivery of, "Thank you for your help."

What assholes! They avoided my question like the plague! Of course they did. Should I have expected anything more? How fucking unfair! In most movies, the detectives would have divulged the story by now.

A detective escorted me back to the waiting room to reunite me with Andy and my family. Drowning in resentment, I asked him how his interview went. He shrugged and was vague in his response. I sighed. It felt all too familiar and given the heartless response of the utterly non-stereotypical detectives, I was hoping for more from my husband. Wouldn't you?

Not letting go, I poked and prodded because I needed to know. My anger made me quiver as I tried asking Andy if the detectives showed him the photo of Arturo too. He nodded. But what did that mean? Jesus! No one was throwing me a goddam bone! Why did this have to feel so impossible? I didn't know if I should hold his hand or not. Nor was he trying to take mine, either. Could this day get any worse?

And like the predictable plot twist, there was a knock at the door. The advocate who had observed my questioning entered, asking if Ally's friend Maddie could join us. Wait? What? *Why* was she at the police station? I didn't understand.

Replying in unison, we said, "Of course!"

When she entered, I gave Maddie the biggest hug I could. We cried in each other's arms, as though nothing else mattered. It reminded me of hugging Ally. Although standing there together, something wasn't right, but I couldn't put my finger on it. Why did she need an advocate to introduce her? She was over eighteen, after all.

Out of the blue, Maddie said, "I hope they catch him."

In desperation, I asked, "Who?" She seemed very ashamed. Looking down, she mumbled Arturo's name. Why would she say that? Does she know something too? But at that point, I didn't give a damn! My pulse went into overdrive, and my head pounded again.

Calmly, I stated, "I thought he was still in jail."

Maddie sighed, and I could see how painful it was for her to share. While she explained how he had been out for almost two weeks, and Ally had been seeing him for the past few days, I stared without remorse.

"I'm sorry, what?" I questioned. As my eyes rolled in the back of my head, I knew. Right then and there, everything became ungodly crystal clear.

Ally's behavior *was* odd that past week. She seemed more dramatic than usual. I could tell she wanted to tell me something. I used every mommy skill I knew, but I didn't want to push her. She would start random sentences blaming Maddie for being stressed out. I tried to be a good listener, offering her a safe place to share, but I couldn't persuade her to continue. I thought with time she'd (as she always had) eventually come clean. Oh, my God! Why didn't Ally trust me?

My thoughts were interrupted as Maddie described the heartbreaking news that she was the one who dropped Ally off at the motel to see Arturo.

She whimpered, "It was only supposed to be for a short while."

After receiving a text from Ally (or so she thought), Maddie went to pick her up. Arturo told her that Ally had gotten another ride home when she arrived. As Maddie sat there confused, he forcefully tried to get into the car, and she successfully resisted, then sped away and went to her house. Holy shit! I couldn't believe what she'd been through already.

Maddie's words were hard to hear amid all her crying. It hurt me to the core, watching her. Maddie then mumbled that she thought Ally had made it home, which is why it didn't dawn on her to call the police. I closed my eyes in disbelief, playing her words over and over. I wanted to be mad at her, but it didn't feel right. I was overcome with compassion, worrying about her as any mother should. What would her family think? Her friends? This poor kid! I hugged her again. I screamed on the inside. But I couldn't let her know – I needed to be strong for her.

It finally made sense that Maddie had an advocate because she held the details we didn't know – it was for her protection. Oh, my God! She was the last person to see Ally, aside from Arturo, and the guilt must have been suffocating her.

I didn't even think about it. Turning to Maddie, I took her hands. I looked her straight in the eye; my voice reflected an "I'm serious" mommy tone. She stood still in her place. It was clear she'd received this kind of direction before. I told her I wasn't mad at her at all, and I was so happy she was safe. And I explained that she embraced the best-friend role as she should. It was perfect, and I would expect nothing less of her.

As I smiled, Maddie profusely apologized. I knew the burden she would carry for the rest of her life. I shook my head, telling her she didn't need to feel responsible. She was stunned by my reaction.

At that moment, Andy took advantage of her silence and screamed louder than I'd ever heard, scolding her like a child. It was predictable. Come on! Did he forget what it was like to be a teenager? I hated him for it. My parents couldn't believe his reaction, nor could Kylie.

Kylie didn't hesitate to scream, "You are such an asshole!"

I didn't think she was wrong. Andy didn't take the criticism well and fired right back, and a mini-world war in our tragedy-stricken family began.

As the volcano kept erupting within Andy, Maddie left the room in pure anguish. Detective Bullock got in Andy's face. She was as tall as him, so their eye-to-eye contact was intense. He rarely backed down quickly for me, so what would make her so special? Her firm posture showed him she wasn't intimidated in the least. She cautioned him to calm down, and his actions weren't helping.

He must have felt everyone staring at him, waiting for his next move. I knew he was in his "seek and destroy" mode. I wasn't sure I could handle much more – did we need more drama?

After taking a few deep breaths, he asked Maddie to come back to the room. I smiled at him. Both my parents nodded at me. As Kylie regained her composure, the room felt safe again. Detective Bullock collected Maddie from the place where she'd been crying. She reentered but was timid as Andy motioned her to come to him. Could you blame her? He seemed sincere in his apology as he hugged her. My heart warmed. It was moving that he recognized the situation (whether he believed in it or not, he did the right thing).

Retaking her hand, I resumed my mommy's tone. I explained that if she hadn't left the motel after trying to pick up Ally and

Arturo tried to get into the car, she'd be dead. I was also so proud of her for telling the truth, and no matter what, I said, I loved her.

Within a few minutes, the advocates suggested we go home. The detectives told us to expect a call from the county coroner. I kept thinking *because it's my daughter, right?* I mean, why else would the coroner call me? It felt cruel and unnecessary. Why not tell me now? I wondered why they wouldn't bend the rules for me. Could this day get *any* worse?

I hated that the detectives wouldn't give in, but on the other hand, I'll give it to them for following their protocol – it was impressive. As strong-willed a person as I am, I'm not sure I would be skilled enough to withhold such a critical fact, especially from a grieving mother who just wanted confirmation if her child was dead.

Heading back down to the car, I didn't even understand how I could function. My body went limp and felt numb as could be. My mind yelled at me to act on anything – but I couldn't. I didn't have even a tiny ounce of energy left.

We exchanged goodbyes with Detective Bullock and the advocates. As I turned to leave, one of the advocates stopped me in my tracks. Her eyes were soft as she handed me the paperwork for the Victim's Advocacy Group. She whispered I should fill it out right away. I looked down at the packet and back at her. Mother of God! I needed this to be over. All I wanted was to hold my daughter. Instead, I held this cold, lifeless unwanted packet of information. It was the last unspoken hint, and my hope faded to a black nothingness that Ally was dead.

IT WAS NOW NEARLY TWO O'CLOCK, AND I WAS FURIOUS AFTER THE DAY we'd had. Wouldn't you think the police would escort us home? How were they protecting us from the public, and ourselves too? Did they really think we were OK to drive? I still get a raging headache thinking about it all. I wanted to give Andy shit for how he was acting like a race car driver, but in a way, I hoped we would get pulled over – I'd love to hear what the cops would say. You can't make up the shit we'd been through so far.

My family and I discussed contacting friends and family. Were all the nonverbal hints enough? I mean, it wasn't official yet, so were we moving too soon? I was shocked. Our debate was short – how could we all be unanimous?

I didn't want to believe Ally was dead but running from the truth was impossible. There was no way it was real! Why wasn't I able to save my baby? Why did this happen? Oh, my God! Did she suffer? This question would haunt my dreams like no other. My life no longer had a PG-13 rating; it went to "R" overnight, and I was in a living Hell.

Coordinating with my folks, we each took charge of a telephone list. I was worried because I didn't have any formal training; none of us did. Why didn't the advocates provide any direction on this topic?

What was I going to say? "Ally is dead, *maybe?*" Does that not sound utterly ridiculous?

Being responsible for destroying the lives of loved ones was absolutely horrible! I chose Ally's other grandma, Barb (MawMaw), to be first – I owed it to her. Even after the divorce from Ally's biological father, Eric, she and I remained very close. She participated in Ally's life as if nothing had happened, taking Ally almost every other weekend and on summer trips. From the first day I met her, she showed me that families could stay together regardless of turmoil. My God, I knew this was the biggest test of all.

My heart raced in anticipation when I dialed her number. I cleared my throat, but it didn't help the fact I was speechless. My cottonmouth didn't help, either. Distracted, I wondered if I'd had anything to drink or eat. Had I even used the bathroom?

Sitting on our front porch shaking like a leaf, I dreaded Barb answering. I watched the cars drive by, wondering if they saw me. I was jealous. Why do they get to go on about their typical day? And there I was, collapsing by the second, blown away by the thought of what I had to say. Could I even say the words, "Your granddaughter *might* be dead?"

Barb answered, and I candidly stated, "I have news." Her tone shifted, as any parent's would. I took a deep breath and said, "Ally is 'presumed' dead." The anticipation of her response was grueling. No one should have to deliver such news!

Her sobbing split me in every direction like shattered glass. God, it was so uncomfortable! I practiced silence in every sentence, allowing her to catch up; in those seconds, I found relief not speaking. I shared some of the details, the big ones anyway. She, too, acted similarly to Petra while assembling data. I loved that they both could compartmentalize their opinions to assess the situation.

As I continued, my voice flattened. I was becoming more emotionless with every word I said. I'm sure I sounded like a cold-hearted bitch. But I was protecting myself from the truth. Who wouldn't?

Seconds felt like hours; I wanted this to be over so badly. I couldn't even imagine what Barb was thinking. Who would she tell first? Would she present the news as calmly as I thought I was?

I thought I had shared everything I could, and a gentle silence embraced us. I closed my eyes and saw an orange glow through my lids from the sun, and I gasped. I'd seen it a million times before, but this time, it was different. It consoled me.

Somehow, our conversation came to a natural end. Barb then offered to be the telephone tree for that side of the family. Thank the Lord! That woman was such a trooper. I wasn't sure if I ever realized how thankful I was to have her in my life. I hoped our relationship wouldn't change because of Ally's death. *Would it? Jesus, I hope not!* What about everyone else? Did they value our relationship, or would we fade apart? The thought made me want to curl into a tight little ball.

My head was pounding, but I was relieved that I had survived the first call. I wiped away the sweat from my brow, there was so much. I wondered if it was because it was hot outside or from all the adrenaline. Regardless, I realized how much I despised everything. Every inch of my body hurt, and my skin began to feel tight from anger. It was as if I was bloating like a balloon stretching beyond capacity. Someone, please pop me and release me from this nightmare.

Wanting to keep the momentum, I did what I do best – pushed myself into fifth gear without self-care. There's no time like the present, right? Who could criticize me for that? One by one, I checked off my loved ones.

After a few phone calls, the conversations became so predictable – scripted, even. They all reacted the same, stunned in disbelief.

Getting to the bottom of my list, I was a statue. I felt so lost in my house. I didn't know where anyone was, and I didn't care. All I wanted was to see Ally walk through the front door. Was that too much to ask?

Resting my heavy head on my shoulder, I played with the bill of my favorite hat, thanking it for being there. Looking down, I'd never noticed the broken veins around my ankles before. Had they always been there? Huh, then it hit me like a thunderbolt, and there was nothing else to say. Nothing would be the same after that day. It was the last time my life was typical and the weekend predictable.

CHAPTER 2

Lost Within the Familiar

JULY 3, 2017

I didn't even know how I was awake, let alone how I could fall asleep – I bargained that it was best not to question. Finding my bearings in the dark, I noticed how quiet our house was – the ghostly kind. I never knew that silence was my worst enemy.

The hard, piercing questions crept through the quiet, stinging one by one. Why didn't Ally call me? Was she afraid I would be upset because of her reconnection with Arturo? How would I have reacted if she had told me? What was her last thought? Did she feel my love as her life ended? I was resentful. Her choices were putting me through Hell, not to mention everyone else.

Desperate for solace, I went to Ally's room. She still hadn't come home. Standing at her door, I hated seeing her space untouched. I debated a few minutes – do I dare disrupt the perfectly made bed, or would I somehow bring bad juju if I did?

When I finally sat, I took her decorative white studded pillow from the stylish trio and hugged it as if it were her. I was careful not to let my old mascara run on it. My God, I missed her. Was there still a chance she could walk through the door? There was no way any of this could be real, right? No fucking way!

Feeling defeated, I let my head hang until my neck hurt. I rubbed it, letting my head fall backward. I was so out of it. I began to slump from my deep sighs.

As my eyes wandered, I couldn't help but stare at her senior picture, and of course, she was smiling at me. Ally was a second chance and wasn't my first choice. The devastation of being pregnant at twenty was too much for me to handle. Becoming a mother at that age wasn't on my checklist. Then after Ally was born (I did suffer from postpartum depression for a while), we bonded, and there was no turning back. I never knew how much I could love that girl. She became my focus, my world.

Feeling her soft duvet cover, I took in the room. The way she decorated represented her style and "old soul." Her space was a retreat based on calm and charm. The black-and-white artwork allowed her to be the "pop" of color and soothed her drama-queen tendencies. Her accessories sparkled on her black ladder bookcase, reflecting her simple elegance. The only thing missing was a hanging chandelier. It would have complimented her metal-tree ivy candle holder above her bed.

I grinned at the melted abstract crayon canvas Ally proudly displayed above her desk. She made it on my birthday the year before (I love a good DIY project). The different shades of pink and purple complimented her room with a subtle radiance.

Hanging off the dark-metal desk frame was her red graduation mortarboard. I sniffled and shrugged. Her relationship with Arturo put such a strain on her senior year – she almost didn't make it. Ally worked her ass off and graduated on time, and I'm not sure I'd ever seen her so proud of her hard work. We all were.

I returned to her bed, wrapping myself in her fuzzy white throw. I couldn't believe how good it felt to hold her girlie blanket. Sitting in my usual spot, I reflected on so many priceless conversations we had over the years. From boy crushes to school challenges, we tackled them one by one.

At that moment, the song she picked for her dance-recital debut, "In My Mind" by Tiësto, popped into my head. Out of the blue, the words played just like I'd heard a million times before. I smiled. Ally's dance recital was (and still is) one of my favorite memories with her.

The hip-hop group Ally danced with selected her to perform a solo at the upcoming "2013 Music from Around the World" presentation at the local high school. She would get the opportunity to choreograph and perform her dance on stage. We were both so excited and yet a little nervous – it was such a big deal. She was going to be a celebrity, after all.

Ally consulted me for advice (that was a proud-mama moment for sure). We'd go back and forth, like a metronome. She'd let me stay on my soapbox coaching her while she'd fiddle with her fingers and express a few eye rolls. Then the tables would turn, and she'd go to town. I would then listen and validate her concerns. It was teamwork.

Ally practiced for weeks to get the dance the way she wanted. She used *Step Up* (her favorite movie) as inspiration. On the day of the show, she was pacing in her room. She was either pumping herself up or beating herself down – something I'm sure she learned from me. Wearing my armor, I went to talk to her.

Sometimes, well, *most* times, she would be so overly dramatic. As predicted, her screeching voice was in full swing. Who knew what she was saying? I'm not sure it was even English. It was quite the scene. I knew she needed to get her feelings out, but still – it was hard not to laugh. I sat on her bed in my usual spot, waiting till she'd come around. And eventually, she did. Ally dried her eyes, and she thanked me for being her mom. She touched my heart in a way that radiated from head to toe; I'll never forget that moment.

I heard the footsteps of Nikki coming down the hallway. You couldn't miss her nails on our vinyl floor. She knew how to make an entrance. Looking into her golden eyes as she approached the door, I could see that she knew something was wrong. It's as if she were nodding in acknowledgment of how bad that morning sucked. Coming to my side, she plopped herself next to me, sitting directly on my foot. Was that accidental or intentional? How did she know I needed her at that exact moment? It's not like I called her or anything.

While I was rubbing behind her ears, my eyes locked on to my favorite art piece from Ally's junior year, next to the window. I admired the modern mix of shapes blended like a kaleidoscope. Variations of black, white, and blue connected the harmony. Can you visualize it?

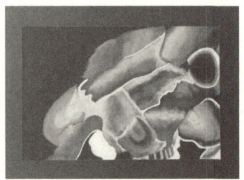

Facing the art piece, I ran my fingers over it. Feeling the colors made me cry. I remembered the day she sat at the kitchen table, dangling her cute legs with her artwork in one hand and writing the paper for that assignment with the other. We were having hot tea while she was telling me her concerns about her drawing. She was reluctant to have it entered in the school art exhibition. I didn't understand why she felt that way. Everyone knew her talents as an artist.

Ally said with doubt, "Mom, it doesn't look like anything, and it's not good enough to show."

My reminiscing was interrupted as I wondered if the paper from her assignment was still in her room. Racing to her closet, I couldn't believe I had found it! I hugged it so tightly. It was right on top of a giant handmade manila portfolio sleeve she made in art class. Huh, it seemed a little too convenient, but I'd take it.

The words were in her handwriting; I stared at them and admired her penmanship. I smelled the notebook paper, but it reminded me only of something old. I held it to my heart, and I sobbed till it hurt. I didn't know if I could read it. Would it upset me more if I did or more if I didn't? I sat there for a moment, scared and unsure of what to do.

Drained, I rubbed my temples. I finished my last double inhale, blinking extra big to refocus. I began slowly, studying each word, one by one.

"Some of my struggles were being able to keep a little bit of my taste into the requirements given. I got a little stressed towards the end if the colors would not be able to blend. My accomplishments are being proud of my piece and still being able to continue my imagination."

As I read Ally's paper, a section spoke to me; it left me in awe. She wrote:

I reread it a few times, each time embracing her message. Did Ally know she was capturing her essence as a person? Not only did her words represent her art piece, but it was also a metaphor for her life. How could my kid be so brilliant?

Ally's words left me stuck in a nightmarish daydream wishing my life away. I couldn't stand how overwhelmed and powerless I felt. I wanted her to walk through the door so badly, but all the signs wouldn't allow me a moment of hope. My baby *might* be dead – what the fuck! I would never be able to help her like that again: no more dance recitals, no more art pieces and no more moments to be a proud mama. I sobbed, wanting to scream out loud. I wish I could have, but I didn't have the energy to make a peep. I never knew I could feel such agony.

Nikki licked my hand. I stared at her, puzzled. How could she sense that I needed my furry friend to be there with me? I thanked her as if she could understand me – well, who knows, maybe she could. I felt silly, but I didn't care – it was perfect. Looking at her and back at Ally's artwork again, all I could think was how much I loved that art piece.

THE NOISE IN MY HEAD WOULDN'T STOP. I SAT ON MY COUCH, WISHING my life away. What else could I do? Now, ten o'clock in the morning and neither Andy nor Kylie was anywhere to be found. Needing comfort, I wrapped myself tightly in my blanket, almost to the point of suffocation.

Was it irrational to have a shred of hope that Ally wasn't dead? Should I let go and accept the possibility it's her? But what kind of mother would give up so quickly? Once, I believed I could change anything; I was that powerful. I despised the truth, learning in such a twisted way that I can't change everything and that controlling anything other than myself was an absolute delusion. I reminded myself that we couldn't make healthy decisions without the facts. But why do we need to learn the most profound lessons the hard way? Is this how unevolved we are?

I flipped through the channels trying to take my mind off things. "Poltergeist" was on. How can anyone forget Carol Anne? Having watched the trilogy a hundred times, I never noticed before that they were probably the unluckiest family on Earth. Although it was silly to compare, I felt a close second.

Not knowing what else to do, I began searching for funeral homes. I mean, we hadn't even received confirmation Ally was dead yet. What in the hell was I thinking? The wishful side of me wanted to wait, and the planner side was lost and needed something, anything to control. No one else was holding out hope she was alive, so what was stopping me? What was the worst that could happen if I looked?

I needed Andy more than ever. Yet, getting on the same page with him took a back seat to all the moving pieces between us. It had been only one day, but it already felt like we were light-years apart. I tried to hold it together – I did. I'm sure Andy was attempting in his way, too. But maintaining our marriage while dealing with everything, emotional and physical, was downright exhausting. Grief was blinding us to each other's pain and talking about it was impossible.

Instead, we defaulted to being individuals. The idea of planning the perfect service for Ally was now, by far, my number one priority, and his need to be the badass protector took charge for him.

Andy's focus to coordinate extra surveillance around our home seemed ridiculous. Yes, I knew Arturo was somewhere, still on the loose. Duh? Isn't that why we have the police or was it a guy thing? Did he take a back seat because he was a stepparent? Or does none of that matter, and moms are supposed to handle the hard stuff? Why wouldn't he want to be a part of making this one-time event beautiful?

I know, deep down, Andy wanted to be the man he thought I needed, but I didn't know that then. I assumed that as my partner, he could handle anything. We signed a contract and exchanged vows as everyone does. But just because we say we'll be there for each other doesn't mean we know *how* to show up.

While I was fully aware of Andy's strengths and weaknesses during our everyday life, neither of us had experienced a trauma-related event. He acted like a ferocious grizzly bear, and I appreciated his protection. But I struggled with feeling an inexplicable disappointment because what I wanted more from my husband was my teddy bear. I was afraid he couldn't take off his alter ego, even for me.

Petra, who was now by my side, asked Andy if it was OK if she acted as my confidant. I loved that she did that, and with him agreeing, she embraced the task of funeral logistics with me.

We didn't even know how to choose a funeral home; would you? At first, we searched the internet for ideas, and I was relieved and admittedly bummed that I didn't find anything on Pinterest.

Seriously, could you imagine? I then turned to the paperwork from The Victim's Advocacy Group. There were several facilities in our local area. And then I found a surprise – the crime against Ally warranted funding from the county. Thank heavens. My money tree in the backyard was short a few thousand dollars to bury my child.

On the list was Horan & McConaty, a crematorium next to my favorite Starbucks. There's nothing like getting your morning coffee on the way to work and seeing the building. It feels out of place. While it didn't look like a funeral home, aside from its visible sign, the building itself seemed more like a million-dollar Country French-style home you'd see in the Parade of Homes magazine, but what did I know? For years, I'd driven by this business thinking nothing of it, until now. On every selfish level – the location was perfect.

With Petra holding my hand, my footsteps became heavy approaching the door. My reality punched me in the gut – I hated stepping inside. We met Alice, the funeral director. Her calm and well-poised demeanor showed me that I wasn't the first parent she had helped. Imagining other parents going through this same heart-wrenching experience was torturous, and yet there was a comfort in knowing I wasn't alone.

During our meeting, I struggled to think straight and couldn't form intelligent sentences. Petra filled in my blanks and took notes – it was a breath of fresh air.

Pulling her aside, I gestured to the coffee shop. Jokingly, I asked, "Do you want to grab a beverage when we're done?" as if we were about to check off the funeral home from our typical to-do list. Thank God for our dark humor. We shared a wink, holding back a giggle. Those little seconds felt like an hour of rejuvenation.

Alice then showed us the beautiful cremation garden at the back of the building. It was full of ponds with koi fish and decorative shrubbery. It was such a surprise – I had no idea this concept existed. It was perfect for Ally. She was never a fan of the traditional cemetery idea anyway.

Everything felt right, as if the details had already worked themselves out. And at the same time, I was still holding on by a thread, wanting to believe Ally wasn't dead.

After a brief consultation with my family, thankfully, no one questioned my hopes, but we went ahead and scheduled Ally's service with Horan & McConaty anyway.

CHAPTER 3

Reality Has No Mercy

JULY 4, 2017

Opening the fridge that Tuesday morning reminded me it was Independence Day. The week before, I had intended to decorate pancakes like flags with blueberries, strawberries, and whipped cream. Now, I could give a rat's ass about the stupid holiday. The *only* thing I wanted to celebrate was Ally walking through the door.

Day two, and still no word from anyone if it was Ally. I couldn't function. My cereal became mush in the milk, and my coffee was cold. If I'd had long fingernails, they would've been stubs from all the tapping on the counter.

I couldn't stop thinking about Arturo. Did he do this? No way! He'd been in our home, for fuck's sake! I treated that kid as my very own.

I adored their young puppy love. I'll never forget seeing him the night of Ally's junior prom. His eyes twinkled in excitement. It was his first time going, too. He scrimped and saved to rent a tux and buy her a corsage. He looked so dashing – he could have been a model for a magazine. I loved watching him treat her like a princess before they left. It really was a fairy tale come true for them both.

I didn't want to believe the possibility that Arturo was a part of Ally's murder. Yes, their yearlong relationship had its issues, but come on, whose doesn't? Theirs however, ended with Ally having Arturo arrested for domestic violence. They got into a struggle, and he punched her in the face with her left eye taking the blow, among other things. I would have never guessed their relationship had come to this. Plagued with remorse, I wondered if there were signs I should have seen. Did I fail my baby? Would she have listened?

Feeling empowered after his arrest, Ally dyed her hair red and got a rose tattoo on her arm. It all happened so fast – it was like she was proving a point, but to whom? Within days, Ally signed up for the Navy. Yes, helping others was a top priority for her. But I wasn't sure if she committed for the right reasons. I thought it was all too reactive, resulting in several yelling matches about it. That damn kid, though, once she had an idea, there was no changing her mind.

If Ally was so adamant about her new future, why would she reconnect with Arturo after his release? What in the fuck was she thinking? I felt guilty for being furious at her and yet overcome with empathy for her good-hearted nature. Did she think he'd changed? I cried so hard, there was no sound. *Of course* she did. Ally saw the best in everyone. It sounded like something I would do. I guess apples really don't fall far from the tree.

Stomping around the kitchen island, I tried to play detective. Fine! So, the two of them hung out for a few days. They were even caught on camera at McDonald's by the motel. It made sense; I mean, they must eat, right? I suspected they probably fought over her new look and choices, especially signing up for the Navy – I could totally see that. But murder? Come on!

I was in denial that such evil could happen to either of us. My inner voice screamed, *"What did I do to deserve this? Let alone me, what about Ally?"*

My phone rang, disrupting my rage. Seeing the number on my screen made my heart stop: "Unknown." I almost dropped it as I panicked. I whispered, "Please, God! Let them be wrong." Answering with such trepidation, it probably sounded like I was going through puberty.

The coroner's voice was flat as he returned my greeting. After a short pause, he bluntly told me that the victim was, in fact, Ally. Anger amplified the darkness I carried inside. How can someone deliver such devastating news with such ease? For God's sake, it's the most tragic sentence a parent could hear! There wasn't even a hint of emotion.

I was cold as ice while the coroner continued talking, and closed my eyes as if it helped. A single tear fell from my cheek as I listened. How could this be real? The fleece jammies that would comfort me didn't make me feel any better. From all the hints I received, it was obvious Ally was dead. But as I heard the coroner recite the official report over the phone, my heart shattered. It was too much to digest, and I wanted to die.

Ally's certificate would record her death with three components: Manner of Death, Date of Death, and Cause of Death.

First, her murder would be considered a homicide. Duh, I thought. That was easy to understand, and I felt like I could handle the pace we were going. Although, as I scribbled my notes, my stomach began to turn.

Second, the date of death was July 2, 2017. They would use the morning of her discovery because they could not determine the exact time of death. Really? It happens frequently enough that they need a procedure for this kind of thing? I couldn't help but feel pity for them. Although it seemed fair, I guess.

Lastly, the coroner stated her cause of death was "ligature manual strangulation." My head spun out of control, and I needed to understand what that meant, like a child. "Just tell me if she suffered," I said as politely as I could.

He was sympathetic in his delivery that death by strangulation can take only seconds. Oh, my God! I then remembered how many times I wanted to choke Ally myself. Jesus! I even thought that at the crime scene. What kind of shitty irony was this? Seriously?

To make matters worse, I flipped through the Rolodex of every movie I'd seen, trying to find some reassurance. What else was I supposed to do? It wasn't hard to pick one, since choking scenes are so damn ordinary nowadays, regardless of genre. I analyzed all the scenes I could think of, and they seemed to agree with the coroner. In turn, I was incapable of relief because I focused on the actor's portrayal: the animated body movements, their pained faces, and the punished sounds they made. It was absolutely awful to think my baby had suffered like that.

Sighing deeply, I offered that my family chose Horan & McConaty as the funeral home. I wanted to be such a bitch, but I kept reminding myself it wasn't the coroner's fault. His voice perked up a little as if I had saved him from another grueling topic. He confirmed they would transport Ally to the funeral home for our service. I was civil as I thanked him and said goodbye, holding back my tears.

Hanging up the phone, I wobbled from all the disgust oozing out of every pore of my body. Almost everyone has heard the adage "Be careful what you wish for" at some point in life. Though I desperately wished for the truth to be known, I hated it! The words screamed at me without remorse. Who could prepare for such a reality check?

Anxiety gripped my every move, and my heart was palpitating too loudly for me to focus. I had just received confirmation of my worst fear: that my baby was dead. At that point, it didn't matter who fucking killed her. Why would someone do such a thing? Did they at least try CPR? I prayed Ally's death wasn't painful – and that she didn't suffer.

I finally dared to raise my head and saw Andy standing there. He took me into his chest, and I attempted to translate what the coroner said. I slurred my words in a manner that didn't make any sense. No matter, my tears said it all. My inner defense system must have triggered as I got his shirt wet with drool. All I saw was the light around us fade to black. He whispered comforting words in my ear, and I slipped into a virtual reality of nothingness.

CHAPTER 4

Witnessing the Unforgettable

JULY 5, 2017

My phone rang, and it was Alice, the funeral director, of all people. My mind concocted an elaborate mini-movie with a Disney ending within a second. *What can I say?* As a mother, I'd defend to the bitter end my wishful thinking that I would see my baby alive again. Sigh. If only that were the case. No, there are still plenty of pages left to read, a fairly good indication that it didn't happen.

Alice was calling to share that Ally's body had arrived at the facility and we could visit her. Oh, my God, really? She warned us that Ally would have minimal makeup on and wouldn't be in her outfit; she would be covered only by a white sheet. Well, at least one part of the movies would be accurate. On the bright side, it wasn't identifying her in the morgue – I guess.

Alice hadn't mentioned seeing Ally before the viewing during our meeting at the funeral home, or I missed it. Regardless, I didn't know what to think. Of course, I wanted to see her, but I was terrified. I told Alice how I felt, but she still recommended spending time with Ally to minimize the shock. It seemed she was going out of her way to be supportive and provide me with guidance. It was the right thing to do. I told my family, and they didn't hesitate to support me in seeing her and going with me. I was surprised, or maybe they were good at hiding their reservations like I was.

Walking through those doors again pained me in every way. The anticipation of seeing Ally was eating me alive. Wasn't I a good mom? Why was this happening to us? My posture looked as though I was an old lady, I'm sure.

Alice was ready for us – she was warm and sympathetic. I didn't know what to expect. My heart was racing, and finding words was impossible. I wasn't sure I could handle what I was about to see.

Already exhausted from my raging internal war, I took a deep breath and pulled up my big-girl panties, commanding my feet to start moving. My daughter is in there, for fuck's sake! As Alice took us through the hallway, I didn't understand how she could be so calm. Everywhere I looked, death surrounded us. When she spoke, all I heard was an untranslated alien language. Instead, I focused on her smile and let it guide me. Opening the door, I swallowed what felt like daggers, and pure agony took over my body. She then left us, and we stood inches away from my dead daughter.

Ally was lying there in front of me. I couldn't breathe. I heard sniffles and gasping from my family. Seeing Ally's lifeless body was my first viewing of a corpse (that I can remember, anyway). She was perfectly placed on the table, as Alice described. Ally looked so pale yet peaceful. Murmuring under my breath, I begged anyone who would listen. I swore I wouldn't be mad at her. Shouldn't this be the predictable scene from almost every horror film: She'd sit up, and the terrible prank would end? Oh, wait, how could I forget? It isn't like the goddam movies.

I cried and was inconsolable, and my blurry vision gave me peace for milliseconds from witnessing Ally's wounded neck. I hated it. Seeing in person how the coroner described Ally was downright awful. I could no longer hide from what I kept denying. Right before me was the truth of how she died. My baby didn't ask for this! How could she be dead? Why was she lying before me not saying my name? All I wanted was to hear her voice, music to my ears, one more time. Was that too much to ask?

The cries echoed throughout the room. Each of us was in another dimension, trying to grasp the reality we were facing. Ally was everything: a most beautiful daughter, a loving granddaughter, a trusted sister, an adored niece and a friend to so many. How would our lives ever be the same? None of us would get the opportunity to make new memories with her. Shaking uncontrollably, I began to feel ill. The more I grasped the idea that a cherished eighteen years was over, I wanted to die.

It was in that second that I had the worst epiphany. Oh, my God! My lineage was also over. Was I the only one who realized this? Should I say something? There is no way I was the first to recognize this. As I thought it through what it meant, all I could conclude was how cruel the truth was.

Afraid I was missing some other "aha" moment, I stopped myself from thinking anymore. I shifted my attention back to Ally in front of me. Despite being surrounded by so many loved ones, I felt alone. None of them could empathize with me or understand what I was feeling.

I needed to know the truth of how she died. At least, from what I could see, anyway. Grateful that I wasn't the only curious one, I noticed my family pointing to different areas of her body. It was fascinating, really. I couldn't help but think our actions could suggest how morbid we were, but I was OK with that.

Ally was so pale; it made the red hair dye even more unflattering than before. Her blonde eyelashes were hard to see – I hated not seeing them doused in her favorite mascara. For the most part, her face looked the same, thank God. Her thinning nose and wrinkled lips stung me hard. But I couldn't dismiss that it would happen to me, too, when I pass. I better understood why the movies make the deceased look beautiful. Unless there's a zombie element, it isn't pretty, not even a little.

I brushed her hair away from her face and noticed tiny gashes on her left ear. Under my breath, I whimpered, "My poor baby! What happened to you?" It didn't make sense, but I knew they weren't from her earring. Pointing at them in disgust to my mom, I appreciated that she didn't throw out a theory. I wasn't sure I could handle that.

Moving down, I noticed her neck was puffy, even lumpy in some places. Hovering my finger above them, I followed the pattern. Human hands did this? I didn't understand. My head fell limp. Who could do such a thing? I didn't let myself visualize what I thought had happened. Did she at least put up a fight? *I fucking hope so!*

It was surreal what I witnessed, but I had to continue. Refocusing, I noticed Ally's swollen arms. They appeared so dang defined from the embalming fluid. I knew she would've loved how they looked. Or been more pissed off that all the working out she did every day was for nothing. I shook my head from my sarcastic thought – what mattered was that I felt better. I knew Ally would have found it funny, and Kylie too. I pointed out Ally's arms to her, and she giggled as if we were on the same page. I knew I could trust her dark humor as so many times before.

Looking up, I noticed Ally's fingernails were not only broken but also appeared jagged. They were cut and trimmed almost to the cuticle – I assumed the coroner did that for evidence. I inhaled and bit my knuckle, trying not to scream. I was livid! Did they need to take that much? It seemed so excessive! How are they going to make her fingers look pretty after that?

I needed a happy memory, anything. Shutting my eyes, I remembered the first time Ally came home from kindergarten, so upset. Because she was a lefty, that poor kid tried everything to keep the pencil smudges from getting on her long-sleeve shirt. She was so devastated because she was different than everyone else in the class. I hugged her so hard and whispered, "That's what makes you my special kiddo." It was the first time I'd ever called her that, and from that moment, it stuck like glue. It was just the smile I needed.

It got me thinking. Shit! I wondered if what so many palm readers have said were true. In checking her dominant hand, Ally's lifeline was, in fact, short. I traced the line, wondering if the length is really an accurate indicator of our years of life. Could this be a coincidence? Not saying anything to anyone, I kept my question to myself.

I'll never forget standing there. I didn't have words to express what happened, and I wasn't sure if any authors had ever written any such words before. During that solemn event, everyone in my loving family shared acceptance of death and an appreciation for supporting one another. It was indeed an incredible moment we would never want to re-create.

We didn't judge one another (at least not out loud, anyway). Why did it take such devastation to unite us in a manner whereby we looked beyond our differences? How could we each practice such respect and understanding without an agreement? It seemed that our harmony connected us perfectly. It was a beautiful experience – a gift from Ally that I'll cherish forever through her death.

I still find it funny how the universe knows when it needs to show up. As my stomach twisted and turned from everything I saw, unable to control what was about to happen, I let out a toot. The sound (and dreadful smell) caused a distraction in the room, and I welcomed the moment of comic relief.

Wiping my raccoon eyes, the sound of double inhales shifted to everyone smiling at one another. There was even some snickering. It was still a strange feeling to be standing over my dead daughter, giggling with everyone. But somehow, it felt appropriate. The room felt lighter; I didn't need to explain it. We all knew that Ally would be laughing too.

It was now early evening. Finally, some alone time with Kylie – I looked forward to it. Granted, I didn't know what to say – would you? Do I dare ask about her feelings? Should I leave it alone and see if she brings it up on her own? Did she think our relationship would change because her stepsister was dead? Was anything ever going to be trustworthy again? For the love of God, how do I stop all this awful noise in my head? Not knowing which way to go, I didn't say a thing.

Kylie and I headed to our favorite store, Walmart. Sure, it gets a bad rap from its unusual shoppers, but I don't think it's *that* bad. I've been the butt of a joke or two because of shopping there, but that's OK. I know it's all in good fun.

We commented on how we didn't make a list entering the store. It didn't matter, though, as Kylie and I had plenty of experience "winging it." Determined to treat this trip like any other, we began heading down the aisles. Struggling, neither of us could make definitive decisions to save our lives. Trying something new seemed like a bad idea. Nothing sounded good at all, not even the reliable depression-soother – dark chocolate. It was nice to be out and getting some exercise, but I thought we looked like wandering idiots.

Thinking we blended in, I was so wrong. It turned out we resembled "that family" who'd been on the news. Fellow customers stared and pointed! At first, I thought I was projecting my insecurities until someone had the audacity to Google our story as if I couldn't see Ally's photo on their giant phone screen. Seriously? Rest assured, jerks. My mommy-ears hadn't gone deaf, hearing as they whispered within earshot. What assholes! Didn't anyone ever teach those Walmart shoppers how to be discreet? *Come on*!

Looking at Kylie, I asked, "Is this what it feels like to be a movie star?"

Irritated, she said, "I don't think so."

They weren't ecstatic fans screaming for an autograph or selfie. Instead, they gawked as if we were freakish mutants. Again and again, aisle after aisle, it was hopeless. I had such regret for coming to a place I'd thought would provide some normalcy, but I had no idea what we'd be walking into. How could I?

Anticipating my next move, Kylie was growing more annoyed by the second. Refusing to cry, I didn't know what to do with my rage and disappointment. These people were clueless about with whom they were messing. Wanting to attack the inconsiderate so severely, this grieving mama bear was about to be hazardous to their health!

Grinding my teeth, I didn't want to create a scene, making me extremely uncomfortable. But I hated feeling this way. Do I say something, or should I leave well enough alone? What message would it send to Kylie? Is this the time to stand up for myself and her?

My patience was wearing thin; I went to my default setting. Proudly taking the higher road, I said, "You're welcome, world. I just saved your lives!" Kylie and I signaled to each other without words, agreeing to leave the store empty-handed.

We talked about our disgust during the drive home and how our trip was a total disaster. It had been a while since I had heard Kylie cuss. Her use of the f-bomb made me chuckle. It didn't fit her to speak like that, but I loved her energy. Her generous helping nature tended to put others first, placing herself last. It'd been a struggle to encourage her to feel comfortable enough to talk about herself and her feelings; she was better at avoiding them. Ecstatic to see Kylie so passionate, I worried about how she would harvest such energy.

Then it hit me. How was the rest of high school going to be for her? Would she get extra-special treatment from her teachers? What kind of gossip would her peers spread? Oh, dear God! I was hoping more for a happy ending. More like a *Princess Diaries* kind of an experience if anything – it seemed more manageable. Both my girls loved that movie; they'd get the reference, anyway.

Kylie's messy bun was flopping around from all her bouncing in the seat. Her hands were extra-energetic as she vented. Between you and me, I was eagerly waiting for her to slap the car window. It would have been funny – well, maybe not to her, but still.

Her venting led us to such an in-depth discussion. We tried to understand if compassion is conditional, and if so, why? Do we really need to know what gets others out of bed to treat them with simple decency?

I was proud of Kylie for admitting she'd typically be the first to get involved in school gossip, and I shared that I'd done it too. So, we agreed, especially now knowing how it feels, that we'd be more mindful of others moving forward.

At the very least, I can say I was glad the Walmart experience happened with Kylie and me being together. We were able to support each other through the ordeal. But plain and simple, this new normal flat-out sucked! How many more life lessons did we need to learn? As if either of us could handle another one? Come on! The weight we were carrying was already heavy enough. Why was life so unfair?

CHAPTER 5
A Mother's Job Is Never Finished

JULY 6, 2017

The laundry list of action items to prepare for the funeral seemed manageable and downright horrible. Write an obituary, gather photos and songs, and find Ally's outfit in three days – oh, that's it? Why in the world would I give myself such a short deadline? Man, if only I could kick my own ass sometimes. I'm not sure, though, even with what I know now, whether I'd do it any other way.

Andy was still too busy to help me, and it wasn't like anyone else from my family was offering. Was I indeed the only one with the ability to make this happen? My resentment comforted me when no one else could. Thankfully, Petra was still by my side and offered to help me again.

Writing Ally's obituary was downright painstaking, leaving me raw and exposed. How could I capture her spirit for others to embrace how special she was? Thank God the facility provided a template. No mother should have to be writing this about her child. I hated it! Each letter I wrote felt like putting a nail in the coffin (no pun intended). Yes, I described my most beautiful child, but I couldn't stand the truth. Bargaining that people who came to the funeral already knew Ally, I kept it short and stuck to the script. I'm sure it read like an assembly manual from an IKEA purchase – but I didn't care.

Collecting pictures for the slide show tested me further. Seeing Ally stuck in time made me cry more than I wanted to smile. I desperately tried to appreciate the unforgettable moments, but I rushed the experience. Why did she have to die? How would the world ever know what it's missing? Ally didn't deserve any of it!

I was exhausted from all the yo-yoing. Could I decide which memories were my favorite? Like most parents, they all were. It was so unfair! Exactly how was I going to be able to tell which had a special place in my heart more than others?

Taking a deep breath, I flipped the pages of the photo albums and searched our digital files. Somehow, I began to grin when I saw the picture where Ally was missing her two front teeth. It was her school photo from kindergarten.

It was quite a celebration when Ally's two front teeth finally fell out. When she was five, she was adamant about riding her bike outside one day in the early fall. Getting her all geared up seemed like too much work, so we compromised and I let her ride in the house (excellent parenting right there). Ally could be quite charming when she wanted her way. She brought her bike in from the garage without a hitch – that girl was nothing short of pure determination.

Ally's laughter echoed throughout the house until the inevitable happened. Right before my eyes, one of the training wheels got stuck in the shaggy carpet, and she face-planted into the oak coffee table. Talk about an epic backfire. Ally was crying so hard there was no sound. Her lips swelled, and there was some blood.

Somehow during my minor freak out, I grabbed some paper towels and a bag of ice, and we headed to the emergency room. Processing all the what-ifs while watching the doctors assess Ally's mouth, I was scared shitless they'd call social services.

I paced the room until I heard the staff start giggling about the accident. They comforted me, sharing that we weren't the first in their experience and we wouldn't be the last. Oh, my God! I was relieved that the doctors didn't classify what happened as child abuse. *They must be parents as well,* was all I could think.

After returning home, we certainly had a story for everyone. There was no way Ally would be able to keep it a secret, and I didn't blame her. How could I? It didn't mean I wasn't already dreading it, though. Thank goodness the story had a happy ending. Ally could share her bravery with the doctors, her teeth were still intact, and she had only a small cut on her inner lip. Nothing a little time and ice cream couldn't heal.

Later, while we were both resting on the couch, Ally was quick to notice her front teeth imprinted on the coffee table. How was that even possible? Regrettably, I never took a picture of the impression. Anyway, as Ally ran her hand over the marks, she didn't know whether to laugh or cry. I didn't either, and her eyes filled with tears.

I hugged her and said, "The table is now a one of a kind, just like you!" She squeezed me back so hard. It was one of my favorite moments I'll never forget.

Within a few days, Ally's front two teeth began to have a hint of grey. Granted, it wasn't something you could tell unless you were up close or seeing her in a black-and-white photo, like this.

There was worry about her permanent teeth, but what could we do? We needed to wait and see the damage. The family had bets on how long it would take before her front teeth would fall out. Most predicted within days after the accident, but we were all *so* wrong. Those suckers were resilient and didn't fall out till the following summer. It seemed her stubbornness ran literally bone-deep, LOL.

Ally always showed everyone her teeth imprint on the coffee table too, as if it were a rite of passage or something. I think she loved that memory as much as I did.

I continued looking at the photos, and one by one, I smiled more and more. I relived them as if each experience were happening for the first time. As I tapped the screen or touched each one, I saw the mini-movie of each memory. Thankful I took as many as I had, I still wished I'd taken more. It's a shame that I didn't.

When the world went digital, I was sad. It wasn't always as fun as going to Walgreens to develop the photos. Watching Ally open the white envelope and sort through them all and pick her favorites was the best. She would take her time studying each one while tapping her finger on her chin. Ally made that movement all the time. I didn't understand her process or what she was looking for in the photos, but it didn't matter. When Ally finally decided, she was so excited, shaking her pics in my face as if she had discovered lost gold.

The torment of this responsibility destroyed me in every way. I resented that Ally wasn't there to help me choose. It was so fucking hard! Drowning in self-pity, I mumbled over and over, "Why did this have to happen?"

Petra softly interrupted and reminded me that the facility had suggested having about a hundred photos for the slide show. Huh, what would they say if I gave them more? Would they even dare? Screw it! So, I picked what felt right. It happened for a reason, and I didn't have to debate it. I ended up with a little over two hundred, which was good enough.

Finding the songs that embraced Ally's essence wasn't as difficult as I thought it would be. Her playlists were plentiful and eclectic. That girl loved her music! As she got older, it was a rare time when she wasn't wearing her earbuds (or taking selfies with Nikki, or both)!

I decided to use a few of Ally's favorite songs. Why not? It felt right. But which ones? Carving out her pop, rap and Christmas music from her playlist was the easy part. I never understood hearing her singing her beloved "Jingle Bells" in August. Anyway, who knew the song "A Thousand Years" by Christina Perri would be perfect?

The song reminded me of how addicted Ally, Kylie and I were to *The Twilight Saga*. Andy even went to every movie with us. Don't ever let him tell you otherwise. It was cool how he bonded with the girls in that way. Our fun debates of whose "team" we were on brought hours of laughter. Whom did you pick – Edward, Jacob, or Bella?

For every smile, my body stung in pain. I couldn't believe she was gone. As I listened to each word of the famous song, I crumbled. Settling for a healthy compromise, I chose the instrumental version in its place.

The final task was Ally's outfit. It wasn't my intention to put her in a traditional black dress, no way! She would have been so mad because that wasn't her style. It was odd. Why was I thinking of her being present and getting upset by my outfit choice? What a strange emotion to have to work through – that my daughter would hate the dress chosen for her funeral. If only she were still here to get mad. Ugh.

Instead, I chose what she wore for her senior picture because she loved that outfit; I loved it.

Her jeans were in the drawer under a few other pairs. Good grief! I am not sure I realized how tiny she was. Her size-zero pants looked like they belonged to a Cabbage Patch doll. How did she pour her cute bubble butt into those? She could thank Eric for that. Did she have to lie down to zip up these damn things like I sometimes do? I appreciated the giggle.

Ally's zipper boots were in her closet right where she last left them. Perfect! I couldn't help but reminisce when Kylie "stole" them from her closet and wore them to school. Ally was so pissed but felt honored because Kylie's toes must have been smushed since Ally wore only a size six.

Slouching, I knew it was time for the tricky part. I couldn't use Ally's original T-shirt from the photo. Her neck was too swollen and would show. Although she also wore a scarf, it was sheer and wasn't enough. For Christ's sake! Why me?

After wiping my tears, I remembered she had a turtleneck sweater with a similar red color; my idea was brilliant. The scarf would go with it too, phew. When I opened Ally's closet, I didn't expect to smell her still. The perfume she loved mixed with her scent circulated the room, blindsiding me. It was so fresh and real; it was the best and worst feeling.

Embracing her clothes as if they were Ally, I knew the smell wasn't going to last forever. I always made a smart aleck remark at her for spraying too much perfume, yet now I wanted to bottle it up forever. Feeling anxious, I scrambled, looking around her room. Noticing that the Victoria's Secret Island Sun bottle was still pretty full, I fell to the floor, helpless. Why did this have to happen? I bawled my eyes out and wished my life away.

Having two daughters of her own, I couldn't imagine how Petra felt. To my face, she was strong, and when I asked, she was "fine." For a response I've used all the time, I knew better. I could tell this part was challenging for her as well. We squeezed each other as hard as we could, the comfort seeming as though we were sisters.

I hoped she and her girls would never fight again and would hug like never before. Would they become closer than they already were, or would this put distance between them? I still wanted her to share their future family experiences. Did she know that, or would we need to talk about it? What if it made her uncomfortable? Oh, my God! What did I do to deserve this? I was torturing myself; I didn't want to think about it anymore.

After what seemed like the heaviest lifting I'd ever done, I couldn't wait to share everything I'd been through with Andy. When I did, he took me by surprise when he contributed a few final suggestions. They were good ideas, and at least he had one, I guess. But I was bitter that he had an opinion in the first place.

While he and his 26-year-old son Alex (who had flown in that morning) were busy managing all the television media, I was in pure Hell. Yes, I understood that Andy wanted to raise awareness about our story; it made total sense, and I was also glad to see them working together.

But when Andy showed me that Kylie and her friend were also with them touring the local television studio where his cousin worked, my veins filled with jealousy. Sure, she got to laugh as she posed as an anchor – probably a real honor to be on a news set, and it was also perhaps a once-in-a-lifetime opportunity, but still. All I saw was Andy's kids were alive and well, and Ally was gone.

Depending on the second, I felt torn over guilt. It was hard to share Ally, but no one from my family was there! Could I blame them? Was I justifying Andy's participation or the lack of Kylie's? What about Alex? Being mad at the world was my right, and that meant including them. It had to be OK, right? The emotional dysfunction I was experiencing wasn't registering on any barometer I'd known. I made myself sick from all the inner torment. Taking a deep breath, I trusted that my family was showing up in their way and let it go.

We submitted everything to Horan & McConaty. Thank heavens, I could check that off my list. That was absolutely awful, but I was proud of what we had accomplished.

Fatigue was setting in, and I didn't think I could go on. However, being the overachiever I am, I committed to writing and delivering Ally's eulogy. What on Earth was I thinking? Could I stand in the spotlight in front of friends, family, and strangers? Would I be able to profess a lifetime of feelings in only a few minutes?

No one challenged me on my idea, and I was glad. It wasn't a question – the mama bear wanted to protect what I could. It didn't matter the cost. Ally's life ended without my permission; my shared memories of her would end on *my* terms.

With the words flowing like an accomplished screenwriter's, it felt effortless. The narrative was a literary masterpiece. For a second, I patted my back for a job well done and almost kissed the paper. Would Ally be proud of what I had written? I toyed with having someone else read it. But this dedication was my way of being authentic. Suggestions would take that away. Dismissing the idea, I shut down the computer, closed my eyes and sighed until I was blue. As my document hit the floor from the printer, I refused to pick it up. I couldn't stomach what it meant. Glaring at the lifeless paper was a cruel reminder that I'd been preparing for the last time I would "see" her.

Before going to bed, I flipped through the slide show one more time; I had to. I stared at this old, worn photo the longest. It's one of my most favorite – what else is there to say? I kissed Ally goodnight, telling her how much I loved her, and cried myself to sleep.

CHAPTER 6

This Only Happens on TV

JULY 7, 2017

Can I tell you how much I was dreading meeting our district attorney? I am exhausted even now, just thinking about it. After everything I'd gone through that week, I was supposed to learn about the legal process, too? Kick me while I'm down, why don't you? It's not that I didn't appreciate what they would do for us, but my bucket was already full.

Arriving at the large, dull-red brick building, I didn't get a laid-back vibe. Nope, we were in a no-fun zone for sure. I'd seen this building a few times before but never thought anything of it. Who knew that the building with all the colorful flags was where the district attorney worked? There weren't even flowerpots outside – what a lack of curb appeal. The employee parking lot had a six-foot metal fence, and it required a badge for entry. Huh, was it necessary? Seeing that didn't bring me warm-and-fuzzies at all.

In the guest parking lot, my extended family was waiting for us. I don't think any of us said "TGIF" to one another. Although I loved receiving their hugs, I was nervous to see Eric, Ally's biological father. For one, I hadn't seen him in a decade. Two, I didn't know if he blamed me or thought Ally's death was somehow my fault. But I was ready to defend myself to the bitter end.

Would he even have a leg to stand on anyway? A few years after our divorce, the court awarded me full custody of Ally. It wasn't my fault he chose a decade of distance. They reconnected only a few months before Ally died, but I'm happy they did. I can't even imagine the kind of regret he carries over missing out on all those years.

Standing there, awkwardly, I couldn't help feeling sorry for him. Obviously, he was uncomfortable. I took a deep breath and hugged him, trusting it was the right thing to do. He hugged me back and whispered his condolences in my ear. I smiled with relief. It told me everything I needed to know; nothing else needed to be said. We shared a different kind of connection – one I wished we'd had when we were married. As we let go of each other, I grinned, forgetting how short he was.

My family couldn't help themselves. Speculations and theories about arresting Arturo and the court process were flung around like rice at a wedding. I sat in the open hatch of our vehicle, sheltering myself from the chaos. I thought everyone looked silly with their animated hands and heads bobbing. It was a welcomed chuckle, but it didn't help my turning stomach or headache.

Their chatter became quiet and subtle. Something told me to reengage in the conversation. Everyone was staring at one another or looking at the ground. What the hell? Someone might as well start whistling to make it that much more awkward. My family knew something, something they weren't telling me. But what? I didn't want to assume anything. Yet I did know how messed up it was! Did they forget I had mommy senses?

My mother approached me in a rather unexpected way. She handed me a printout published the day before at 1:21 p.m., commanding that I read it. Talk about feeling like a child! What was she thinking? It was a news article about Ally.

Stepping away so I could have some space, I trembled as I held the paper. I didn't even want to read it, but she handed it to me for a reason. I cleared my throat as if I were going to read it out loud. I rolled my eyes and shook my head at myself – God, that was dumb.

At first, I thought it was old news until I read further. My attention came to a screeching halt when a paragraph held details the detectives hadn't shared. What? Ally's purse strap around her neck! Are you *fucking* kidding me? My face turned red with blazing fury, and I covered my mouth with my hand, trying to catch my breath.

Growling, I said, "Ally was strangled with her *accessory*? My poor baby!" I wanted to escape, but where would I go? How could this be happening to me?

I could hardly see through my tears anymore. The blurry words whispered another fact I wasn't ready to process. Caught on surveillance video, Arturo threw away a large pillow in the dumpster – a bloody one! Oh, my God! Whose blood was it? I clenched my jaw extra-hard, hoping it would hurt so I'd feel nothing else. Is that where the blood came from – those marks from Ally's ears? I let the tears run down my face.

Each word I read reaffirmed the betrayal I was trying to deny. I hated it! Ally had no idea what she'd gotten herself into with him. None of us did. Would I even know the signs of what to look for anyway? Would she have listened? I screamed under my breath! Could this article get any worse? My head began throbbing – the pain turned into a migraine. What else could there possibly be? I quivered at the thought of continuing.

I took a double-take at the words and shook my head in disbelief. Arturo did what? What kind of stupid idiot also tosses their probation paperwork in the dumpster? Why would he do something so stupid? That seemed like a real rookie move to me. *Thank you* for leaving behind undeniable evidence, but seriously? Did he think no one would notice or be smart enough to look there? It felt ridiculous, like a bad joke. I couldn't understand why he'd be irresponsible about cleaning up the scene. What if the strangulation was a scare tactic that went too far? Maybe he was in shock? I didn't know, but I'd take it, you son of a bitch!

I put the paper to my chest, counting each breath I took – unable to move. I closed my eyes, thinking it would protect me from the truth. My eyelids fluttered so hard; it made my head hurt even more. How could any of this seem possible?

I felt lightheaded and lost control of my senses. My shorts felt damp. Was it from sweating, or did I wet myself? I couldn't tell you. Every muscle ached as if I had run a marathon. I leaned into my car, trying to find my balance. That motherfucker killed my baby!

Turning my attention to my family, I glared at each one of them, wanting to shoot the target they wore. How long had they known? What assholes! They all know I didn't surf the internet or watch the news. All week, I was contemplating the treachery of Arturo and now my family, too? Could this get any worse? I slammed the papers down in the back of my car and shook my head, mumbling how you shouldn't believe what you read on the damn internet.

Storming to the building, I kept visualizing Ally lying there with her purse next to her. I screamed on the inside! I didn't know whom I should be angrier with – my family or that son of a bitch who killed my daughter! *How am I supposed to meet the attorneys now?*

Talking to the receptionist behind bulletproof glass, I tried my best to be kind. That poor lady didn't deserve the fire-breathing dragon, ready to spew. She escorted us through the high-security building, showing us the dull-looking conference room full of a dedicated team of professionals representing the State of Colorado, ready to fight for Ally. It was reassuring.

Staring at them, I felt underdressed. The lawyers' suits had to come from those fancy stores only high-dollar attorneys can afford. And there I was, a slob in shorts and a T-shirt. At least I had shaved my legs – that felt like a win in my book. It didn't matter, though. I found comfort in bending the bill of my favorite hat. Could I have handled dressing up for an occasion like this? No way! I am sure they didn't care what I looked like anyway. If they did, we had bigger problems.

I couldn't stop thinking about what had happened in the parking lot. I didn't even want to sit by any of my family. What jerks! How could they not tell me about the article sooner? I would have! I tried to have empathy – I really did. That must have been awful to carry such news for however long and not share it with me. Did they have a contest to see who would draw the short straw or what? It wasn't fair to any of us to be in this situation. I compartmentalized my anger, trying to focus, but it was hopeless. This room was the last place I wanted to be for so many different reasons.

When I re-read this section today, I knew my family was looking out for me, but it didn't matter – I still carried anger for quite a while. Hindsight is, unfortunately, only good if you've had the experience to look back on. It wasn't until I saw "A Beautiful Day in the Neighborhood" with Tom Hanks for my dad's birthday sometime later that my eyes opened like never before. Maybe if I'd seen it before this meeting, I would have been more open-minded.

Hearing the quote: "Anything that's human is mentionable, and anything mentionable can be more manageable" changed me.

What a beautiful sentiment to remind me to still love those around me despite what had happened. I knew what I needed and wanted to do; it was time. I could finally let go of my resentment, and that was a beautiful gift. Thank you, Dad – and *Mr. Rogers.*

Circling back to the team, they explained the legal process while giving detailed instructions. For the love of God – come on! I don't speak "lawyerese." Could someone dumb this shit down? I watched my family nod their heads, and I wondered if they got it and I was the only one who didn't. All I gathered at that point was that we were in for a long ride and a bumpy one.

The lawyers explained that Arturo was "presumed" to have fled to another country. Huh, that was fast! They then described the process of extradition and court. I wanted to throw up. It had so many different variables, much like paranormal phenomena. Not to mention, the length of the court process ensured that I'd need a walker by the time it concluded. *I'm sorry, where's the positive?*

Wrapping up the meeting, the lawyers asked me if I had any questions. I had only one, and it wasn't about Arturo or the crime itself. All I wanted was to have Ally's ring back. Nothing else mattered to me. I could only imagine what family or the lawyers would think of me, but I didn't care.

One year earlier, Andy and I had renewed our vows for our tenth anniversary. After deciding to upgrade my ring, we gave Ally and Kylie an identical white diamond band from my original set. Ally wore this ring *every* single day. She cherished it more than anything I'd ever seen. It was the only valuable item she didn't pawn during her relationship with Arturo. It meant the world to me that she didn't budge no matter how many times he threatened to break up with her about paying his bills. When she promised to keep it safe and take care of it, she meant it. My sweet baby was wearing it when she died.

Speaking up, I asked our district attorney if I could have Ally's ring back. He was clueless about the value it symbolized for me. How could he know? Looking around at his team, he cleared his throat. He explained that her ring was considered evidence, and if the legal team requested it to be released, it could impede the case. Holding back my tears, I didn't want that, but for fuck's sake! Why does everyone in a suit have such a damn callous tone?

Everything felt hopeless at that moment. Sighing, I somehow felt appreciative that the police at least had Ally's ring. They'd better take care of it and not lose it as we see in the movies. But what if they did? Suing them wouldn't get her ring back. And then I'd be without my daughter and her ring! I absolutely despised this entire situation inside and out – I'd never felt so trapped in all my life.

I WAS CONVINCED THE UNIVERSE WAS PICKING ON ME. I'D HIT AN ultimate low and didn't see how there could ever be a light at the tunnel's end. How could I? One after another, each day gave me a new weight to carry, heavier than before. The strength I once thought I had as a mother was no match for the week I'd been through.

After seeing the lawyers, our lead detective greeted us when we arrived home. Shit! I'd forgotten he was coming over at two o'clock. Was it afternoon already? "He'd better have only good news for me." My inner voice screamed in fear of another gut punch.

Sitting down, he wanted to go over the specifics (that he could) with me. Surprisingly, I got good vibes from him right off the bat. A bit reserved, but I could tell he had a funny side. No matter what he did, I saw Will Ferrell, so Detective Ferrell he'll be.

His first words of advice to me were to be myself – I'll never forget him saying that. Was it training, or was he just that intuitive? It's like he handed me a flashlight to find my way in my nightmare, I couldn't believe it. My ego was also ecstatic, and the gloves were off. I don't remember the first joke I made, but Detective Ferrell laughed. He didn't seem to mind my off-color humor. The jokes helped break down the barriers for a little while anyway.

As I tried to comprehend each word he said, they bounced off more than anything. I explained being at the District Attorney's Office a mere hour ago, and my tiny sponge was already full. He understood what I meant, thank God. But what was important was hearing the melody of his tone, and it was full of passion for solving my case – that's all I wanted.

After a few minutes, I then told him about Ally's ring. He got choked up – I didn't expect that. I could see he understood why I wanted it documented with the lawyers and with him. He opened his letter-size binder and made a note. I joked that I was disappointed he didn't pull out a pocket-size scratchpad from his inner jacket and flip the black leather top over to take my note. We laughed.

As Detective Ferrell was leaving, I mentioned the news article. My intention wasn't to be a bitch, not at all. Only to say I thought learning about Ally's purse should have been shared in person. Acting astonished, he asked where I had heard that. I pulled up the website as if I held some kind of power. He turned to his partner (not Detective Bullock), observed from the corner, and excused themselves outside. I didn't understand, but I knew it couldn't be a good thing.

Upon their return, both of their faces were pale white. I didn't know what that meant. Sitting me down again, Detective Ferrell began apologizing. He explained that the details about Ally's purse and the pillow shouldn't have been public knowledge, and he'd had no idea they'd been published. I didn't know what to say. Well, that's not true, but I bit my tongue. *If this could happen with police paperwork, what's to say that Ally's ring is safe?* I wanted to punch anything, everything.

Now standing, he assured me that he and his team would get to the bottom of it. I wanted to believe him. I did. As I held in my tears, he then stated his apprehension about how this development could affect the investigation. Completely stunned, I shifted my irritation to the media. What assholes! I didn't think of that! What if it did compromise the investigation? Was their big story more important than the case? Who would leak such a thing – and why would someone take it? All stupid questions: I already knew the answers. How am I supposed to trust a penetrable system? For Christ's sake! It was turning out to be like the movies after all.

As they left, I barricaded myself in my bedroom for the rest of the night, scrambling for clarity. These past few days had been the absolute worst I'd ever experienced. I struggled with mean thoughts, but that wasn't me. Some even scared me. I'd never been so angry before. I had to believe that this was a normal reaction. Let's be real. There is *no way* even Buddha could handle any of this shit.

After a worthless shower, heading to bed, I snagged the crocheted part of my favorite slipper on the door handle to the cabinet under the television. Shrugging, about to cry, I screamed in my hands, "Could anything else go fucking wrong today?"

Untangling the knitting with care, I opened the drawer. Huh, there was the journal I received from a friend umpteen years ago – and I just stared at it. Since our move, I hadn't seen that book, and I certainly didn't remember putting it there. It felt like it was begging me to open it. I touched the cover and felt the beautiful binding. There was even a pen next to it. Well, that seemed convenient. I took out the journal and got into bed.

I turned on the television, and my favorite movie of all-time was playing. With joy, I said, "Hello, Ripley, I'm glad you're here."

It seemed an odd coincidence that the movie *Aliens* would be on when I needed it the most. After I turned the volume to low on the television, the room felt peaceful and relaxed. Flipping through the book, seeing all the blank pages, I didn't know where to begin. What if my family read my entries? Would they judge me? Then what?

Would they hold it against me if I said something about them? I was all over the place, scared and confused. Fiddling with the pen made me feel better.

At that moment, the most epic line of all time played. "Get away from her, you bitch." I, of course, smiled.

For whatever reason, I then felt more open to the idea. I knew I needed to do something – anything healthy would help. What could it hurt? It wasn't like Andy was a snooper; you didn't even need to hide things from him. He's the guy who can't find the ketchup in plain sight on the fridge door. Kylie was too busy hiding in her room to go hunting through mine. Deciding I could let go of my fear and not worry about anything else, I began journaling.

CHAPTER 7

Diamonds in the Rough

JULY 8, 2017

I woke up with the worst pillow face ever. Having never had such deep impressions before, on some level I thought it was impressive. And yet when I touched them, they confirmed the dark, winding maze I'd been through.

Walking downstairs, I finally felt refreshed. It was about damn time. The morning felt like any other until I saw the mess from the night before in the kitchen. Nope, there wasn't any waking up from my nightmare. Ally's reminders surrounded me at every step, with every sense. How could I even forget I was living one?

Seeing Alex sleeping on the couch, looking like his dad all sprawled out, made me smile. I wished he lived closer. We were more like good friends than anything. I adored Alex's southern charm, despite the fact his sometimes-slow drawl and choice of words cracked me up. He and I have shared redneck jokes in a way that others would frown upon — we've never cared if we crossed the line. We know it is in good fun.

Finding him a blanket, I became distracted, remembering how much he loved torturing the girls. They were *so* excited when he would visit, but they were begging for him to leave within days. Like clockwork, the girls would try to gang up on him with their concocted ideas, but they were always short-lived. At least they worked together. Alex would then retaliate as big brothers do, and the girls would end up crying every time. My heart warmed a little. Man, those were some good times. I loved all the shit they gave each other.

Sitting in my office, I looked at the day's schedule. Some of the events I was looking forward to more than others. Petra's ex-husband, still a close family friend, booked a paddleboard experience at Cherry Creek State Park. Some much-needed girl time was about to happen with Kylie, Amy, and Petra. The gesture was more than thoughtful, and yet I was also confused. Was this kind of an adventure unusual for such an occasion? I can't say I've seen that in any movie.

Andy and Alex were going to hang out with the boys. Who knew what that meant? Paintball, probably. Maybe some shooting would do them good. Unless it turns into their usual pissing match over who's better; that's all we need.

As the ladies and I headed out, we stopped at Starbucks. Following my typical Saturday routine, I appreciated feeling "normal." For the first time all week, it felt like I could relax. While waiting for our coffee, we realized none of us had gone paddleboarding before. It was exciting to think we would create a new memory together while honoring Ally.

Reaching the beach area in the park was a bit nerve-wracking. The lake has a reputation for its dirty water – it's super-gross. The thought of digesting goose poop made me feel a little green. I couldn't wait to see who would fall in first and have some extra fiber in their diet. My money was on Kylie.

As we stood in a horseshoe formation surrounding our adorable instructor, I took in her instructions. She gave us the option to wear the life jacket or strap it to the board. Not being a strong swimmer, I didn't hesitate. I slapped the vest on as tight as it could go. There was no way I was falling in! I wasn't about hanging out with the fishes.

After the safety presentation ended, our purpose for being there came up. The bubbly instructor called out what seemed likely reasons.

"Birthday, anniversary or special event?" she asked.

My heart dropped – what was I supposed to do? I heard the other groups shout their responses, but I didn't know what to say. Usually quick-witted, I panicked; nothing came to mind. Amy didn't hesitate, though.

She replied with a gentle smile, "We are present for a life celebration." Her response created an uneasy, quiet pause among the crowd. Stunned, even I was a little embarrassed. Embracing the moment, I closed my eyes. In the past week, I could see only my awful nightmare about Ally's death. But Amy's words made me see something else, something *beautiful*.

Instead of continuing to mourn, we were there to celebrate Ally's life, an amazing one at that. I sighed in appreciation – receiving a wonderful gift. Feeling everyone staring at me, no one else existed for that second. I was in a place of serenity. Opening my eyes, I gave her a look of gratefulness while gesturing my hand over my heart. Confused, the instructor grinned, signaling at her watch, and herded us to the water.

Paddling out from the beach was pure comedy. None of us knew what we were doing. Amy even attempted a few yoga poses – she looked so dorky. We had to see who could stand up first. Bragging rights are a big deal, you know. Having a new appreciation for balance, I could get upright easier than anticipated. Everyone else's success wasn't as graceful as mine, not even a little. It felt so good to laugh that hard.

Finding my rhythm, I paddled ahead from the group for some alone time. I sat on the board with my legs dangling in the cold water, observing the birds chirping, fish jumping and the calming silence in between. Soaking in the warm sun from the cloudless sky, I felt joy. Giggling, I also felt sunburned and wondered about my sunscreen situation. The slight breeze created a euphoric sensation that cooled every inch of my body, allowing me to forget my story for a while.

Where did the hour go? Sad that our epic adventure was coming to an end, I sighed. Heading back, we found ourselves racing one another. I loved the unintentional competition as I brought up the rear. As usual, my cockiness got the better of me. Not paying attention to my form, I began to lose my balance, and I rocked back and forth, praying for a miracle. Within a second, I fell in and gulped the poopy goose water. It was disgusting.

Squeezing my vest like a lifeline, I bobbed along, looking around. Did anyone see what happened? Holy shit! I couldn't believe I'd fallen in. Naturally, my paddle looked miles away, and my favorite hat sank in the other direction. I first rescued my hat, giving my best impression of a drunken dogpaddle. Managing to catch my breath, I made my way to the paddle that somehow stayed afloat. Jesus, I was out of shape. Fearing that the "Jaws" theme music was imminent, I pulled myself back onto the board as fast as possible. Then, paddling as if I had a motor, I hoped my speed would dry my clothes before making it to the shore.

Approaching the beach, Kylie motioned that the instructor would take our photo. Dang, how did she get there so fast? I thought it was a super-cool idea until I realized how shameful I felt. I had no choice but to swallow my bruised ego and confess why my clothes were wet. Damn it! I couldn't believe I was the one to fall in. Although, I was glad I could provide a joke at my expense – you're welcome, jerks. LOL.

Exchanging several photos, we noticed a shimmer in one of them. Could it be real? No way! It was absolutely breathtaking. My eyes filled with tears, and I cried. Without words, we all knew it was Ally.

I couldn't believe it – she was there with us! Having an epiphany, I shook my head in disbelief. It was *Ally* who pushed me off my board. That little shit! Even in death, she had a sense of humor and was still a practical joker. What a true testament of her being able to "dish it." She played this to her advantage, though, because in real life she wasn't so great at "taking it." I smiled ear to ear like a proud mama, and so did my inflated ego.

Walking back to the car, I couldn't find my words. I didn't want the moment to end. I couldn't wait to share what had happened but also had reservations as to whether others would believe me. What asshole would dare question my experience? What would I say if someone did? I went from zero to sixty, feeling anxious instead of embracing what I'd just experienced.

On the way home, my worries still consumed me. The last few days had proved nothing but a whirlwind of constant chaos. For every moment that I felt a tiny bit of happiness, sadness stopped it in its tracks. Why did Ally have to die? What did I do to deserve such agony? Realizing how much I smelled like swamp water, I became appreciative of my awful reeking odor. I needed a distraction from my inner turmoil.

UNSURE OF WHAT I WAS EXPERIENCING, EVERY SENSATION I FELT WAS ALL wrong. My racing heart competed with my breathing, and focusing was impossible. Maybe it was a panic attack or perhaps a nervous breakdown. Great – that's all I needed. I didn't know how I would make it through the night. Why did I want to have a public viewing again?

Dreading what was about to happen, I was afraid to ask my family for help. It's not like they' undergone anything like this either, not that I knew of, anyway. For the love of God! *When are things going to feel easy?*

Watching the time get too close for comfort, I slapped my reflection in the mirror, and screamed at myself to pull it together. Not even kidding – I swore I saw myself flinch. After wiping my tears and clearing my throat, doing what I do best, I hid my pain and headed to the car.

We arrived at Horan & McConaty early. Alice advised it was customary for the family to view their loved one before anyone else. My legs felt hard, as if encapsulated in cement. Each step I took counted the seconds until my time with Ally "in person" would be over. Why did this have to happen to her? We'd never get to make any new memories together. Why would anyone take that from me?

Making my way to her open coffin, I sank; seeing her motionless body again was dreadful. My family and I surrounded her, and we sobbed. I felt everyone's love for my baby as we stood united. It was strange how comforting brushing hips could be as we passed tissues.

Glancing through my tears at Ally's overall presentation, I was impressed. Not only did she look close to her senior photo, but the outfit I picked out was also flattering – it hid her wounds well. What can I say? I gave myself a high-five.

As everyone stared at Ally, they nodded with heavy hearts. It didn't take long for my mom to speak up, noticing Ally's hair had changed since her private viewing – it was now back to blonde. Finding the courage to share, I spoke about our first meeting with Alice.

I told her that Ally, in spirit, wished to color her hair back to blonde. When she and Arturo were dating, he disapproved of an artificial look. He believed in only natural beauty (I did appreciate that). When he got arrested and went to jail, Ally felt empowered to rebel and have fun. Not only did she get her rose tattoo, but she was also adamant about dying her hair red. Ally asked for my help to color it. How could I say no?

I shared how Alice touched my hand and nodded with a smile. She then mentioned feeling a connection to Ally because her son had gone to school with Ally; they were friends. How small is this world? I knew at that very moment Ally had brought us together. Damn, that kid of mine is the best! Alice gracefully agreed to accommodate Ally's request; I felt a huge weight lifted. She also suggested I replace her glasses since her own were with the police. And if possible, an identical matching pair would help complete her look, I agreed.

Petra and I visited Sally Beauty Supply. The employees were more than helpful. I showed them a photo of Ally, and they recognized her from the news and insisted on providing all the bleaching products at no cost. No way! I was speechless. I didn't feel judged; they didn't even whisper to one another. These girls were young – how did they know such sympathy? I felt like an ass for thinking most millennials were jerks. Happy to be wrong, we walked out of the store with new hope for humanity.

Walmart Vision Center was also kind. Reaching the counter, I gave them Kylie's name first – she had new glasses to pick up too. Nothing like two birds with one stone. The gal turned pale and began to stutter. Huh, she turned to her co-worker, who was the manager, and pointed at the screen. She approached me and apologized for our situation, saying she saw our story on social media. Are you shitting me? I had no idea.

I didn't know what to do. Did I need to go into detail about why I was there? Is this when less is more? Going with it, I explained only how I needed Ally's exact frames. Without question, she didn't hesitate. She found them with such ease as if they called to her. Her kindness didn't stop there – she gave them to me at a reduced cost. I cried, thankful for their generosity.

My family wept from my story; their tears were full of love. I then gave the caretakers of Horan & McConaty some praise. Ally appeared as herself for the most part. Between you and me, she could have passed as a wax figure from Madame Tussauds. Nonetheless, it was clear that they had compassion for Ally. Even the press-on nails were a nice touch. I never understood the challenges they face, and now I'm forever in their debt.

Ending with a fun fact from Alice, I shared that it took the staff *five* attempts to bleach Ally's hair back to blonde; it wasn't perfect, but close enough. Brushing Ally's hair aside, I pointed out the damaged ends of her hair underneath her neck.

Laughing, I said, "Good thing, she won't mind." I made the ba-dum-ch sound while playing my imaginary drum set. Was my joke too soon? I didn't think so. Neither did my family.

For whatever reason, I looked away for only a second and heard giggling. I turned with curiosity to notice that someone (I'll leave the culprit anonymous) from our family had added their pink lip gloss – it was the plumping kind. They were obviously hoping to make her shriveled lips fuller. Everyone pointed fingers at one another while smiling with bashful faces. Perhaps Ally whispered this idea to "whomever" because her girlie side would have wanted to look her best, I don't know, and it didn't matter – it was one of my favorite moments, and I'll never forget it.

While guests arrived, my family was greeting their cliques. It sadly reminded me of my high school reunion – total yuck. Out of my element, I sat on the bench alone. I don't thrive in large groups. I'd prefer to observe from a corner. I debated finding refuge in the back-family room; however, a few familiar faces stood before me. Blasts from the past were here! Words were hard to find, and I didn't know what to do. The power of social media carries such amazement; I'll never understand it.

Hugging these lost treasures, I cried. I wanted to catch up as if our relationships had never lapsed. But this gathering wasn't about getting reacquainted. The purpose of our reconnection smacked me in the face as I received their condolences.

I didn't think I could be humble in such loss' depths, but I knew Ally had brought these people to me. I knew she would want me to receive as much love as possible. I knew she was everywhere and she was in everything we did that day. And yet, I still struggled to find words. Shrinking and becoming embarrassed, I trusted they could feel my heartstrings strumming a melody of thankfulness.

A few people were apprehensive about coming up to me; they whispered among one another, not noticing I was aware. Did they think they would catch what I had, or did they not know the right words? I felt like an outcast again.

It didn't help that strangers were also introducing themselves left and right. It's like they were compelled to share their memorable experiences about Ally. Yes, hearing that everyone had a similar opinion, using the keywords: "most outgoing," "trendsetter," and " her sense of humor" warmed my heart. But at the same time, I felt obligated to listen while my boundaries stretched. Because in some instances, they were sobbing even more than me, and I was consoling them!

After ping-ponging through emotions; I was exhausted. I couldn't find my ground; I was adrift without an anchor. How was I going to survive another service? The idea of it made me ill. I had no clue the viewing would challenge me in so many ways. How did the event shift to being for everyone else? Was I their host? Maybe I was subconsciously addressing my tendency to take care of others – who knows. But what I did know is that I just wanted the night to end.

CHAPTER 8

The Silent Party Guest

JULY 9, 2017

There wasn't enough Starbucks in the world to make me smile that morning. I'm not even sure that winning the lotto would put a dent in my inner misery. My mind was mush. I didn't remember getting ready for the service or how I made it to the car. I felt like I was somehow outside of myself and watching all of this happen from somewhere else. It's probably a defense mechanism, but it was still scary not remembering the things I'd done moments before.

Arriving at Horan & McConaty, we noticed a posted VIP parking sign for us. Huh, it was a considerate gesture for what felt like a red-carpet appearance. Thank goodness I wore my sparkly black dress – it was supposed to be a celebration, after all.

As we walked up the steps in slow motion, the staff eagerly awaited our arrival. I sighed. It was a cover-up to the tantrum I kept at bay. I had no idea how I'd make it through this. The clock would tick regardless of how I felt, but each second, I wanted to die. After taking our coats, the staff members escorted us to the family room. Geez – we really were like real celebrities.

Debbie, our officiant, would be conducting the service. She was a spunky mature lady sporting a fiery orange pixie and red lipstick. Without a doubt, Ally would have loved to go shopping with her. But I wondered what others would think of her. She didn't have a traditional stuffy funeral look about her at all. Honestly, I didn't care – I loved it.

Her résumé was plentiful, and she was perfect for assisting in our celebration. Her background included being a domestic-violence counselor, and she specialized in traumas.

Having a quick discussion, we agreed on the direction we wanted to go. I appreciated Debbie's adaptability – it was a foreign concept for me to have support like this. Still, her compassionate nature allowed me to lower my guard – I felt safe and relaxed by her side. It certainly wasn't a typical response for me, especially with a stranger. There was something special about her.

My stomach was in knots; it was time to begin the service. I tried smiling, but once Andy took my hand, I crumbled, and he led me to my seat. Not only were the benches full like a can of sardines, but guests lined the walls shoulder to shoulder, and participants were standing outside.

Among the guests was Andy's cousin, covering our story for a local news station. Why didn't Andy tell me he'd be here? Or maybe he did and I didn't hear him. Torn – I wanted to support his idea, and yet I didn't want media people there. Can't anything be intimate? Not knowing how to feel, I focused on all the caring humans (and our dog) present for Ally's life celebration.

Debbie began her sermon, and her beautiful messages carried throughout the room. The crying was infectious as it echoed from the intended audience. Intimidated, I feared following such an influential introduction.

Within minutes, it was my time to address Ally's eulogy. Andy stood next to me on his own accord. Relief enveloped me because I didn't have to ask. Searching the room for Ally among the crowd, I hoped to see her nod her head. She wasn't there.

Trying to find my bearings, I adjusted the podium's microphone and wondered if I should visualize everyone naked. Isn't that what you're supposed to do to calm down before giving a speech? The thought was fleeting (thank goodness – no offense to anyone who attended), and I cleared my throat.

I read every word as a proud mama would. Since Ally's death, it was the first time I had felt strong – empowered, even. My words painted my picture. Speaking with conviction and passion, I shared my thoughts, my way, uninterrupted. My eulogy read:

"Thank you for being here to honor Ally's Life Celebration. Over the past decade, I have grown quite accustomed to large gatherings for Ally's amazing accomplishments because of our blended family. Today, for me, especially acknowledges how large Ally's family really is.

Like any parent, I could mention a gazillion proud moments. Still, some of my favorites: earning her white-belt ceremony in karate, her numerous gymnastics recitals and her own choreographed cameo with Aurora Dance, Ally NOT trying out for 'American Idol' (I did you all a favor), and most recently her high school graduation. Not celebrated yet: Ally's acceptance to join the U.S. Navy to deploy in January.

For Ally's birthday parties, I often felt we needed a bigger house because of all the family and friends bumping elbows. Still, Ally insisted on having at least part of her party at home, and I didn't always understand but agreed. For Ally's 18th birthday, our house was packed up for our move, and she chose the Golden Corral. (I was sure that's NOT a suggestion on Pinterest for the big 18, but that's my Ally.) After our breakfast, she shared her party was good, and I asked, 'Not great?' She replied it wasn't the same as being at home – at that moment, I truly understood what she meant.

I know that Ally wholeheartedly is and will continue to be grateful for being surrounded by so many remarkable friends and family. Today, as her mother, I want to thank you each personally for taking the time to honor my special lady once again.

Moving forward, I will take Ally with me on new experiences, find confidence and strength when there are challenges, and, most importantly, to continue to love. Ally will want all of us to continue with practical jokes, find ways to better ourselves, give back to others and simply laugh. Let's together fulfill her wishes because she IS watching over all of us. Thank you"

I couldn't wait to sit down after placing the paddleboard picture in Ally's casket. Exhaustion took over. Public speaking is, for sure, not on my list of favorite activities.

Debbie then introduced Maddie to the podium. Shit! How could I forget? As she walked up, I took a breath, and Amy and I stood next to her. Maddie carried such worry that the world was mad at her (some had even blamed her for Ally's death). It was my way of sending a critical message to the public about my everlasting support for her.

Maddie opened her paper; she hadn't prepared a speech, and there were only a few jotted notes. At first, I wasn't sure if that was a good idea, but I trusted she'd speak from her heart.

Standing there, she looked so frail, so nervous. Giving her a little squeeze, I reminded her I was there. After that, she didn't hesitate and began her beautiful dedication to Ally:

"Ally was the kind of person who always wanted to be strong. She constantly sought strength and sought to be the pillar of light for those in the dark. And of the many lessons and the experiences she instilled in me, I remember three the most.

One, never be afraid to love yourself. Like many times in our lives, Ally had trouble loving herself in certain moments. And, to remember that you are enough. You are loved, and you deserve all the love in the world, and no one can ever take that away from you.

Second, to be grateful for things every day. Write three things down that you are grateful for every day, whether it be the sun, the clouds, and a simple bug on the sidewalk that made your day maybe a little brighter.

And the third is to celebrate life every day. Celebrate old life, celebrate new life, celebrate the present, and always know that you are loved, and thank you for showing the love and support in being here for Ally today."

Peering out to the crowd, I wanted Maddie to receive a standing ovation. Was that wrong? I knew people wouldn't clap, but hopefully their positive energy would embrace her like a hug. I was so proud of her for being brave. Everything she said was so spot-on about Ally, too. What I loved most was hearing about writing down what you are grateful for as an exercise. I'd brought home this idea not that long ago, and for Ally to share it with her best friend touched my heart. My God, Ally really did listen to me for once! I couldn't be happier at that moment.

I hugged Maddie, and there was some shuffling to get seated. Surprised that Amy stayed at the podium, I saw her pull out her paper. She too was trembling, but her appearance was confident and rather composed. She spoke for work all the time, but I was a little taken aback. Perhaps because this was more personal, it made her uneasy. It made sense. Smiling to the audience, she delivered this lovely dedication to Ally:

"My Perfect Pumpkin. My absolute favorite memory with my two favorite nieces was taking them to Anderson Farms for our annual pumpkin patch day. It would start with us stopping for Starbucks to grab your favorite Frappuccino. Don't forget the extra whipped cream, please! We would sip on our frappes while the cool aunt played some probably not age-appropriate rap music! Then we spent the day in hayrides, barrel rides, farm-animal feedings, corn mazes, and the finale – picking out the perfect pumpkin in that huge pumpkin patch.

Watching you smile in amazement of all the pumpkins lights my heart. Ally, you will always be my perfect pumpkin. 'Beauty is not in the face; beauty is a light in the heart' – Kahlil Gibran.

I would like to say to my brother and sister-in-law that my heart goes with you. You are to be commended that you raised such a beautiful daughter. I hope the presence of the people who are here today proves to you the high regard in which she is held in this community. She made a difference. She touched our hearts.

My prayer is that your grief might move through you gently. May you hold in your minds forever the truth we know today: Ally lives in the arms and in the mind of the universe. Keep your hearts and minds open to receive her. She shall yet communicate her love for you, for she lives on in spirit and shall never be forgotten. I love you! Live, Love, Laugh.

Man's inhumanity to man is the hardest to understand on this planet and definitely when it impacts someone you love and someone so innocent and so beautiful. I am holding the love and light for justice and always believing that it will happen in this lifetime or in the next that justice will be served. We are in a very just and loving universe. Heal the past, live the present, dream the future!"

I squeezed Andy's hand, and my eyes filled with tears. It felt like only yesterday I was listening to Ally share her adventures at that pumpkin patch. The memory made me smile. I dabbed my eyes with care, realizing I wasn't wearing waterproof mascara. What was I thinking? Of all the times I could forget such a thing! Jesus! What an idiot! Even though I knew Ally would be laughing at me, I needed to learn how to give myself a break.

Kylie approached the podium, inviting Ally's older half-sister, Becca, to join her. I was so glad she came. I didn't get to see her as often as I'd like once Eric and I divorced. Although because of Barb's dedication, our paths would cross when she'd take the girls for a grandma weekend or summer getaways.

I remember like it was yesterday when Eric's younger sister, Kristin, got married. Andy, Kylie, Ally, and I were all invited to attend. Becca took Kylie under her wing as her sister, too. They were the cutest trio I'd ever seen, running around like best friends the entire night. I knew that day it didn't matter who came from what mother or father. They bonded in a way that kept them connected through the years.

Seeing Becca again, I was full of questions and concerns. How would her life be affected? Would she stay connected to Kylie still? Was her last time spent with Ally a good one? What if they were fighting? If anything, I hoped that Becca knew how much Ally adored her big sister.

I could see that Becca was shy and hesitant to join Kylie, creating giggles from the audience. It didn't matter to me, though. I welcomed smiling. It looked like unprepared stage fright – can you blame her? It was more than obvious they didn't plan this together. Kylie was looking for support and put Becca on the spot, but she joined her anyway. Standing together, they held hands. Their bravery was evident as Kylie delivered her dedication:

"For Ally. I want to first start by saying thank you to everyone who has come to support my family and me today, as well as those that have sent food and flowers to our house. My family appreciates everyone's generosity so much.

Ally had such a contagious smile and a way of getting people to laugh. Ally, although she made some mistakes (just like I have too – trust me, you can ask my parents), she was my biggest role model. She always had a helping hand and wanted the best for everyone and made sure that everyone was taken care of.

What saddens me the most is knowing that in the future, when the time comes that she will not be in the audience of my high school graduation waiting for me to walk out with my diploma, getting to see me start college and experience things like being an aunt to my future kids or being by my side if I chose to get married. She also doesn't get to experience those monumental life moments herself and travel the world like she wanted to. I know that even though she isn't physically here in person, she will always be by my side in heart and in spirit.

Just a few days before Ally passed away, she pulled me aside to have a conversation, and she told me that one day she wouldn't always be around to take care of my parents and me and when she wasn't, that job would become mine. She told me she knew I would do a great job; I just never expected that job to start so soon, but I will not let her down.

I will miss the moments where we didn't get along and had stupid fights over things that didn't matter because, at that moment, I knew we were together. I miss her so much, and I will miss so much about her, and I know everyone else will too.

I believe that this experience will open everyone's eyes, teach us how important and precious time and family are. I miss you so much, Ally, and I hope you are flying high and resting in peace. Thank you."

Kylie's words were touching. I was unaware she'd put a tribute together; it was incredible. Whispering to Andy, I asked if he knew anything about it, and he confirmed he didn't. I knew she meant every word; I was so proud of her.

I was thankful she could express what Ally meant to her in this horrific tragedy. I wanted to thank her somehow for the gift that she didn't even know she'd given me. The relationship between her and Ally was more like frenemies. But when the hair-pulling was over, they were sisters, and it filled me with love and happiness to see that bond. As her stepmom, it was an honor to witness.

As they both returned to their seats, I became distracted by Ally's Navy recruiter approaching us. He presented me with the United States flag – a most thoughtful ceremonious gesture as Ally hadn't even served yet.

Ally had only recently committed to join the Navy, after all. Ally desired to serve and protect. It was (and still is) her mission to look out for everyone else. She was so excited when she enlisted. Nonstop, she wouldn't quit talking about boot camp and her future travels. She couldn't wait to see other countries and for us to visit her. Without a doubt, it was to be a new and exciting chapter for her after a complicated relationship with Arturo.

It felt strange to receive such a prestigious award on her behalf. As if Ally's desires to help people would somehow become my responsibility – so her death wasn't in vain.

I laid the flag in my lap in awe. Accompanied by the recruiter were three retired veterans. Did they even know Ally? They wore their uniforms and accomplished medals with pride. It was beautiful as they ceremoniously saluted Ally as their own. I knew she would have loved that. Their contribution truly made her celebration special.

Debbie resumed her position and continued her sermon. Her words were powerful, and they shook the room (in the right way). She was wise and respectable. That lady had a skill for keeping the attention of the room; it was impressive.

With that said, I did tune her out at times, focusing on the weeping I heard. I was so humbled to have been a mother to such an awesome kid. Better said, Ally may have been a kid in so many ways, yet her maturing independence turned her into a young lady. One who had influenced so many.

As we watched the slide show, I tried to be fearless. Proud to see Ally's growth through the sequential photos. What parent wouldn't be? Being reminded, again, I would never get to create a new memory with Ally (the way I was accustomed) was shattering. I tried practicing gratitude as the pictures were advancing, but I couldn't hold my head high.

It didn't help seeing Ally on display in her open casket. Not because I chose it, because we were here in the first place. Why did this have to happen to her? Struggling with back-and-forth emotions, I wasn't even sure I had names for them all. What I did know was that I was becoming exhausted by the second. Each moment seemed filled with a lifetime of memories, happiness, pain, and agony.

Stuck in anger, I inwardly growled. I didn't understand how only days ago I wasn't that upset when I put this slide show together. So why now? Was the numbness lifting? Weak and dizzy, I questioned whether this was what grief felt like.

As the last instrumental song, "Happy" by Pharrell Williams, played, I sighed in relief. Did anyone notice the music? Would they think it was in poor taste? I couldn't imagine hanging out any longer, and yet we still had the celebratory reception to attend.

Alice escorted us to the reception building (across the parking lot). I looked for the paparazzi. Was I going crazy? Yep. I thought so. Greeting the staff, I saw that they were beyond polite. I quickly excused myself and raced to the bathroom. My makeup was still intact; I couldn't believe it. I had no idea how it stayed put. After taking a few deep breaths, I peeked at my watch and promised myself that I was leaving early. For once, I wasn't going to stay to the bitter end of an event and help clean up.

I made a small plate of appetizers and sat in the corner. Petra and her family were by my side, and my family was nowhere in sight. The room began to fill, and my heart raced. Guests surrounded me like cattle within seconds. I felt like I was on a pedestal, but not the right kind.

One by one, it was a never-ending shower of condolences. Same as the night before, my boundaries stretched beyond comfort. I listened intently and tried to smile as guests shared so many lovely memories. Of course, there were – my kid is incredible.

My attention span was fading fast, so I encouraged guests to put their thoughts on Ally's memory-box cards. I wasn't sure where the confidence came from to direct them, but I was relieved.

A natural breaking point presented itself. My co-workers took me outside for fresh air, and I admired the cremation gardens with them. In my silence, I wondered when I would find the courage to dismiss myself on my own – hopefully, sooner than later. It was a nice change of scenery, though.

At that point, I would have preferred to discuss work gossip anyway. We did exchange a few stories of what I'd missed; I loved the distraction. Those lighter moments were exactly what I needed.

Walking around the gardens, I felt more at ease under the warm sun. I pointed out all the beautiful flowers surrounding each engraved brick along the pathway. The choices to design them seemed endless. We saw some with quotes, and others with butterflies and flowers.

They gazed in amazement. I then showed them that Ally's brick with her name and the quote "I Am Enough" would be at the entrance of the pergola that takes you to the serine Coy Pond. They smiled at my choice.

The crowd was winding down, and I avoided socializing as much as possible. I didn't keep that stupid promise I made to myself about leaving early. Damn it! Reluctant, I asked the staff if they needed help cleaning up. The manager was quick to dismiss my assistance. Thank God, I dodged a bullet there!

As I was grabbing my things, the crew stopped me. They gestured to the bouquets and house plants decorating the room behind me. I didn't understand. They explained that they were all gifts and we needed to take them home. Are you serious? What was the point of giving clear directions not to send them then? Why don't people listen?

The thoughtful gesture felt more like a trick to test my patience for humanity. What the hell? My stress level was already through the roof. The staff must have recognized my inner turmoil and smiled. They offered that we could donate the foliage. What? I had no clue. A group that worked with the facility would take them to hospitals and nursing homes. Melting at the thought that other people could receive enjoyment from them, I cried.

Thinking I was in the clear, my mom assured me I could manage to keep a few alive. Ugh. I felt pressured. Begrudgingly, I picked out a few smaller plants to take home. For crying out loud, when will I learn to stand up for myself?

Heading back into the room where Ally was resting, it was time to finally address my last goodbyes to my daughter of eighteen years. This moment would capture and represent the last time I would be able to touch her.

I didn't want to leave her body – this wasn't how I envisioned her life-ending. I wasn't supposed to outlive her! Her death was out of every sequence I'd known. I wasn't ready to accept I'd never see her again and that our relationship would now change to a spiritual form. I hated how fucking unfair this felt.

Admiring all the sentiments within her casket, I studied each one with grace. Every thoughtful item was a gift full of purpose and love. I cherished how these trinkets would remain with Ally, and they'd forever bind her with those who left them.

Aside from that, here comes a morbid truth. I was also appreciative of the extra items because they would create more ashes along with her casket. What can I say? Ally was a pretty tiny lady. I had every intention of making a memorial keepsake (my vision was still unclear) for immediate family members, and we also needed some ashes for her burial urn. So in my mind, this was the case that size did matter. I didn't mind or care what the ratio would be – I knew there would be a part of her regardless.

I kissed her forehead softly and whispered how much I loved her. She reminded me of one of the many sleeping princesses under a spell. I'd never wished so hard for a fairy-tale ending.

Smearing her makeup, I shook my head, making an "argh" sound like a pirate. Oh, my God! Seriously? I stopped breathing when I saw that her skin had already begun turning black. It was so shockingly sad.

Trying to touch it up, I didn't know whether to laugh or scream. As I struggled, a passing staff member must have noticed. Did they hear my pirate sound or what? They assured me not to worry and that they would take care of it. *Does this happen all the time?* I didn't know what to say. I found it refreshing they understood the level of vanity we can have even for the dead. Especially before a cremation, it's kind of silly if you think about it.

As the staff left the room, I was alone again. I adjusted Ally's scarf and fluffed her hair to make it perfect. I kept her glasses and one stuffed purple bear to put in her bedroom. I hated seeing her like that! I couldn't leave her, but I knew I needed to. No parent should have to say goodbye this way!

I didn't know how many more times to say I love you. How do you make the parting moment as perfect as it can be? There is one chance to have no regrets.

With every second passing, I felt my heart becoming empty – an infinite black hole. Ally didn't deserve to die, and I didn't ask for a dead daughter! The anguish was unbearable. Why wouldn't she wake up?! Couldn't I have this one wish? I was a pretty decent human, after all! I knew I was bargaining, but I didn't care.

Andy, Kylie, and Nikki approached and stood on each side of me. I was thankful for their presence. They seemed to know that I needed to be alone, but with them. They understood the roller coaster of emotions and the irrational anger I felt. I tried to stretch my arms around them; it was terrible. My intention felt more like wet noodles dangling over their hips. I'm sure it looked like it, too.

Time paused as we embraced one another. Each one of us was staring at her with pure compassion. Andy then pointed at Ally's smeared forehead and looked at me. I wiped my tears and sighed. I giggled, lowering my nodding head with ownership; I was finally ready. It couldn't be any more perfect. I'll never forget that last moment we were all together – all five of us, as our family, for the last time.

As they walked away, I didn't move. Our perfect moment as a family was complete. But as Ally's mom, I needed to be the last person to say any final words to my baby.

Closing my eyes, I touched her chest and said, "Mommy loves you, kiddo." I was at peace.

"... I believe that this experience will open everyone's eyes, teach us how important and precious time and family are. I miss you so much, Ally, and I hope you are flying high and resting in peace ..."

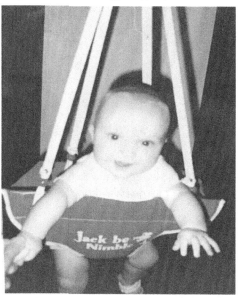

April 1999: "Playing peek-a-boo while babysitting Ally at six months old." – Nana (my mom)

July 2000: "Cutie Ally and sweet Pete (and Mommy's legs)." – MawMaw

May 2001: Ally unexpectedly sang to Nana for all to hear in our neighborhood.

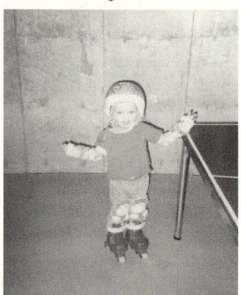

November 2001: Determined like no other, by the end of the day, Ally was zipping around my folks' basement.

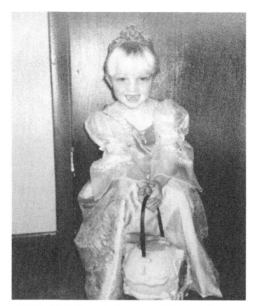

October 2002: Ally's first Halloween. We'd trick-or-treat in the neighborhood.

October 2003: "Ally and Papa (my dad) being goofs at Eagle Park." – Nana

November 2003: "There wasn't anything Ally couldn't
do" – Nana

June 2004: Ally is on vacation in Oregon with the Raber's. Oh,
the look.

August 2005: Ally was thrilled to participate in a safety presentation at school. She was always being helpful, and I think this catapulted her desires even further.

August 2006: The cutest trio. Becca, Kylie, and Ally at Auntie Kristin's wedding.

June 2007: "Kylie and Ally spending an afternoon walking the Platte River with the Starrett grandparents." – Grandma Starrett

November 2008: "Ally with new baby cousin Emmy." – MawMaw

August 2009: "An enjoyable afternoon with my nieces Becca
and Ally in MawMaw's pool." – Auntie Erin

October 2010: "Running the Scream Scram 5K Race at
Washington Park with my Fancy Fairies – Kylie, Ally, Jake and
Ellie." – Aunt Amy

May 2011: "First Boulder Bolder with my nieces, Kylie and Ally, and my fave-sister-in-law, Tiffany, in our homemade shirts. We had 'LIVE, LOVE, LAUGH, and RUN' on the back." – Aunt Amy

November 2012: Ally's 14th birthday. What is she trying to say by wearing a shirt that says, "If you think I'm CRAZY, you should meet my MOTHER!"?

August 2013: "Ally's one-on-one hip-hop class with Rico, owner of Streetside in Boulder, Colorado." – Aunt Amy

August 2013: "Dinner overlooking Niagara Falls with Ally, Becca, and Auntie Andrea." – MawMaw

December 2014: Ally's first-time snowboarding. I'll never
forget what she said: "OK, it's harder than I thought. I loved it,
but I don't need to do it again. LOL."

July 2015: Ally, Me, Kylie, and Andy in Los Angeles touring the
Warner Brothers Studio and sitting on the set of the tv show
"Friends."

April 2016: "I loved working with my girls for our annual 'Giving Back to the Community Day.' Everyone was impressed with their teamwork, including me." – Andy

November 2016: Ally took a selfie during her art class. She promised she was paying attention.

May 2017: Ally's graduation. Such a proud mama moment.

July 2017: Emmy drew and colored this picture without
anyone influencing her. Her breathtaking interpretation of Ally
now sits on a shelf on the ladder bookcase in her room.

CHAPTER 9

A Bit Of Sunshine

As you've probably guessed, Andy is the strong, not-so-silent type who typically tasks himself to control a situation. He's also not a fan of feeling vulnerable; he feels it's a massive sign of weakness. What can I say? He often reminds me of a stereotypical hero. Aren't they always coming to terms with their identity somehow? So I was surprised to learn he had set up a meeting with a medium.

Days before our appointment, Andy let me in on a little secret: He'd received an unexpected email from a friend a few weeks after Ally's death. It contained an endorsement for a credible resource who could help us. I jumped up and down to meet an authentic medium and travel to the other side. My heart warmed at the thought of knowing this kind of connection was possible. Would I be able to "talk" to Ally? What would she say? Getting to be with my kid was all I wanted, even if it meant needing someone else's help.

When I'd been to metaphysical fairs, Andy was usually my plus-one. I thought Andy was only supporting my fascination, not that he necessarily believed in it. Andy explained his skepticism but was willing to go out on a wing and a prayer to meet her. He was also looking to find out if Ally was at peace and thought it would comfort me. Talk about wanting to hug this guy – I couldn't believe it. For sure, this gesture was going on the list of the most thoughtful moments of our marriage.

Immediately researching her website, I was shocked to see she didn't have a long, ornamented scarf wrapped around her head. Her outfit didn't contain a lick of lace or dark crushed velvet, either. Huh, her website suggested quite the opposite of the classic Hollywood image. Not to mention that she didn't look like most of the ladies at the fairs, either. No, this gal could have passed as a polished corporate-America businesswoman. What made her so different? I didn't know what to think.

It took only a few seconds to read to understand – leaving me intimidated. This medium was a well-recognized psychotherapist offering counseling, executive coaching, and intuitive readings. She'd also assisted investigators in finding suspects and criminals, along with solving cold cases. She was also featured on many talk shows; her listeners have left moving testimonials. In the world of Fortune 500 companies, her name wasn't uncommon either. For Christ's sake! After reading all that, was she at least missing a pinky toe? I knew that wasn't nice, but seriously?

Mapping her address, I kept telling Andy there was no way it was right. We were meeting her in a strip mall, of all places. I still half-expected to see an old converted house with a large sign outside with a crystal ball. Jesus! I was such a jerk for stereotyping. After all, did Ally look like a teenage girl who'd get murdered? And do I look like the mother of a murdered child?

Before I made myself upset, I shifted my focus to appreciate the day's convenience. We could grab lunch, do some shopping, and then meet this lady who could change our lives. It seemed like a pretty perfect day to me.

As we sat in the food court in the strip mall, Andy and Kylie overlooked my growing concern. They were whispering to each other about who knows what. Looking around, I watched people going about their typical day. And here I was, wondering if this woman could talk to dead people like the boy in "The Sixth Sense." Didn't I deserve a happy ending like most movies?

Stuck in my thoughts, I sensed I should look up. Standing before me was a sophisticated Barbie doll in her prime. Her pink dress with open-toe heels complimented her tan skin and curled long blonde hair – she glowed with an aura of class and kindness. I immediately looked down, and yes, she had all ten toes (wink). I was in total awe; she was even more attractive than her online photos.

She didn't hesitate to say my name with such conviction – I felt like a real celebrity.

"Hi, I'm Karen." Her smile was genuine.

I didn't even know her, but I had respect for her. Without saying a word, I already trusted what was about to happen. How did she know it was me? Could she see my invisible wounds? *Duh, maybe because she's psychic?*

She invited us to the second floor, where she'd rented office space. Walking up the stairs, she explained that she had recently moved out of state and didn't keep her local office, as she works by phone. I enjoyed the small talk – it reminded me that she was human too.

As Karen looked past me, she noticed my family had fallen behind. Gazing straight at me, she prefaced she had a secret. I was all ears – what could it be? The winning lotto numbers? Not quite. She mentioned that Ally had visited her that very morning.

I stuttered, "I'm sorry?"

Karen's excitement reminded me of a giddy schoolgirl. "As I was making coffee this morning," she said, "Ally showed up wanting to introduce herself to me."

I didn't know what to say. Does that kind of thing happen to Karen all the time?

Thank God we finished walking up the stairs – my footing became unstable. My mind went blank, as if someone had hit the delete key. How could this be real? Is that her normal? How did Ally even know to meet her earlier? Did Karen have a universal appointment book that the dead were privy to? Was this how she knew who we were? Did Ally tell her? I wanted to whisper to Andy what she'd said, but we'd already reached the door.

Gesturing us to have a seat, Karen was easygoing and encouraged us to be as relaxed as possible. Trying to arrange the chairs to face her was chaotic and a little embarrassing in the tight room.

I was full of anticipation and yet so nervous. We were about to talk to Ally in a strip mall, of all places. Really? Thank goodness my T-shirt was a dark color. My deodorant wasn't helping me at all. Did Andy and Kylie think it was weird to connect with the dead this way too?

Sitting down, Karen explained the process of how she calms her mind to raise her vibration. Even though it sounded complicated, I giggled, thinking it seemed more like an oxymoron. She told us her eyes would remain closed and that she could be silent for moments at a time. She then elaborated that she would say whatever she got but that some messages could feel random and messy. Her intentions were clear that she'd help walk us through the conversation and our questions. Appreciating the introduction, I felt that my curiosity had been eased – for the most part, anyway.

Wrapping up her outline, Karen offered to take notes if we thought it would be helpful. What a smart idea! I was already feeling like I wasn't keeping things straight.

I desperately searched for my pen in my purse, but my heart stopped as she mentioned that we could record our time together.

I whispered, "Are you shitting me?"

If Karen wasn't legitimate, would she offer to let us record her? None of us wasted a second. My family and I slammed our phones on the table, all tying for first place. It was a rare time I was thankful for technology.

I blurted out, "Should we hold hands?"

Andy and Kylie both got theirs out. Amused, Karen quickly assured us we didn't need to do a thing – only be. Oh, my God! What kind of stupid comment did I make? Did I demoralize her craft? We were all blushing a little. I tried to reassure myself that she must get that all the time.

As we settled, she asked if we were ready. Were the lights going to dim or something? We all nodded at once.

Smiling, she took a deep breath and went silent. At that precise second, time slowed to a snail's pace. Comprehending my emotions was impossible. My anticipation was in overdrive, and patience seemed out of reach. But I didn't make a peep or dare move a muscle, even though I was about to burst at the seams.

From the morning of Ally's life celebration, that day marked a new beginning for her and me. It started a clock that measured a constantly increasing magnitude, the longest time I've been apart from Ally. I despised counting the forever-growing tally that I didn't ask for or want. Sure, on a good day, it did confirm how long I'd been a survivor. Touché. But at that very moment, I wanted only one damn thing. I didn't give a shit how selfish it felt. I needed to speak to my daughter!

Through our nineteen-year relationship, including pregnancy, Ally and I were side-by-side. No, it wasn't every day as she got older (we both needed space), but it was the right balance. We practiced the unspoken vows like a married couple. I used to joke with Ally how silly it was that there wasn't a ceremony for parents and children in that way. Yet Ally always found a way to try.

Whether by texting, calling, or hanging out in person, we connected. Even during her teenage growing pains, Ally did her best to show up. I'll always love her for that. Was she going to be able to do that today? Would she have words of wisdom? Could Ally help ease my suffering and comfort me? I had trouble sitting still and didn't want to wait any longer.

When Karen opened her eyes, I almost gasped out loud – seeing her genuine excitement validated mine. Turning to me, she described how easy it was to talk to Ally and how much she liked her. She loved her "sassiness" while relating to her "old soul."

Karen wasn't theatrical like I'd envisioned. Nor was she performing like a ventriloquist, and I was glad because there was no way I could handle either of those. Instead, her tone seemed caring and authentic. I could hardly contain myself.

I envisioned how Ally and she could be interacting. Were the two of them sitting at a park bench with coffee having casual chitchat? Did Ally talk normally or sound more like whispers? How did Ally look? Did she appear as herself when she died or was Ally more ghostlike or even a glowing orb? Should I dare ask? Trapped in a spiritual web, I didn't know how to process whether my growing questions were rational.

Feeling a twinge of jealousy, I struggled with the fact that a stranger could talk to my daughter and I couldn't. I'm her mother, after all. Shouldn't I have the power? I tried to compartmentalize my negativity and circle back to feeling grateful, wondering if Karen would be able to sense my inner struggles.

Karen looked at us, eager to share.

Ally spoke about "not being in her right mind."

I almost wet myself from hearing the expression. In that very instant, I traveled back in time to the week before Ally died. I replayed the conversation that Ally and I had over and over about her being more dramatic than usual. It didn't matter what I did; she wouldn't confide in me. I begged her to look up so I could see if her big blue eyes were filling or not. When she did, I could see her mascara was smudging her glasses. Good Lord, that girl had the longest eyelashes.

Ally rarely said bad things about Maddie. Each sentence that she started about her, she failed to complete it. While Ally ran her fingers repeatedly through her hair, she kept muttering how the stress wasn't helping her anger issues and that she wasn't in her right mind. I'd never heard her use either of those phrases before.

There was *no* way Karen could know that! I never told anyone – no one. I was in total, utter shock! Should I reveal that Karen was right among my family, or even out loud? I couldn't fathom what was happening.

THROUGH HER MOTHER'S EYES

Karen then described getting the chills, saying it was a validation of her communications with her target. The hair on her arms moved. Each blonde hair stood straight up, stealing my breath away.

Only Ally could have shared those words with her. It wasn't like any one of us pointed Karen in a particular direction, and she wasn't throwing out questions. What I saw wasn't a hoax; it couldn't be.

Karen winked at me before closing her eyes and resumed talking (in silence) to Ally. My heart was beating so hard, I thought for sure everyone would see it, if not hear it. A few seconds passed, and Karen reopened her glistening eyes.

Ally mentioned "her anger issues," Karen said.

Oh, my God! I wanted to scream out loud. Tear after tear ran down my cheeks in awe. What were the odds Karen could have guessed another exact word-for-word statement? How was any of this possible?

As our conversation continued, I was keeping score of all the accuracy. I'd tap Kylie's leg when Karen said something spot-on. I couldn't help it. It was exciting when Kylie did it, too.

Andy's arms laid across his chest more often than not; he was battling his skepticism. I am sure Andy was scrambling to figure out if personal information had leaked about Ally. He wasn't the only one. Was there any way Karen could have investigated our family? Yes, Ally's death was easily searchable on the internet, but what about everything else?

Karen ensured we were doing all right with constant care as her priority. I am sure she knew this was a lot to take in. I was more than OK; I was communicating with my kid! The happiness was more than awesome. Although for every smile, the evil twinned emotion wasn't far away. I kept chanting to myself to be in the now, but it was hard to stay focused.

Looking at the table, I saw all our cellphones recording every word. I was indebted because I didn't know how much more I could absorb. I guess what they say about having too much of a good thing was real.

Thirty minutes into the conversation, Karen brought in the support system she called "divine guidance." Was that even a thing?

All I could think was the more, the merrier. What did they look like anyway? More angelic, I presumed. How many were there? Had Ally already met them?

We all agreed, and as we did, the room felt different – it was weird. There was an instant feeling of universal support. I couldn't explain it. I looked at my family, wondering if they were experiencing the same. Their faces seemed to be in amazement of some kind. I knew they had to be feeling it too.

What happened next blew my mind.

Karen curiously said, "Divine guidance said – do you know what I am talking about, there is a lost ring?"

Her question blindsided me. My adrenaline kicked into high gear, and I was sweating again. I dreaded the crash I would have later.

Stunned, I had a hard time coming up with an intelligent response and stumbled to find words. Did they mean the ring Ally was wearing when she died? Was it because the ring was in evidence and it was "lost" to me for the time being? I didn't know what to think.

Kylie then spoke up. I turned to her in confusion. She stated the ring could be the matching wedding band to Ally's that was "somewhere" in the basement in a storage tub. Shit! I'd forgotten hers was missing too.

Kylie would clean and rearrange her room like clockwork when she was upset. Items would get packed away and later resurface again. It seemed like a never-ending effort to me. Maybe it was her way to find harmony – I wasn't sure. But it didn't make sense to me why she would pack away a precious gift like that? Why not display it on a chain, at least? I tried to be understanding, but the thought of both rings missing destroyed me.

As time passed, Kylie's attempts to locate her ring were unsuccessful. Coming to terms with the thought it was gone was devastating. What else could I do but work through the disappointment? She was a young teen then, after all.

All the pain came flooding back like a tidal wave. But I didn't think it was appropriate to call Kylie out in front of Karen. Regardless, both ladies' scenarios fit the question from divine guidance.

I shook my head, desperate to make sense of the situation. Not many knew I wanted Ally's ring back – only my family and the police. And I certainly didn't think it was public knowledge about Kylie's missing ring, either. She was too embarrassed to share for misplacing it in the first place. It also wasn't our place to tell anyone. Well, I may or may not have said something to Petra and my mom in confidence.

Karen mumbled how weird it was for her to get that. We all agreed and talked about different scenarios. It was surprising to see Andy joining in the discussion. He was active and seemed passionate about figuring it out. For the first time in the meeting, his facial expression softened with the look of acceptance. I sent loving vibes his way as I studied him, thanking him for this gift.

I slumped in my chair; my poor little sponge was *so* full. Would it be appropriate to ask for a break? I mean, Karen kept asking if we were all right, but time is money. I didn't know if Ally would get exhausted too. How often would I get the opportunity to talk with my kid? I didn't want to miss anything, just in case. But what else could there be? I was already so blessed with everything so far. I should have known Ally had more to say; she could talk your ear off for hours when she wanted to.

As Karen returned to us, her face was somber yet hopeful this time.

Ally said, "He is going to be put in jail."

Oh, my God! How could she know that? Could she see the future, or was she trying to make me feel better? I was, for sure, taken aback by that comment. Andy perked up, puffing his chest. Karen explained that Ally kept saying it again and again. Each version was different, but the message was still the same. No way! I wanted to believe it, but it was confusing. I'd not seen souls predicting the future in any movie before. Could this really be happening?

Karen then shared her psychic opinion. She sensed that the police would locate Arturo in a school of some kind in Mexico. Huh, what did that mean? What did she see to get that impression? I scrambled to make a note of the time on the recording. I didn't think that information was enough to give our detective, but it gave me hope. I wondered if our detectives would even entertain the idea of a medium helping them.

Within the silence, I started thinking about the school. Would Arturo go back to school for further education? That didn't seem up his alley, though. He was a skilled concrete worker, so maybe he would be helping to rebuild a run-down building? He was also a talented guitar player. Would he volunteer to teach the youth or the elderly, perhaps?

Internally, all I heard was his life was moving forward in some way. How was that even fair? Why did he get to do the things he was good at or loved? On the flip side, I knew he couldn't hide forever – he was too social to become a hermit.

I wanted to believe he carried guilt for everything he did to Ally. And if he gave back to the community, it was his way of apologizing. Was it abnormal to think that way? Because I had optimism for my daughter's killer? Why did it feel like I was the only one who could still admit his good traits? Just because he did an unspeakable act, does that wipe out all the good? Did I have to get on the wagon and grab my torch and pitchfork? It didn't feel right to me. An eye for an eye? Not this gal.

My focus then shifted to his family. I couldn't imagine being the mother of a murderer. Jesus! That thought made my stomach turn. What a heartbreaking situation for them. How do you even determine loyalty at that moment? I mean, you have to wonder if they believed what he did was wrong, or were they still thinking that he didn't really do it? How could his mother, or any female relatives, look at him and not feel so much anger that he was so violent?

My heart went into overload, feeling empathy for his family – they didn't deserve any wrong because of their son's actions. Were their friends and family shunning them? I could only imagine how many blamed them, also! Shaking my head, I couldn't believe how fucked up the situation was for everyone.

Karen then giggled out loud. Talk about switching gears, but I welcomed it – the room was feeling heavy for me. Karen described how Ally "showed" her a fun pose that she and Andy shared in a particular photo. As Karen reenacted Andy draping his arms over

Ally, I watched him attempt to keep his stern face. Thrown off his guard, Andy was obviously uncomfortable. I wasn't sure what photo Ally was referencing, but it was clear he did.

Why couldn't Andy budge and at least smile? But I knew that his armor was mighty. Karen, speaking for Ally, asked him to keep this photo in our bedroom. Andy hesitated – something happened. Because he then responded to Ally. He said he would keep the picture on his phone, which he sleeps next to every night. Holy shit! I wanted to hug him right then. It was so beautiful to experience.

Karen then turned to Kylie.

Ally said, "You should be a guidance counselor."

That seemed out of left field. Without hesitating, Kylie confirmed that Ally had mentioned that to her before. Really? I had no idea. Kylie sniffled, and I took her hand. Karen even showed us the chills she got as a result. I could tell it meant so much to Kylie that she and Ally connected.

After a moment of awkward silence, Kylie asked Karen if Ally had suffered. I was so glad someone else brought it up. It must have been plaguing her, too. As Karen went universal, I realized Ally might tell us she *did* suffer. Oh, my God! What if she did? What if there were grueling details? I was shitting my pants in anticipation, worried it could be another "careful what you wish for" example.

When Karen opened her eyes, I gulped so hard it hurt.

Ally said, "I knew where I was going, and I got out of my body." I slumped from gratitude.

Relieved, I said, "Thank God."

I watched Andy and Kylie sigh too. It wasn't quiet, by any means. How did Ally know to leave her body? Having so many questions, I didn't know where to start.

I'd been dreading for weeks learning if Ally had suffered and felt pain till the bitter end. But now, I could release the weight I carried. Even if there was the slightest chance our meeting with Karen wasn't authentic, I didn't care. Those very words were the exact thing I needed to hear, and I hoped it gave Andy what he was looking for too.

Shifting gears, Karen asked Andy if he was carrying guilt.

"Oh, God – here we go," I mumbled to myself.

I wasn't sure if she'd overstepped or not. To my surprise, Andy opened like a floodgate. He told her that yes, he did carry guilt and rage because, as a protective father, he felt as though he had failed. He loved Ally as his own, regardless if they were blood-related. It was painstaking to hear him admit his burden. It's not like we hadn't talked about it in private, but to hear him in front of others was something else.

I felt torn because, in a way, it felt like we were airing our dirty laundry. I mean, Karen is a professional and all, but in front of his daughter? I wasn't sure she needed to be a part of it. Although, it could be useful for Kylie to hear her dad's stance too. Andy had already made comments about doing background checks on all of Kylie's new boyfriends. I wasn't sure that was fair to her, and I didn't necessarily agree with that. Hadn't she already been punished enough for Ally's mistakes?

From what I saw, Andy took the platform to reiterate that he had predicted Ally's death. He wasn't shy about saying he thought Arturo was a "piece of shit" from the start. Andy pointed out many examples of how Arturo mistreated Ally and me, too. Andy was adamant that he could have stopped it all by making Ally end their relationship. Or, he thought, beating him to a bloody pulp would do it. Yes, it was his right to say his feelings, and none of this was news to me. Except for this time, his words felt like an attack saying it was my fault Ally was dead.

As Andy proclaimed his regret for doing things "my way"; I didn't understand. Every situation we faced with the ladies, we talked it through together, ending with a handshake before handling it. Proudly, we shared that as parents, and now I questioned what I had missed. Was that not indeed the case?

Staring with disgust, I felt backstabbed by him. So, based on his theory, if we had done things "his way," Ally would still be alive? Is *that* what he was saying? It took me a minute to wrap my head around his comment. Did he hear how he was sounding? Or was I misinterpreting?

I felt abandoned; grinding my teeth was all I could do to keep quiet. My mama bear was ready to pounce. I knew Andy's perception wasn't accurate, not even a little. But would he ever recognize that? Ally was on *her* path, one that neither he nor I could control, plain and simple. She had a one-track mind, and all we could do was plant a million seeds for her to water.

Desperate, I tried to let his words roll off my back. I knew it was his anger talking. I wanted to believe it wasn't personal – I did, but it still hurt.

Karen quickly noticed the tone and asked me if I was all right. I wasn't. My face had to be every shade of red. She asked how I was feeling as Andy was sharing.

I didn't want to lie, so I said, "I thought we would end up divorcing." What else could I say? I hated feeling that way, and it sucked, speaking that in front of Kylie. But I didn't know how we could stay together if he blamed me in some way.

She looked at us with such empathy, stating she could see the built-in conflict as a disaster. She offered her thoughts about my role as the peacemaker between Ally and Andy. Not only did I need to support Ally's path as a love-crazed teenager, but I also had to balance Andy's dislike for Arturo. Man, she was so spot-on. Was our situation that predictable? I had absolutely no idea how Andy and I would get through this. How could a marriage survive such a tragedy, particularly when our opinions differed so much?

Karen went silent, asking Ally for her thoughts.

"You and me both, Dad," she said.

I loved hearing that she was relating to Andy about his anger. He smiled.

"But I wasn't going to let you win because I was also in love with him." Her thought finished so sweetly, confirming what I already knew.

My God! I was so proud of her for admitting that. What was Andy now thinking? Did he get it? What about Kylie? Was she at least learning something from this? Although I still wondered if Ally was embarrassed or ashamed that she was in love with Art? Is that why she hid the fact that she had been talking with him more recently than said?

I couldn't believe what a turn the meeting had taken. One minute we connected to Ally on a beautiful level, and the next was pointing out our dysfunctional marriage. Was it always going to be a roller-coaster ride with everything we did? Why do there need to be constant reminders that there are two sides to everything? Am I going to get a damn break? All I wanted was for Ally to come home and the nightmare to end. Was that too much to ask?

Our time with Karen was wrapping up, and I was sad. Her vibe was one that I connected with well. At the same time, I felt anxiety because I didn't know how to express my gratitude. I am sure, being so popular, she's heard it a million other times from other families. But I needed her to understand the impact she made in *my* life – my experience was transformative and unique. Would saying "thank you" be enough? Panic set in while the clock counted down the remaining minutes.

After we spent an hour and a half together, Karen asked if there was anything else she could do for us. Andy told her there was a lot of useful information. That was polite of him to say. He also said he knew this would make him and me closer. Excuse me? I didn't expect that at all. But I wondered if he was only saying it, or did he mean it? I was so beat; I couldn't tell if he was authentic or not.

Andy further stated he was looking forward to Arturo getting caught, and Karen reaffirmed that he would. If divine guidance and Ally both saw it happening, it had to be real. It was good enough for me. What else would you need? A little faith and trust, I suppose.

Karen went universal for the last time, asking Ally what she had to say.

"I know I walk on water," she said all girlie.

Jesus! The tone sounded exactly like her. We laughed out loud – what a fantastic way to end the meeting. Ally, being her princess self and all.

Karen then proposed keeping in touch. My heart warmed at the idea because it felt genuine. She also offered her agency contacts to help support our outstanding court case. I liked the idea of having that in my back pocket. I found comfort in knowing my support system was growing. I didn't know when I would talk to her again, but it didn't matter – our connection felt timeless. Karen and I hugged each other like sisters. The depth spoke for itself.. As I walked away, I wondered if it was it a coincidence that Andy's friend would send him the email, and he would setup the meeting? And Karen to be available to see us while in town? What about Ally knowing to meet her that morning? I am unsure whether I had more questions than answers after that meeting, but I felt complete. Everything I should know, I did. There wasn't a doubt that my experience was real.

CHAPTER 10

There is No Easy Button

AUGUST 31, 2017

We were mindless, drooling zombies almost two months after Ally's death. Thankfully, none of us started hunting for brains, but it didn't seem too far off. Someone had to do something. So I did what I do best. Playing the almighty mother card, I declared it was time to find reinforcements. Andy and Kylie weren't kicking and screaming about my idea, so I had to believe they were on board. Days after my ruling, we met a healing resource, a therapist specialized in grieving.

Walking into our therapist's office was scary. Was I the only one who was dreading what was about to happen? Should I even ask?

The thought of explaining my story to a therapist made my skin crawl. How does someone decide to do this for a living? What if I have a mental breakdown? I was already feeling the pressure build. The last thing I needed was a straitjacket. Does this therapist have any idea what they're about to walk into, or was it possible it's the other way around?

From left to right, the communal area had multiple families. There were different shapes and sizes, ages and genders. Everyone looked "normal" to me (as if I knew what abnormal looked like). I would guess even we looked like a typical family. But everyone knows you don't come to an office like this for fun. What were their circumstances requiring them to seek guidance? Can you even imagine the stories you could create from this place? This office was a cesspool of drama – a wet dream for the nosey or gossipy person.

I could feel their eyes doing the same as I was studying them. Did anyone recognize us from the news? Man, I hoped not. Even if they did, would they dare say anything? I am not sure I could've handled any further anxiety.

No one was pulling out their phones; it seemed we were in the clear. What I noticed was there was a quiet level of respect among us. It was refreshing not to feel treated like a freakish mutant, as seemed to be the case on so many previous occasions. I found comfort in seeing other families there in an uncomfortable, twisted way. I mean, I knew they must have heartbreaking stories too. But they were here like us, trying to find their way. I loved how brave we all were.

Looking around, I noticed several pleasing decorations. They captured my aesthetic, and somehow I began to feel comfortable. There was an affirmation chalkboard on the wall for display, and it was hand-designed with the phrase:

"Oh, that's a good one!" I said, turning to my family.

Would they buy into this concept? Did they already feel that way, or would they scoff at such a statement? They both nodded with smirks – it wasn't enough direction for me to conclude anything. I'm sure they were carrying enough apprehension for being there rather than taking in a meme.

My amazement was interrupted. A lady walked up and introduced herself.

"Hi, I'm Beth."

She motioned for us to head back to our official meeting place, her office. How did she know who we were? Did she have a gift like Karen's?

The room was contemporary and looked as though I had decorated it. It appeared more like a tiny living room from IKEA than an office. Her artwork reminded me of pieces I'd created. Could we be this in-sync already?

Beth was a mature brunette with a trendy outfit and heels. She also wore a messy high bun (Ally would indeed have favored her style). She didn't appear to be the stereotypical sweater-vested therapist. I could tell her questions were going to be more involved than the typical "How does that make you feel?" Thank goodness –

I couldn't handle that. I wondered how Andy would address such a question.

Beth pulled out a worn notebook and pen, ready to get down and dirty. Adjusting her cute reading glasses (they didn't have a beaded neck strap), she took a deep belly breath. Thankfully, we didn't need the uncomfortable formal introductions.

Days before our meeting, my mother had offered to research different therapists. After using the list from The Victims Advocacy Group, she found us a match. I was thrilled to hear she'd set up our first meeting. Not to mention, we learned we had an allotted budget for mental-health care, too. It was such a relief.

Beth began by asking a few basic questions about Ally's death without hesitation. They seemed like warmup questions. But I suspected they were enough to point her in a particular direction. As I spoke, I realized my mom and Beth might have already talked, but I didn't know to what extent.

I was getting uncomfortable, and then it dawned on me. I had no clue what my mom had told Beth about us. Sure, she could have searched for Ally's death, but that wouldn't tell the survivors' story. So what was my mom's interpretation of my story, anyway? Was my mom projecting her feelings about me (us), or did she offer what I had shared along the way? What was I thinking? I should have followed up with her; I had instant regret.

When I described the specifics about Ally's death, it sucked. I already felt like an outcast with everyone else (including my family) who knew the story. I was either calm or comical, treating my account like a typical first-world problem. Talking with a stranger made it all that much more awkward.

Beth guided the conversation with a smooth touch; her comments resonated with me. One after another, I saw her brilliance, and I was at ease. It was clear her style was one I could connect with on my terms. Huh, I've heard many sad stories of people struggling to find "the one." How could I be this lucky on the first try? Kylie also seemed taken with her. Turning to Andy, I noticed he wasn't feeling it. I wanted to cry. He became guarded and hesitant, not knowing what to expect.

Looking at the clock next to her, I sighed. The hour flew by, and it felt like we barely had introduced ourselves. Yet, for the second time since Ally's death, I believed I had found another person capable of understanding me. It's not that friends and family hadn't been supportive. Of course they had, in their ways. But the weight I was carrying was more significant than any of us put together. I needed coaching from a professional, and fast. I didn't know what would happen without Beth.

After looking at her phone, she invited us to schedule another appointment. I whispered, "Thank God!" It meant she felt a connection as well – I was sweating bullets.

Our time moving forward would be a mix of individual and family appointments. Agreeing, I was eager to schedule my first meeting. The first date she offered me was over a week away. I snarled in disappointment. I got that she didn't cater to the severity of content, but hadn't I been through enough already?

Oh, goodie – another life lesson. Everyone knows the phrase "Good things come to those who wait," right? The thought of actually having to follow through and practice patience sounded downright awful. It made me want to throw up.

As we left, I didn't know what to think. But I knew what I was feeling: excited, nervous, and hopeful. Man, I was already getting tired of all the ping-ponging emotions. But seriously, did I make the right decision? Would Beth be a good fit for me? Would Andy and Kylie divulge their deepest, darkest secrets to her too?

Trying to keep my cool, I slowly walked behind them, taking in the waiting room again. As I turned the corner, I noticed a vase with a sign hanging around its neck. It was priceless. I loved the sarcasm, pointing fun at human nature. Of course this was the right place for them and me.

CHAPTER 11

A Single Echo

JANUARY 6, 2018

I'm not sure what it feels like for other folks, but being an only child means I am the sole receiver of family heirlooms, whether I want them or not. It's the polite honoring of my mother's intentions. Fine China, furniture, and various decorations live in our basement. Over time, I've donated some pieces but kept the ones I had a deeper connection with.

My great-grandmother had a shoe-box-size jewelry box that I'd suspected was once white. Now, it had discolored to a dingy yellow. Kind of like an old newspaper that sat too long in the sun. I wasn't sure of its age, but there was something about it I liked.

Could it be the rectangular box-like design that spoke to my geometrical appreciation, or was it the row of tiny gold circles that ran along the entire base? A gold filigree pattern also framed the top with swirling stems and leaves that resembled symmetrical and lovely hearts. The brass fastener reminded me of a treasure chest, and it even had a lock – so secretive.

Shiny, soft, red satin fabric lined the inside of the lid. On the material, a scene painted in gold told an artist's story. It was a street full of tightly knit houses and a streetlamp next to a tiny metal carriage full of foliage. I had no idea what street it captured, maybe one in Paris? Red velvet covered the interior: a single shelf, multiple variable-sized compartments, and the entire bottom.

The jewelry box seemed so proper. Not a typical item I would possess at all. A small metal music player hid underneath the shelf in the right corner. It was the wind-up kind. How could such a tiny mechanism play such a tune? Those engineers who design these kinds of devices are exceptionally talented in my mind.

When my mom "offered" me this jewelry box, I was about ten. I didn't have one at that time, so it made sense. My appreciation for its beauty took time for me to understand. Having it for nearly three decades, I'd played the music only a handful of times. Some for fun, but mostly after moving to a new house ensuring it hadn't broken. The song was unlike anything I had heard before. It was a melody designed for a grand ball. It wasn't something that one could forget.

Since our latest move, the jewelry box lived on top of our built-in, six-foot shoe rack in the master-bedroom closet. One afternoon, I retreated to the walk-in closet to cry in peace. This space felt like a sanctuary at times. I could shut the door and smother my face with my clothes to further muffle the noise.

The early-eighties design meant the closet was short and narrow. Better said, it was for only a single person at a time. However, when I needed alone time, it felt comforting being in a tight space. As if the surrounding clothes could hug me.

It had been only a few months without Ally, and I was miserable. My nightmare was relentless as it tormented me regardless of the hour of the day. Nothing could cheer me up. I hated everything: work, my hobbies, and also my people. I didn't even find pleasure in drinking my favorite Starbucks drink. That should have been a real sign for most to understand my state of mind.

Sitting on the hard tile floor, I rocked back and forth, drowning in self-pity, and crying till it hurt. How was I going to survive? I tried reciting every positive meme I knew, but nothing was working.

"Why the *fuck* did you have to die, Ally?" I whispered, hoping she could hear me. My face began to itch from all the snot, and my eyes hurt.

"Someone better explain why this is happening to me." In my mind, I expected an answer.

By now, the tears were running down my legs. Jesus! Why didn't I bring in a box of tissues? I grabbed a shirt from the laundry basket and blew my nose. I didn't care.

What was I saying? Was I blaming Ally? Did I *just* wipe my face with dirty clothes? I shook my head. Is this what I've become? I took a deep breath, realizing something had to change.

Giving myself a few minutes to stand up because my leg had fallen asleep, I sat there running my hands along the floor, hoping what I touched was a dust bunny. Laughing at my ridiculous worry, things didn't feel so heavy anymore. Finally, feeling them again, I brushed myself off to signify, making a mental shift. Before reaching for the door, I apologized.

Sincerely, I told her, "Ally, I'm sorry for being angry with you. I love you, kiddo."

Slowly opening the door, I could see the light from the bathroom window. The sun was warm on my face. It wasn't from the heat itself but from the healing light. Taking a step forward, I basked in the radiance, smiling as time stood still.

Within the very same second, the music player made one loud chime. Holy shit! My heart stopped, and my adrenaline went into overdrive. The note echoed long enough that I knew what it was. I couldn't believe it! I snapped my head around and looked at the jewelry box still in my closet. No way! How did the handle get turned? Nothing was touching it.

Stretching on my tippy toes, I pulled it down to investigate. My only thought was a bug or a spider had gotten into the mechanism. It seemed like a lame thought, but I wanted to be real about what happened.

My heart was pumping out of control as I clicked open the latch on the jewelry box. I opened the lid in slow motion, peering through my squinted right eye as if that would protect me. I was fearful that something creepy would jump out and land on me. That was all I needed.

I gave one final snap to force the top open. I jumped back like a frightened little girl, although I didn't screech. I was pretty proud of that.

On the bathroom sink, it sat. The jewelry box was wide open, and nothing came flying or crawling out of it. I studied it from afar until I got the courage to step closer. Shifting around the jewelry at the bottom, I made my way to the corner music player. Holding the box to my ear, I thought this would be the perfect time for a little creature to attack. Stupid movies! I didn't hear anything rustling around, so I gave the box a good shake: nothing. I shook it again to see if I could trigger the music player. It was silent.

Baffled, I wound the handle on the back. I didn't let go because I was afraid I'd made it all up in my mind. I wasn't sure I could handle a letdown like that. But what else could it be? I let the handle go, and the music played its song as intended. The melody echoed throughout the bathroom. Validated, what I'd heard was the one note.

I sat the jewelry box back down on the sink and said, "Thank you, Ally." I was smiling from ear to ear.

Speechless, I replayed over and over what had happened. Would anyone believe me? Did I want to tell them or keep this moment for myself? My daughter had reached out to me from the universe! How did she even do that?

I loved that it didn't take a medium to connect with Ally. I hugged myself from all the joy. Was this our new language? Could we communicate this way in the future? I didn't want to get overzealous, but I was excited like a kid in a candy shop.

Embracing our moment, I said to Ally, "I am open any time you want to talk, kiddo." I kissed the jewelry box and put it back in the closet, bracing for one more chime. Nothing happened. Giggling at myself while looking in the mirror, I told my reflection that the experience was real. It was empowering saying that to myself.

So, has the music box chimed again to answer your big question? Sadly, no.

CHAPTER 12

Behind the Curtain

FEBRUARY 8, 2018

When all this began, I believed the concept of my island was scary. Wouldn't you? It wasn't my fault I'd landed at this location because of a circumstance out of my control. Does the movie *Cast Away* ring any bells? Yes, my life changed without my permission, and I understood that managing my future was my responsibility. I did. However, I wasn't sure which was worse – strapping on heavy scuba gear and diving right in (Beth's motto) or using the raft I'd built out of debris as a product of survival.

I would never have predicted the need for Beth and me to understand my past behaviors and habits to work with my current loss. We needed to work together to rediscover a few key highlights from my earlier timeline. Grasping my youth would mean having a better understanding of my blueprint – it was time to roll up my sleeves and get to work.

Beth offered me the direction to begin when and wherever it made sense. Using the usual chronological order wasn't necessary, and whatever I thought would provide value for her would speak for itself. Really? I didn't expect that.

I'd never talked about myself this way. Was that normal? I appreciated her guidance, but what I was about to do was foreign. Would she judge me? What would it mean if she wrote things down that I said? Was I prepared for her opinions? What if she diagnosed me as crazy?

Starting my journey without a passport, I traveled deep within myself. My words felt effortless as I described what came to mind. Believing my conceptual thinking was a little less standardized from a young age than most, I loved the feeling of power. I was both Darth Vader and Princess Leia from *Star Wars* for Halloween (no, not the same year). What does that tell you?

My school résumé was a mixture of unusual ingredients – my prouder moments included being an artist and musician. I lettered in academics and athletics. And yet, I was also a heavy cigarette smoker. Explain that one to me.

My music varied from Metallica to Cher, and based on that, I dressed according to my mood. I didn't fit into any clique; however, I could relate to most of them. In saying that, I wasn't popular, but I got along with most peers – there was a level of respect. Labeled unique quite often, I wasn't sure it was always a compliment.

My mom and I would have what some called "word battles" day-in, day-out. I would have agreed to call them that when I was a teen. In retrospect, I am pretty sure the description wasn't accurate. Being heard was all I wanted.

On top of that, I didn't always understand why others didn't think the same way I did. I solved problems quickly, as they unfolded before my eyes. It always felt like a moral obligation to do the right thing when no one else seemed to be doing the same. I strove to be the best – period.

I also enjoyed country line dancing. Petra and I stomped our cute cowboy boots, dressed in our flattering Rockies butt-hugging jeans and oversize belt buckles. I was always facing the opposite way of everyone. What better safe place to test the steps of conformity? Not to mention attracting Ally's father as well (wink). I discovered just how much I loved pushing the boundaries by adding my personality and style to everything.

I thought my description of my rebellious self pretty much covered it; I was a misfit. Did any of it make sense to Beth? Why did I choose those memories to share? I'll admit, I felt pretty high on the pedestal at that point. Well, that is until I saw her reading note after note. What did that mean? I wouldn't say I liked feeling vulnerable.

Thanking me for sharing, she assured me I was in a safe place. This exercise was a precursor to many things to come. Smiling, she stated she was excited to join forces. From that moment on, our relationship evolved into a real partnership.

The growth I experienced kept me coming back for more. I found myself challenged in one way or another, but that's what I wanted. Her knowledge of self and relationships was beyond profound. I often needed to remind myself this was her craft because I felt inferior a time or two from her wisdom. This gal seemed to have it all. I'd make tally marks in the air when she wasn't looking (at least I hope) and I felt like I'd said something insightful.

After a few meetings, I sat and cried in my car, wondering why I had come back. Was I taking on too much too fast? Oh, I'm sure the perfectionist in me was coming out. My mission to be a survivor took precedence. Someone must do it, and it couldn't be anyone else. Why did I wait for shit to hit the fan to make this choice? What can I say? I like to do things the hard way, but it's better late than never, right?

If Ally hadn't died, I wouldn't have ever known looking in a mirror could be so hard. It meant I was growing, but man, some growth spurts hurt way more than others. Is this one of those times when it's fitting to say it's happening exactly how it is supposed to?

As our time continued, I identified decades of defense strategies I'd created. It sucked!It was hard to admit that the strategies I created decades ago wouldn't still work for me now. But how could they, I'm not the same person. It was hard to understand that my tried-and-true patterns had a shelf life. Ugh, more work to do. This process reminded me of how much I don't like onions and peppers. Coming to terms with myself was precisely that, gross! The board outside her office had the phrase: "We repeat what we don't repair." If only that saying had hung on our family fridge growing up! Who knew what kind of shitty behaviors I wouldn't have formed? Let's be honest, though. I am sure I was too busy playing outside to care anyway.

To allow myself to move forward, I would need to accept that we, as evolved humans, can't "change" our coping tools overnight. Each one was individual, and we would have to first "work" with them for a positive outcome. I heard this as a learning opportunity (a common phrase I use and practice), and it clicked.

One of the resilient behaviors we discussed was how I swallowed my resentment. She explained that instead of addressing my feelings with others, I'd allow them to stew, resulting in a rotting pit of emotions. God, that was hard to hear. I couldn't believe I carried that toxicity and didn't think my voice was of great significance. How could I do that to myself? I thought that I was taking the higher road more often than not. But in hindsight, I was allowing others to walk all over me. Seriously? Beth would (again) remind me I can't change the past; we needed to focus on what I could do about it now. I'd be curious to know if she felt like a broken record, having to work hard to continue to help me focus on my goals.

My work also revealed that I look for approval from others when, in fact, I needed it from myself. Really? It didn't make sense. Even though I always seemed to set out to be the best, it never felt "good" enough. My parents would reward my good grades, and they took me out to celebrate after a victory or loss in a soccer game. My teachers had nothing but good things to say. My reviews at work were full of compliments. I couldn't figure it out. There was always someone better, something more.

I understood that I'd created an internal critic, a nasty one, by digging in the history trenches. I nurtured this relationship every day, like washing my face. Until, at some point, I set her free. No longer requiring my permission to flourish, she was relentless with concocting self-doubt. That bitch constantly crippled my confidence.

Admitting that I doomed myself all the time was downright awful. Beth coached me to begin a new path – I needed to forgive myself. Are you kidding? How do I *not* let my internal critic judge that? This shit was getting harder by the day. I couldn't recall a time I was so desperate to quit something. Even giving up smoking when I got pregnant with Ally was less complicated than this.

The vicious cycle seemed impossible to unlearn. I felt blind finding my way through my never-ending mess. Beth assured me that I could trust myself to get there with patience.

Doubtful, I'd often reply, "If you say so."

It was about that time she offered self-awareness testing. We began by identifying my fundamental principles. It was an excellent warmup exercise to reveal my highest priorities and most sincere beliefs: growth, joy, wholeness, wisdom, empathy, creativity, and gratitude were my core umbrella – it made sense. I thought I sounded pretty darn great so far.

As my puzzle took shape, Beth then shifted gears to the Enneagram. A reliable tool used since the 1960s. Huh, I'd never heard of it before – you? She explained the definition as spiritual psychology, which was right up my alley.

Now, as a seasoned self-discoverer, I, of course, was ready to take the test. I am a #1/Perfectionist/Reformer with a Nine-Wing (the Peacemaker/Optimist) of the nine personality types. Oh, my God! It was the literal interpretation of my life. Self-controlled and principled, eh – you're darn right I am. No wonder no one can push me harder than me! It said I also calmly strive for constant harmony while easily seeing both sides of an issue – true story.

Consequently, it also revealed some truths that were hard to read; that shit stung for a long while. Others can find me harsh and critical at times. *Really?* In my mind, I am only trying to improve things. I guess others don't see that? It also stated I needed to permit myself to be messy. Are you shitting me? What do you mean I need to relax? Not to mention, the section about needing justification slapped me still.

Like it or not, the Enneagram provided the clarity I needed to start understanding who I am. The detailed descriptions read as though the authors had already met me – validating that I wasn't the only one wired this way. Appreciative of this awareness, I would proudly add it to my new tool kit. I was sad, though, for all the others with whom I share my number who live in constant inner misery with their critic, as I have.

I wasn't the only one having self-discovery. Andy also took the Enneagram test with Beth. It turns out he's a #8/Challenger/ The Leader with a Seven-Wing (Enthusiast/Adventurer). My jaw dropped from the accuracy of his description. As with my number, of course, things made better sense. I'm sure others would agree.

A gallant crusader against injustice – yes, please. A sense to accomplish something significant – music to my ears. And the desire to be independent – we were a match made in heaven. It was clear what I found attractive, and what I didn't.

Just as I had some hard truths to digest, Andy did too. Having the fiercest personality of the nine, he didn't have any problem owning it, not even a little. What about acknowledging that his domineering tendencies could be overbearing? He could also go too far in his self-interest, unaware of the destruction it caused. Eights are also prone to anger – how could Andy deny that?

I didn't know if Andy would be open to the idea of even talking about the printouts from Beth. I think he took the test to appease me more than anything. I was desperate for him to understand and step up. Because the work Beth and I were doing was making a difference, I wanted that for us. I could feel it, and others could see it also, even him. So why wouldn't he be on board?

As predicted, when I offered him his packet, he scoffed and downplayed it. I was so pissed! In that hasty moment, I made a snarling comment, using the material as ammunition for an ultimatum about saving our marriage. God, I was such a dick! So I left a sticky note on his packet and put it on his desk – not one of my finer moments. Guess whose therapy took a back seat. Ouch.

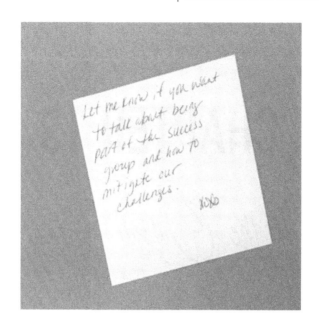

CHAPTER 13

On the Outside Looking In

MARCH 24, 2018

I earlier said my story is like a movie sometimes. Each time I've traveled down a metaphorical yellow brick road, I've uncovered "feel-good" moments in the unlikeliest of places. And just when I thought I'd found my way through disaster, without fail another antagonist would lurk in the shadows stalking me, once again, for the opportune moment to take advantage of me when I least expected it.

What I am talking about is two things that intertwine with each other daily. That is, being part of a blended family and having surviving children.

Five months or so after Ally's murder, even though things felt blah, I couldn't shake feeling like an "outsider" because half of "my team" in the Starrett bunch was missing. My devastation became an obsession, one that clouded my perception, filling me with jealousy that Andy's daughter and son lived. Not so much with Alex because he wasn't in my forefront. But sadly, Kylie wore a target.

It's not like Andy and Kylie didn't include me in everyday things. For the most part, they did – business as usual. And Kylie continued spending one-on-one time with me. So you'd think I'd be fine. Instead, my hypersensitivity was on overdrive, searching for things to substantiate my claim that I didn't belong.

Case in point: We were at Walmart, as usual, getting our groceries and extra school supplies for Kylie. After paying for what I thought was everything, I noticed Andy had separated the school supplies and paid for them. I didn't understand. It's been "my job" to pay for things since we got married. Don't get me wrong – Andy would pay for an unexpected trip to Dairy Queen if I didn't have my wallet, but Walmart? What made this trip so different from the past decade?

Let's be real. I'm sure I would've questioned it in a normal circumstance – it was just odd. When I asked, Andy justified using money he'd received from his ex. Trying to process his logic and move on was hopeless for me. I'd already planted the seed that they didn't need me anymore.

As you can imagine, it only went downhill from there. Or uphill, depending on your viewpoint. Nonetheless, my jealousy spread like a disease. It was awful. There wasn't a day that went by when I didn't envy their relationship, and the thought of leaving them seemed more manageable than the daily torture.

Every moment Andy and Kylie interacted together made my stomach turn. Whenever I watched them laugh, do chores, or even watch a movie, they appeared perfectly content without me.

Meanwhile, we continued to play family. I'd call it more like walking on eggshells. Kylie's intention to be the best-behaved daughter won her the Miss Congeniality sash for sure. Make no mistake about it. I appreciated her efforts to avoid getting in trouble – a parent's dream. Still, I'd be lying if I said her good intentions sometimes didn't feel like a suck-up. It's unnatural for a teenager to obey the rules (all the time).

Of course, Kylie's plan could last only so long. Her efforts began to fade in month six, and she started making up for lost time. It was then that Andy became a stranger to me.

I don't think anyone would deny Ally was the first to stretch the boundaries on almost everything. Some showcased her incredible talents, and others, not so much. If anything, it was the best gift she'd given Kylie. With a perfect bow, Ally handed her a manual containing detailed sections on how to "see things through" and "what not to do" growing up.

Unfortunately, it didn't get better when Ally met Arturo. Things spiraled out of control faster than a New York second. It was a year of constant yelling and fighting between Andy and Ally. He was the typical protective dad, and she was the defensive daughter about her dearest love. Neither was right or wrong, but goddam, it was exhausting.

It wasn't till Arturo went to jail that things began to settle down, and we had a brief interlude of calm as a family. Even to the point where Andy and Ally became close (again) after having a few heart-to-heart discussions. Sigh, finally.

Anyway, seeing Kylie make some of the same mistakes that Ally had, I noticed that Andy's predictable tendencies were utterly nonexistent. There was no yelling or even any mention of punishment. In all fairness, we'd discussed a million times having a "calmer" approach, but seriously? To all of a sudden become a pushover? I'm sorry, but it seemed unfair that Kylie didn't face her dad's wrath as Ally had. Does that sound like a shitty thing to say? Probably.

Yet the one thing Andy and I agreed on was making sure Kylie was involved like usual, if not more so than before. The last thing we wanted was for her to feel "forgotten." It was a rare time he and I were effortlessly on the same page since Ally's death, and I'd take it.

Kylie and I continued our girlie routines like clockwork. Facials, pedicures, and Starbucks – our time was enjoyable. Noticing she wasn't talking about Ally, I feared that she'd feel "no longer important" if I continued. So I stopped talking about Ally in front of her altogether, and my grieving became more like whispers when

I was alone. It didn't help that Andy didn't mention her either. In thinking about it, hardly anyone brought her up – only me. Perhaps they thought it would be too painful if they did, I don't know.

Three months had gone by, and something was missing. The guilt I carried walking the tiniest tightrope of my life between my ladies left me feeling like less of a mother. To the point I didn't want to be one anymore, period. I became distant with Kylie, and even my rituals to honor Ally became less and less frequent, and eventually they ended.

Swimming in self-pity, I looked forward to one of my calls with Karen on Thursday. You can't help but smile when talking to her. As my frown turned upside down during our session, everything was all well and good until Ally called me out.

"Mom, why don't you talk to me anymore?"

I'll never forget my gum falling out of my mouth; I was in such shock. What the hell? I'd never seen *that* happen in a movie before. I had *no* idea Ally could be *that* aware! It didn't matter. Her question cut me like a knife! Dropping my head in shame, I wanted to die. Asking me if Ally's question made sense, Karen reiterated that she says whatever she gets and doesn't edit it at all. There was no need for her reminder. I already knew there was no way she could know. Taking a deep breath, I said, "Yes, it does."

I would've gladly admitted to anything other than this. I hated explaining what's been going on and why I'd hadn't talked to Ally. All I could envision was her screaming, "Mom, I've been calling you. Why aren't you picking up the phone?" Jesus! What kind of mother would let that happen?

After I embraced one of the worst wake-up calls of my life, things became clear during our discussion. Rather than dealing with my loss, I had projected my jealousy – it was nothing more than a nasty symptom I'd created to avoid the unbearable guilt. I love Ally and Kylie both more than anything, but the truth is that there is a connection with your maternal child like no other, and I missed *mine*!

And that wasn't all. I admitted another truth, one I'll have until Ally and I reunite. Things will never be the same for an innocent sister who didn't ask for this to happen. Now, for every accomplishment

Kylie has, that gloom will forever be bound to the joyous experience because Ally isn't physically present. Talk about another double-edged sword for my tragedy-stricken psyche.

When I took Kylie to Chick-fil-A that Saturday, my nerves were all over the place. Was it the most intimate place to discuss a deep, dark secret? Not really. Although, I wasn't going to pass up when Kylie decided where to eat. It's not that often she does. Usually, I got the frustrating and classic "I don't know" teenage response. Besides, it was Ally's favorite. I thought she'd be there, providing us extra comfort.

After thirty minutes or so, awkward silence surrounded us. Staring into Kylie's concerned big brown eyes, I'm sure she had to know something was coming. Dread filled every cell of my body. I didn't appreciate having this kind of conversation in the first place. I sure missed having the abundance of first-world problems like we did. I would have given anything to talk about that trivial bullshit instead.

In one fell swoop, I shared the torment I'd been carrying as if I were sitting in Village Inn with my coffee and cheesecake talking to Petra. I thoroughly explained to Kylie what I had witnessed at Walmart, my jealousy over her connection with her dad, keeping my grief to myself and no longer wanting to be a mom.

As I hesitantly finished, all I could think was "Thank God!" For what I assumed would be brutal, I patted myself on the back. My words came out better than I had practiced in the mirror. I wish I would have recorded myself between you and me – it was that good. Maybe all those years of training talking about problems at Village Inn with my best friend had finally paid off.

Studying Kylie's flushed face while blowing my nose, I worried that I'd overshared. After all, she wasn't Petra, and we didn't have a history of twenty-five years through thick and thin behind us. The last thing I wanted was for anything to change between us. But in my mind, Kylie deserved every detail to understand truly what I'd been going through. Still, I braced for impact.

I looked past Kylie, and everyone around us became a blur; all the screaming from the indoor playground stopped. It was strange sitting there with her and everything around us on pause. I couldn't help but think how powerful this moment she and I were having was – like it was meant to be.

Unexpectedly, Kylie opened up like a floodgate. She expressed feeling sad and guilty through her tears because she didn't want to make me feel that way. And maybe if we spent *more* time together, I'd feel better. My heart broke – she'd taken responsibility for my jealousy.

She continued that she understood what I was saying and where I was coming from at the same time. It took me by surprise. She didn't sound like she agreed to try to shut me up, as I've experienced before. Not at all. Instead, she spoke with a mature authenticity that made me believe she understood.

While she was dabbing her eyes, I jumped in, addressing the unnecessary blame she had taken. I touched on spending more time together. I said that realistically, we aren't supposed to be in each other's back pocket – all we need is a healthy balance. Then, I clarified that my jealousy was simply the hurt from missing Ally, which wasn't Kylie's fault. Using her mom as an example, I reminded Kylie of the biological bond they share too. Nodding, she smiled.

Man, I was on a roll. The energy I felt between us gave me the go-ahead to explain how my pain stemmed from another dark place – that my bloodline lineage was over. I didn't mention it to be mean, nor was it personal, only a fact. Nodding again, I did what I do best. Jokingly, I smirked and said, "Guess it's all on your shoulders, kiddo. *No* pressure." We laughed. Kylie mentioned that we shouldn't forget about Alex. After a second, rolling our eyes, we both laughed again, even harder. We loved picking on him.

When we got home, I told Andy how Kylie and I had shared our most profound connection to date and that it was beautiful. I hadn't felt this happy since hardening my heart after buying the extra school supplies. Smiling, Andy looked at me in a way I hadn't seen in forever. Taking my hands, he described how he'd had a similar conflict with Ally. Not the jealousy part but the biological-bond piece, yes. His eyes became teary as he told me he could never fully understand what I was going through but that he'd support me all the way. And for the first time in nine months, I believed we'd make it through this nightmare stronger than before, and that's what I wanted.

CHAPTER 14

Monsters Are Real

MAY 2, 2018

Staring at my phone under my plush warm covers, I dreaded thinking about work. Huh, I must have a severe case of the Mondays. Even though, since Ally's death ten months ago, it was now the one place I could feel like me. Well, I only had to wear one mask, at least. For eight hours, I had an escape from my "real" life.

My ass was dragging as I got ready. I couldn't understand what was so different about that chilly morning. Thankfully, my office isn't a pain about the dress code. Pulling my blue jeans out of the dresser, I could only hope the stretchy material would somehow comfort me. I didn't care that it would be in the seventies later, so I picked my warmest gray sweatshirt and pulled on my black Skechers boots. Quick to justify that it would be a "hat day," I chose my favorite winter hat with a light-gray puffball to compliment my top.

Ally used to borrow mine all the time until I made the joke that she should get her own before she wore mine out. Deep down, I was flattered that she would wear something of mine. It must have meant I had good taste, right? She eventually went to Kohl's and got her own; I loved that we were twins; I have tremendous regret that we never took a picture together in our matching hats .

After a doom-and-gloom train ride to the office, reaching the final stop made me cry. What the hell? I was so damn bitchy – maybe I was getting sick? Yes, that must be it!

On the nine-minute walk to work, I decided to let Starbucks in our building take care of me. Once I got there, I ordered my regular blueberry oatmeal and my favorite drink.

Riding up the elevator, instead of doing a few usual squats to race myself before reaching our floor (if I'm alone), I watched the tiny television share fifteen-second news stories. Sometimes, there are important ones, but not that morning. I was also glad we didn't have elevator music. I probably would have been cynical about that, too. I heard the computer voice announce "34th floor," and I rolled my eyes. It felt like I had gotten there in no time, ugh.

Shuffling my feet to my workspace, I stared at it, wishing I had stayed home. It looked exactly like any other day, but man, I wasn't feeling it. I set my Starbucks down and put my bag in the drawer – I got a little winded. Are you kidding me? I shook my head, dismissing what I'd experienced. Reconfirming that I was getting sick.

By then, my co-worker, Rachel, had arrived, and I went to her desk for our morning catch-up. Thankfully, she was on a roll talking about her evening, so I didn't need to exert much energy. The conversation switched to me, and I was pretty robotic, but she didn't seem to mind. We wished each other a great day, and I returned to my desk.

Taking a deep breath, I stood there for what felt like minutes, dazed and confused. I persuaded myself to sit instead of stand. Oh, my God! What is wrong with me? I've used my standing desk for almost two years now. Everyone knows I bop around throughout the day. Because of all my standing, there was even some worry about me compacting my spinal column – it was a running joke. But today, it felt wrong. I lowered my desk, picked up the coat in my chair and looked around for a communal hanger. I felt silly not knowing where the closest one was.

There wasn't one person who didn't comment that I was sitting throughout the workday and then asked, "Are you OK?" It was like a broken record. How can one minor change bring such attention? I replied with different jokes, trying to lighten my insecurity. At the same time, I kept checking in within myself: No fever, my tummy felt OK, and I didn't have hot or cold flashes. It still didn't make sense, but something was off.

The following morning, it was the same thing. Except for this time, I hit snooze a few times. I couldn't move. I felt fine except for the lingering anxiety of the day before. I ended up having to drive in to make it on time. Pissed, now I had to pay to park. What a waste of fifteen bucks, not to mention my gas! There was a reason I started taking the train. Not only did work reimburse local transit, but I also made a pact with myself to save money for a trip. It was a win-win. Why couldn't I get my shit together? I settled that one day wouldn't hurt.

I made it to my desk, but the desire to stand still wasn't there. I bargained that I'd try after a few hours. Maybe I needed to warm up or something.

As the day progressed, I didn't even try, not once. Instead of letting my music play on shuffle, I intentionally picked heart-thumping songs to see if that would make a difference. Nope. I may have smiled now and then, but nothing I did was working. Some moments, I was able to shrug it off. Others, it nipped at my consciousness.

After a long car ride home in incredibly satisfying rush-hour traffic – not – I had plenty of time to self-reflect. I scolded myself that tomorrow would be different. I talked through the steps I'd take, one by one. I agreed with my plan, feeling optimistic. Don't you love it when you coach yourself bouncing back and forth between first and second person, especially out loud? I could only imagine what the other drivers were thinking. Laughing at myself, I chalked it up to everyone having a few bad days.

By the end of the week, I was swimming in disappointment with myself. Every day was still the same, running late, driving in, not standing, and now I wasn't working out, either. Come on! I was sleeping OK according to my Fitbit, and eating healthy, so why didn't I have the energy to do the things I used to do?

"I'm worried about you," Rachel said to me by that late Friday afternoon. I freaked out, honestly. My internal barometer dial immediately shifted to concern.

Over the weekend, I talked to Andy about it. He was supportive and suggested I give myself a break. He had no idea how on fire my inner critic was. I wanted to listen to him – I did. Keeping her at bay, I opted for a lazy weekend, which was not in my character. I felt like a zombie most of the time, staying in my house clothes. Everything I touched felt heavy, and I didn't know who I saw when I looked in the mirror.

Good or bad, I knew myself. I always had an answer, but not this time. I'd never experienced anything like this before. I knew I wasn't sick – this was something else. Trying to ride the wave, I ignored myself and tried making my staycation as good as possible.

Fast-forwarding to the end of May, the victories of feeling accomplished lessened each day. I survived on the basics, and even that was questionable. Did I brush my teeth? How about washing my face? Between you and me, not always. Mascara can last two, three days if you sleep on your back and don't shower, just saying. So this is what my life was boiling down to, gauging a good morning on my "MacGyver" skills to appear presentable? Who was this girl?

I also developed a worry I'd never had before. I became fearful I was showing up late to punch a timecard that my work had never required. My anxiety didn't make sense, but the math for racking up unnecessary charges to my credit card for parking did, and yet it didn't stop me.

Standing at work still wasn't a thing despite trying a few more times. Although I did notice that the comments from co-workers finally stopped, that was nice.

As each workday transitioned to nighttime, I became more intimate with laziness. I felt so guilty for not being active. I hated it! Instead of taking advantage of the weekends, I felt lost in my home – nothing was mine. But who else would I ask permission from to use my stuff?

When I looked at my exercise equipment, once trusted friends, a soft layer of dust was resting on them. Walking by my art studio, my supplies stayed adequately organized from the last piece I made before Ally died, awaiting my command. The beauty I had made with them seemed like a hundred years ago.

Don't get me wrong – I did little things here and there. OK, let's be honest – I made dinner. That's something. However, I'm sure my family got tired of the repetitive meals: spaghetti, chili, and pulled chicken. Each made in a giant pot for the gift of leftovers. I justified it as efficient, enough said.

The once-upon-a-time advice from friends and family began contradicting itself. Their diehard directions to stay busy changed to saying I should now rest and relax. Are you fucking kidding me? On top of that, hearing how tired I looked was a real confidence-booster; I couldn't win. I mean, I was relieved, and yet I felt abandoned by my loved ones. I was so damn confused. How do we truly know when to push through the tough times versus permit ourselves that much-needed break?

Let me guess. You have a loved one with the cure-all for everything, regardless of whether they've practiced what they preached? Good news – me, too.

At the time, my funk didn't seem life-changing enough to share with Beth; we worked on so many other things. Good grief, there wasn't enough time in the day to touch them all, but I felt like we were hitting the most important developments. Instead, I relied on other resources to talk through my observations of what I was going through. The advice I received was almost unanimous: I needed to try meditation. So I did.

I hate to say it, but it was downright disastrous after using the Calm app a handful of times. Another unfortunate setback in my journey. It wasn't the program, by any means. There were plenty of options for beginners. It was user-friendly, and I received an inspirational meme after completing a segment as a well-deserved reward. What more could someone ask for, anyway? It's a tool designed to hold my hand, with which millions have found great success. It should have been the answer, right?

When I started the program, I knew it would have its challenges, of course. I let Andy and Kylie know my plans, and they were surprisingly supportive. Practicing in the morning didn't fit into my routine at all. I already get up early, which only meant going to bed sooner. My bedtime was already eight – I didn't want to give them any more ammunition to make fun of me that my transition to becoming elderly was nearly complete. All I was missing was eating dinner at four o'clock and wearing white New Balance tennis shoes with Velcro straps.

The first night, I sat in my pitch-black bedroom, following each instruction described by the guide. I chose my comfy bed, sat upward against my headboard and began relaxing my body. As I listened, it didn't take long for my mind to wander about paying bills or things I'd forgotten to do. Coincidentally, the narrator then noted that fleeting thoughts were healthy. Thank goodness! They reiterated this message repeatedly; I felt comforted, as if they knew what I was doing.

After a few minutes, they directed me to sit in stillness. At first, this seemed like a good idea. I thought I'd find clarity and wisdom by looking within. As I stared into the darkness of my consciousness, I patiently waited to receive something, anything. Within a second, I saw glimpses of Ally's crime scene. The yellow tape, the patrolling police officers, and the overwhelming fear I felt flashed like an explosion, piercing me with shrapnel from all directions. My heart raced, and my body was uncontrollably shaking. Panicked, I ripped out my earbuds and stumbled in the dark from my bed to find the light switch. Desperate for safety, I clicked on the button and looked around my bedroom, confused and scared.

Sitting back down on my bed, I held my phone, rocking back and forth, contemplating how I'd never experienced anything like that before. Turning off the app, I thought enough was enough for one night, and I lay down with Ally's matching hat (it's been on my nightstand since she died). Squeezing it tightly, I had no idea how to fall asleep after something like that. But somehow, I must have.

I didn't share my experience with Andy or Kylie the next day. I was too afraid of what they'd say, and it wasn't like they were asking anyway. Instead, I did my best to compartmentalize the anxiety that surrounded my every move, pretending I was OK – my favorite mask, of course.

As the day progressed, I felt better after I justified that it must have been a fluke of some kind. Maybe I was tired or ate something spicy. Many say food can affect your dreams, so why not meditation? Although everyone knows I eat bland food, but whatever. It didn't matter what I came up with; I wanted to forget that it ever happened, so I bought my lame-ass excuses.

Waiting a day, I decided to try again. I generally preach, "Take a no-thank-you bite," to just about everything new. And that's what I did. Why give it another go? It already failed once. Why try again? I guess my desperation in needing something to help my old self return took precedence. I hoped more than anything that this time would be a positive experience.

So, in the meantime, I made sure to have a flavorless dinner beforehand. It wasn't hard. I wore my *extra*-soft jammies, thinking they would comfort me. After getting a chair from Kylie's room, I again sat in my pitch-black bedroom. I'll admit that her metal chair wasn't as cozy as my bed. Like before, I intently listened to the predictable guiding instructions, following each step one by one.

This time, I made it a minute or two before my mind wandered again to my to-do list. Nevertheless, I gave myself a little pat on the back for staying more focused on this go-around. I was smiling, and I thought I was on the right track. Then, the voice invited me to sit in silence again.

I cleared my mind and welcomed the clarity to arrive, taking a deep breath. It took only seconds. My body tensed, and I felt total pain. I saw what I assumed was the horror of what the motel room resembled. Disheveled sheets on the bed, furniture pushed over and papers littered on the floor. It was evident a struggle had happened; I gasped out loud.

Limp from the fatigue, I fell to the floor. Is that how Ally died? Oh, my God! I didn't see Ally in my vision, but I knew she was there somewhere – waiting for her mama to save her in real life. I cried so hard there was no noise, exhausting myself to the point of turning blue before finding my breath again.

I curled into the fetal position, not able to make a sound. My pulsing heartbeat throbbed everywhere I ran my fingers. The app was still talking in the background, but I didn't have the strength to turn it off; I didn't care. Frozen, I was stuck thinking about my poor baby as I fumed. I missed her so fucking much! Plaguing questions stabbed my heart one after another. My draining wounds began morphing into hatred and fueled my thoughts.

I was in a nightmare, and yet I was wide awake. Concentrating on anything was unbearable. Everything felt hopeless, and for a split second, the thought of killing myself seemed like the cure.

I wanted to be with Ally, wherever she was. I longed to see her again any way I could. I knew my family was downstairs, but so what? It didn't matter, the millions of ways I tried to explain it. They could never understand what I was going through; how could they?

The thought of feeling this pure isolation any longer made me sick. I wanted to end my misery.

Staring into the blackness of the room, I lay there, aching. I'd never thought in a million years that I would ever consider such a thing. No way! I despised people who took their own lives; I thought it was *so* selfish. However, at this moment, I believed that I understood their motivation, relating to it with every cell of my body. The act itself is about being in control. Their world is in such disarray; this choice seems like the only one they can manage. No one can take it, and it would be on their terms.

To this day, my imagination had never let me down like this. Every option I considered, I hit a wall like a crash-test dummy. Was it a sign? Scarves only looked like beautiful accessories giving me an edge of sass. My bedsheets were my silent friend that embraced me unconditionally. The blade in my shaving razor provided the undeniable sensation of sexiness I felt after running my hands along my soft legs.

After what seemed like forever, I bolted straight up from the floor, fearful that Andy might come in. How would I explain the puddle of tears on the floor next to my phone? Beats me.

I convinced myself this had happened for a reason. Yes, I wanted to be with Ally more than anything – without a doubt. But I didn't want to die, not yet. Maybe this was the universe reminding me that I had the chance to choose. I still felt so lost, and my options were bleak. Nonetheless, the few I had were mine, and no one could take them from me.

Putting back Kylie's chair, I realized my family had no idea what had happened, and I didn't have to tell them. I was glad; I didn't want to. It wasn't because I was embarrassed – well, maybe a little – but more so because I was afraid. Now, ten months afterward to the day, I began adding up all the ways I hadn't been myself since Ally died, and I hated it. I couldn't see hope and the positive in everything like before. I was one way to face my friends and family, and when I was alone looking in the mirror – I was another. Now, I saw only a monster.

CHAPTER 15

Layers Are Invisible

JULY 10, 2018

Walking into Beth's office that afternoon, I was eager to share my photo of us remembering Ally's anniversary. Andy, Kylie, and I returned to Cherry Creek State Park as before and went paddleboarding. This time, we brought Nikki.

Sharing a giggle with Beth, she wondered if the spot in the lower-left corner of the photo was an orb of Ally. It was priceless because, sadly, it's my finger. I always enjoy a good laugh with her.

Continuing, I described how we had a balloon release at Ally's grave with the entire family afterward. I proudly explained how triumphant I felt having made it through the first year of Ally's death – as if it were a rite of passage to say the world hadn't gotten the better of me. Raising her eyebrow, Beth asked me to repeat what I'd said. I'm not too fond of it when she does that. Taking a pause, I spoke each syllable with the most precise enunciation.

"I-feel-victorious-for-surviving-the-first-year-since-Ally's-*murder*." I stared at her as we sat in awkward silence. Was I supposed to have an epiphany or wait for her guidance? My chest beat like a drum replaying the words over and over in my mind. The more I stared at Beth, the more I felt I'd said something horrifically wrong.

The pain hit me like a shotgun blast. It wasn't like I didn't know Ally was dead or I hadn't said the words before, but something was vastly different. My world turned inadvertently upside down again, and I sobbed in front of Beth for the first time.

Having no idea what had just happened, Beth sympathetically reassured me that I was in a safe place through all my double inhales, trying to catch my breath. Can I tell you that was a first for me? Not only did she not interrupt or rush my experience, but she also thanked me for finally sharing a good cry with her. Who does that, anyway?

Beth agreed that yes, I did "survive" through the first year. And at the same time, I shed a layer of numbness, leaving me raw and vulnerable, exposing a hurt that couldn't possibly be worse, and yet here it is.

Knowing me all too well, she questioned my definition of the word "survivor." In my condensed version, it's someone who can acknowledge that they were victimized and not let their tragedy define them.

Looking at me with her squinted eyes, she said, "And have *you* acknowledged you've been victimized?"

It was true. I'd been fighting with myself since Day One between being a survivor and victim. It's not much of a secret that I despise those who bathe in self-pity. Please don't misunderstand me. Everyone has shit happen to them, of course. It's when the "oh, woe is me" label defines them instead of becoming a victor to thrive in life again and help others. I'll never forget when a friend told me that they look and sound like Beaker from "The Muppets" after a while. You must admit that these people do exist.

Offering this idea, I hoped I was wrong: "I probably raced through the first milestones to check them off the list." Sigh, I wasn't. Beth validated that it's common with the newly bereaved.

In retrospect, for Ally's 19th birthday, only months after her death, the entire family honored one of her favorite indoor glow-in-the-dark mini-golf activities. Although without the photos, I don't remember a thing about it. I focused so much on her empty place setting at Thanksgiving and Christmas that I couldn't share any other meaningful memories. The same applied to my birthday and Mother's Day, too. Holy shit! It *did* feel like a blur.

After giving me a minute to process, Beth asked if anything out of the ordinary had happened.

Wishing I could disappear, I said, "Yes."

Beth mentioned I had depression due to my complex grieving process when describing my recent funk. Really? Was it predictable to everyone around me that I'd hit an ultimate low? Probably. But it wasn't for me. What was I missing right in front of my face? All it took was her reminding me how standing at my desk became a burden for the light bulb to go off. Huh, all right.

I then told her about the horrible meditation experience that led me to the thought of suicide. Becoming overly anxious, I waited for Beth to hand me a straitjacket. And yet there was a sense of satisfaction in having been honest with her.

Looking at me like a best friend would, she said, "What you experienced is normal."

Speechless, I hung on every word. Beth explained that I'd developed post-traumatic stress disorder due to the situation's trauma. Jesus! Was there anything else we could add to the list of how fucked up I am? I didn't ask for any of this! You know that phrase "You are only given as much as you can handle"? It was about to get the middle finger! Who decided what a person can handle, anyhow? If I'd been "weaker," would Ally be here? It's not that I disagreed with it – but I was overwhelmed. Could *one* thing in my life stay the same and not need a makeover?

With snarky regret, I said, "I guess I should have asked before trying meditation." Beth recognized my frustration and reassured me, again, that what I had experienced was normal.

She explained that recent studies have shown it can be more harmful to relive your traumatic experience without supportive measures and resources in place first. Because the brain can generate a protective biological barrier, accompanied by my numbness lifting, deep meditation could exacerbate symptoms (i.e., worry, making irrational decisions, and memory loss) whereby I could actually dissociate as a result. I mean, I get it. Escaping reality is bad and all, but you must admit that if your symptoms involve creating an alternate identity, is that *really* any different than a superhero having an alter ego?

Anyway, she clarified that she didn't recommend continuing until we worked more on my recovery and resource me up a bit. I suppose my mind didn't understand that the actual trauma was over. In that case, everything I was experiencing in the present was only a trigger, followed by a trauma response – meaning it could basically retraumatize me. Well, that sounds like fun.

Overcome with fascination, I nervously asked if this was why she avoided bringing up Ally's murder. For the previous ten months, we had talked only about my perception of how *I* was coping.

She replied, "Yes."

I'd thought she'd given me a get-out-of-jail-free card, when in fact (I didn't know until recently) she used "Prolonged Exposure" to treat my PTSD. I'd describe the event in detail, in the present moment, with Beth guiding me. It's a reframing and recalibration technique, which in turn allows healing to unlock itself.

After months of work, I understood that my reactions from meditation were a sequence of trauma responses, leaving me paralyzed and giving my body no choice but to shut down. That's cool and all, but instead, I'd like to choose my response, wouldn't you? Now, when shit hits the fan, I use the "Double P" technique: Practice patience or practice pause; they are interchangeable, if you ask me.

If we default to using only our emotional mind in times of stress, we are more than likely only bringing fuel to the fire. Instead, we need the handshake with our thinking brain because it's rational. Together in unison, they clear a pathway to our wisdom, allowing conscious problem-solving to take place. Of course, it's easier said than done, but my energy reserves aren't as depleted when used regularly, giving me a chance to reframe the situation. Besides, it's fun to say, "I need to go PP now," and watch people's reactions.

Meanwhile, using these techniques were helpful for many situations – even though they didn't "fix" (I hate this word) my relationship with depression. Grappling with the idea of antidepressants when Beth first mentioned it, I insisted talk therapy would suffice.

It took almost two years before I succumbed to the realization it wasn't getting better. I slowly continued losing interest in just about everything else, one by one. I should've known when movies became daunting. OK, this might be more because seeing *Atomic Blonde* changed everything. For the first time since Ally's death, I witnessed what I believed was the most accurate depiction of her murder.

Sure, like most action movies, watching all the ass-kicking and name-taking was exciting. Then, the film took a turn, as it should. Now in a motel room, a beautiful young lady was tossed around like a limp doll fighting for her survival. Even though she got a few good hits in, it didn't matter. She gruesomely died from a cord choking her.

Still not knowing any details from our case, this movie forever imprinted the idea of Ally's death in my database. As a result, I despised seeing new ones. The possibility of another strangulation scene held me hostage. It didn't matter if you watched the trailer or read the synopsis. Nothing protected me.

Not ready to subject myself to future torture, I began watching the same movies over and over, thinking they were safe and predictable.

Although many I adored took a back seat, as I had forgotten that they, too, had a strangulation scene. Sadly, my Rolodex of movies became relatively minimal, and my favorite pastime became my worst enemy.

But I digress. Let's get back to why I dragged my feet about medication. Much like everything else on my journey, I had another hard-hitting lesson.

My mom's sister Peggy, whom I share a birthday with, is my favorite aunt of all time. She *really* got me. Our styles were the same, our behaviors – you name it. I idolized this woman from head to toe, probably because I was her doppelganger.

In my preteen years, I witnessed her becoming a hot mess. Weight gain, weight loss, mood swings, and crazy hairdos – completely situationally lost. But one thing was consistent: her sadness. Not understanding, my family would explain it as best they could, using kid-friendly words and, of course, downplaying the truth.

Long story short, nothing seemed to help, one medication after another. My Aunt Peggy was in a downward spiral and suddenly died at forty-two.

Now an early teen, I took her death hard, but not in the way most would expect. Because my family did not reveal the truth until decades later (I don't blame anyone), and hearing "she'd given up" from so many, I labeled her as weak. In my twisted kid-logic, I concocted the belief that because we shared a birthday and were so similar, I'd end up unstable and doomed just like her. Planting a seed like no other, I set in motion every strength the Enneagram said I had, and probably a few weaknesses, too.

I carried this belief around for thirty years, and you could say I developed strong opinions about many things. Beth once challenged me to look at my situation differently. What happens if, on a massive spectrum, we only have loyalty to the past? Wouldn't that be like creating a living memorial? Meaning our present-day life is now insignificant. Interesting.

When Beth mentioned antidepressants for the second time, I gave her the stink-eye. She knew how I felt about them, so why bring it up again? Sitting with the idea for a few days, I had an epiphany strike me like lightning. It all made sense. I realized what I'd done. I feared, in every way, that my fate would be the same as my aunt's. I had faulted her choices instead of giving her credit that she did the best she could, and that wasn't right. It was time to accept that each human's experience is truly their own.

I've said all along I didn't want Ally's death to define my existence – it's only a part of my story. So why wouldn't this apply to my Aunt Peggy's death, too? As a result, I've committed to trying an antidepressant. Wish me luck.

CHAPTER 16

An Empty Space

JULY 21, 2018

From the very beginning of Beth's and my therapeutic partnership, she coached that grief's effects can make situations more awkward for anyone. Meaning some relationships would even have an expiration date, and I might need to find a new tribe. I heard what she was saying, but I thought for sure it wouldn't happen to me. Although, once I started thinking about past encounters, her warning or wisdom (you decide) was already in motion.

The ever predictable, "What did you do over the weekend?" question was downright dreadful. Did anyone genuinely want to hear how I sulked most of it? They didn't. More often than not, if I tried to share my feelings, somebody would dismiss them with an interruption of some kind, or they told me to look for only the positives. It became predictable. More and more, it fueled my desire to wear my favorite "I'm fine" mask.

Then on the flip side, if I would ask about their weekend, their answers felt guarded, even scripted. People didn't want to talk about their kids in front of me. I hated it! Does my tragedy mean I'm any less your friend? I'd hope not. If we had a relationship, like a real one, wouldn't that mean I already knew about your kids? But if you choose to stop, aren't you taking yourself away from me too? Isn't one loss enough?

My other favorite was when people would forewarn me that they wanted to talk about Ally. Seriously? They would either ask if I would be OK or preface the subject. It even once happened with Petra, my best friend of all people. Yes, I understood they thought it would be painful, but couldn't talking about her also be a gift?

I *want* to talk about Ally. She is one of my most favorite people on the planet (now universe)! With each story I tell about her, she lives on through happiness, laughter, and love. It was a way for me to see and feel her warmth. I can visualize her as I remember her, and that's what I want.

So how was I ever going to get shit off my chest if my audience was limited? It's not like I can hold it in, waiting for Beth all the time. I was descending into madness. Jesus! What's next?

Meanwhile, I was so tired of feeling invisible. Is that why I saw myself as a monster? Is that why I was beginning to notice that the world around me, even my family, was moving forward and I wasn't? Is that why I felt more alone than ever? I was devastated yet again. When was I going to catch a damn break? Seriously?

Maybe it was time to find that tribe Beth talked about earlier. Was that even a thing? Were there other bereaved mothers feeling like they were going insane too? Between you and me, that sounded downright awful! I've never gone on the hunt to make new friends; I sense stranger danger in most cases. All my relationships have "just happened" – I liked to believe it was as nature intended, even including my parents.

I found the packet from the Victim's Advocacy Group, and within it was a phone number for the Parents of Murdered Children. I gasped. I stared at it gratefully and yet hatefully – there was no way I belonged to this group! Was this indeed my future? My capacity to digest the flurry of emotions was running thin. I sat in denial for a good hour, wishing my life away.

I tried talking to Andy. He was in such a different space from me – another disappointment. Our conversation only reiterated what he told me for the past few months: that he was feeling fine and didn't need support. How could that even be possible? What made his statement more confusing is he'd chosen to continue counseling with a different therapist – never in my life did I see that coming. I certainly don't want to belittle his efforts, because I'm super-proud of his choice, but what in the world did they talk about then? I didn't know if I should be more pissed or feel sad for him. Nonetheless, he said that he would go to a group meeting with me if I called.

It was something, right? I most certainly didn't want to go by myself. In my mind, I was already concocting the idea that by going, it could open Andy's eyes to his feelings. It sounded like a win for both of us.

I shook, dialing each digit in the phone number. For every hopeful thought of feeling united in my tragedy, I also hoped it was disconnected. The phone rang until the voicemail greeted me. The message was clear that I'd dialed the right phone number, ugh. Is this really happening? I was relieved and yet so scared to leave my information. But I did, leaving the shortest, most awful non-rehearsed voicemail of my life.

I paced around that morning full of anxiety about receiving a call back. What would the caller say? Were they a parent like me or some poor volunteer? Why had I not checked them out more thoroughly? Talk about an idiot.

I found their national website, and I didn't know what to think. My first impression told me to run away, hard and fast. Flashing in the top right-hand corner was a slideshow of deceased loved ones. As they appeared on the screen one after another, my stomach became queasy – some were so young. Could this be real? I clicked around the various sections: Murder Wall, Parole Block, and Survivor Support. I began comprehending just how real this was.

Phil, the Front Range Chapter leader, called within a few hours. As he introduced himself as the father of his murdered daughter,

I got chills on my arms. Dear Lord! There were two of us! I didn't know what to say.

Walking around our upstairs, I listened in awe as he shared bits of his story. I'll spare you now and throughout the rest of the chapter from the gory details. The bottom line is that his oldest daughter's boyfriend murdered her after months of unreported domestic violence. Morbidly, the similarities we shared gave me comfort.

Phil shifted gears and explained about the meetings and how they worked. Every word he said felt so surreal. I couldn't believe I was having this conversation. All I could hear was that there were other families and that they were available to help me. For God's sake! There were more like us? I never dreamed of such a thing. Has my head been in the sand, or what?

The what-ifs started building unwanted anxiety, but it didn't matter. I was ready to jump into the car and meet these people. He cautioned that the meetings could be intense. Some people share only a little and are quieter, and others, well – they tell every little detail and can be rather explosive. He said it could feel like a "POMC hangover," to be exact. I appreciated that warning, and yet I didn't fully understand or care, honestly.

I told Andy about the news and the meeting being that night. He was in full support. I appreciated his willingness to go – it didn't feel like pulling teeth at all. He didn't seem too worried about the dynamic of the group setting, either. It didn't surprise me; he thinks he can handle anything.

In saying that, we decided not to invite Kylie until after we experienced the meeting for ourselves. The last thing we wanted to do was cause her any further trauma. In talking with us, she was OK with that. Besides, she was content staying home with Nikki anyway, declaring she would throw a party while we were gone. Oh, the poor dog.

Andy and I walked hand in hand from the parking lot toward the double doors, not saying a word. The building looked more like a prison than a corporate telecommunications office from the outside. The drab concrete structure lacked any personality at all. Thank goodness for the mature trees surrounding the grounds. Why were there no windows? That seemed odd.

There was a tall tower next to the main building, and it looked more like a perfect vantage point for monitoring inmates than anything else. It was connected by what I could only assume was an interior bridge also encased in concrete. Why? It didn't make sense. What were they trying to protect, anyway?

I kept asking myself if we were in the right place. Could it be any more ironic? In a way, this location seemed very fitting for us. I related to how lifeless the building looked and felt. Maybe for Andy, the concrete structure represented the hard-shell guy he portrayed. And perhaps the high walls provided safety and yet forced isolation for me.

Wanting to throw out my metaphorical realization to him, I didn't bother to say anything. The last thing I wanted to hear was a tough-guy response shooting me down. What I needed more was a vulnerable validation. It was rare if I heard him say, "Me, too," when

I'd throw out what I was experiencing. I couldn't understand how we never overlapped in a similar grieving emotion at the same time.

I ached in desperation to bond with someone, anyone, so I wouldn't be alone and going crazy with each step I took. We walked by the front desk, and the security team greeted us. A switch flipped in me, and I became nervous and even more insecure. Is the staff this nice to everyone, or do they know why we are here? Did Phil tell them to look out for "newbies" or what? A twinge of sickness rumbled loudly in my stomach. Practicing the properly trained response, I smiled and returned the gesture.

The inside of the building was dark and outdated. I couldn't spot one thing that provided any inspiration: no plants, no exciting pictures, nothing. All I could think was that the employees who worked there had to be sad all the time, and the energy to produce a smile had to be exhausting. I have to tell you, the interior only put a bow to the metaphoric packaged moment I had outside.

Walking toward the bare employee lunchroom, we approached about twenty or so chairs placed strategically like a crescent moon. I, of course, had a million critical things to say, but I held my tongue. I found the table with Phil's sign-in sheet from our call. I stood there in awe, seeing the other names of those present.

Holding the pen, I stared at the columns: Victim's Name, Relationship, Date of Birth and Death. I already hated being there and wanted to cry. I looked around for Andy, and he was busy introducing himself as if we were at a company function. My jaw hurt from my grinding teeth. I looked back down at the sheet and saw a single tear hit the paper. After filling out our name tags, I found a seat at the end of the circle.

I adjusted my purse under my seat, over and over. Was it necessary? Not really. I think I was just fiddling with it because I was anxious. I couldn't recall a time I was so uncomfortable in a group setting.

As I pulled out my notebook to take notes, Phil approached me and introduced himself. Could he tell I was nervous? This dad certainly wasn't what I had expected. Although I wasn't sure what

I thought he'd look like when we were on the phone. It didn't even cross my mind.

In front of me was a guy who looked like everyone else. OK, he did have a touch of Santa Claus going on, glasses and all. Aside from his salt-and-pepper hair, he would have a real chance at being the best mall Santa ever. He didn't seem much older than us, so maybe in a few years, anyway.

Everyone began to settle and take their seats – it was a full house. Looking around the circle, I was speechless. It didn't matter the age, gender, or relationship to their loved one; it seems violent crimes can happen to anyone.

I *so* didn't want to be there. More than that, I didn't want to *need* to be there. My foot became restless and wouldn't stop shaking. I kept looking at Andy for solace, but I felt more confused about his behavior sitting next to me. He crossed his arms behind his head while slightly rocking back and forth in his chair. A peculiar mannerism in front of a group of strangers, I thought. How could he appear as relaxed as he did? I couldn't say I'd seen this before, and I didn't get a good vibe from it at all.

Phil began the meeting by going over a few safety moments just like we do in corporate America. I have to say I felt a little more at ease – I enjoyed the usual schedule. He then went over the remaining logistics, and I could tell he'd been doing this awhile. He was a natural leader, and I appreciated his style.

The next moment took me by surprise. Phil "welcomed" Andy and me – it was the strangest thing to hear. I realized that my life wasn't ever going back to the way it was. I now had a lifelong membership with the most painful dues that would never expire.

The group took a deep breath, as if they were anticipating what would happen next. Sure enough, the pleasantries were over, and the room felt heavy. A spotlight might as well have highlighted Phil while the saddest song ever played in the background.

Phil began sharing the story of what had happened to his daughter. He shared the details, which I had heard on the phone already. I peeked over to Andy to watch his reaction. He sat like a statue, motionless – not surprising. Then, Phil told more gruesome specifics that made my stomach curl. Oh, my God! That poor, poor family! Could this be real? What words could provide comfort? It then dawned on me. Is this what it was like for everyone else around *me*?

Eyes wide, I stared at my paper, trying to put aside my feelings to write down some questions. Jesus, it was hard. Phil had warned me that you couldn't "unhear" things, but damn, it was awful.

Looking around the room, I tried to comprehend how many more people would share their stories. I had no idea, but I understood it would be a long night. I wasn't sure at that point if I wanted to come again, so I needed to focus on the purpose of why I was there. How else would I know if I were going crazy?

I jotted down some notes for Phil. I wanted to understand better how he and his wife had lasted ten years with a surviving daughter. Did they attend counseling? How did they grieve as a couple? What advice could he have for us? I felt so connected to him; he could hold my family's salvation.

One by one, the other members shared their stories. I was so numb by the time we made it around the circle. It was like watching a marathon of the most disgusting movies ever. But I kept writing down details that related to me. It sucked because there were just too many. Nevertheless, I couldn't deny that these people in front of me were the bravest humans I'd ever met.

The world has no idea what they've been through, and yet here they sit. These parents are alive – OK, maybe not all well, but I was sitting among survivors, for the most part. Yes, a few came across as more victimlike, but rightfully so. Unfortunately, one family had experienced almost a remake of *The Amityville Horror*, not even kidding. How is that possible? All I could do was internalize how grateful I was for Ally's death, compared with what they were going through. Is that not the *most* messed up thing to think or what?

I looked at my watch; it was almost eleven. I felt drained from all the gruesome storytelling, and I began to understand Phil's earlier caution more clearly now of the "POMC hangover." Interrupting the room's silence, Phil asked me if I wanted to share my story. My adrenaline went into overdrive, and I looked at Andy.

"Please, God, let him take one for the team and speak up," I wished. Besides, I wanted to see how he'd talk about it. I hadn't heard him do that before. My facial expressions and eye contact weren't persuasive enough.

"You go ahead," he said. I wanted to die, right there. I was full of disappointment and anger. I didn't think I had any capacity left to feel that night – boy, was I wrong.

Clearing my throat, I didn't know where to begin. I uncrossed my legs, shimmied myself up in my chair and found a comfortable posture, trying to buy time. I realized I hadn't shared Ally's story out loud with strangers in months. I was scared shitless.

At that moment, I did feel Andy's hand take mine. I squeezed it, pretty dang hard, too – not knowing if he understood why. I was relieved that he supported me. At the same time, it seemed like he had pushed me in front of a firing squad.

I saw everyone staring at me, and I couldn't stand it. But within a flash, I noticed their empathetic faces, and it was real. This entire night, none of them talked over one another, they didn't judge one another (out loud, anyway) and they listened intently – no matter how long anyone spoke. These people got it, more than anyone else I'd known. Why did it take my daughter dying to find such an incredible group of people I never wanted to meet? The respect they had for one another was unprecedented, unlike anything I'd ever witnessed.

"Ally was eighteen, and her boyfriend strangled her," I said, sounding like an auctioneer. The realism of what I'd just said paralyzed me. Again, I knew it was real – but the hard truth struck me like a lightning bolt.

I sat there, watching everyone nod their heads – I even saw another mother tear up. They all became blurry, and I sobbed deeper than with Beth. I was so embarrassed about crying in public, but I couldn't stop it. Thankfully, the circle had boxes of tissues everywhere, and I grabbed one, shoving my face as deep as I could, letting the darkness surround me.

Andy rubbed my back as I cried for what felt like forever. What was he thinking and feeling? What about the group? I am sure they'd seen it before.

After I wiped off my raccoon eyes, my sniffling sounded ridiculously loud, but I didn't care. I blew my nose a few times, feeling exhausted more than ever. I looked at the group as they patiently waited for me to continue. Noticing Andy was still holding my hand, I felt supported. I politely asked Phil if I could shift to the questions I had. He didn't hesitate and agreed.

I asked if anyone had suggestions for our marriage. Joe, a member for almost thirty years, chimed in. He described how he and his wife, Kaye, had had a dry-cleaning business that kept them together. A customer would come in whenever they would fight, forcing them to settle and put their happy faces on. They looked at each other and laughed.

Everyone in the group smiled and listened as he shifted gears to explain that they closed the business after a while and started a successful nonprofit, Voices of Victims. He further told us about the foundation and the post-sentencing services provided for violent-crime victims.

The group provided their gratitude for their work, and the room went silent. It was clear they held high respect for the couple and all their efforts. That's all well and good, but I have to say Joe's story didn't exactly point me in the direction I was hoping. I think I had more questions than anything. Nonetheless, I thanked him and appreciated his sharing. I was too tired to redirect my question or pry any further.

Now, it was almost midnight. I acknowledged the group as a whole. I needed them to know how much they had validated me. Even though each story was unique, I found relatable references and how I could learn something from each one of them.

Getting choked up, I noted how alone and crazy I'd felt through this journey. And through the group, I witnessed kindness, determination, validation, disappointment, anger, compassion, hope, and empathy. I concluded that I wasn't crazy and that the one feeling I'd been honestly longing for was in this group. And although I didn't want to belong, I'd found my missing piece.

CHAPTER 17

Accept the Unacceptable

SEPTEMBER 13, 2018

How does your family react when things go south? Mine? It's like being at a masquerade ball. It's true. For the first two months after Ally's death, there was a sense of feeling connected. But for the past year, not only was I hiding behind a mask – so were they.

Desperate for normalcy, we fell back into our routine of having my folks over for Sunday Family Movie Night. For an event we'd done for years, I thought we were as close as it gets. Although in reality, our time together became more superficial than anything. In our defense, we didn't know any better. There isn't a book called "Working Through Murder for Dummies" – that I've found, anyway.

As my newly identified numbness began shedding, it became obvious that the pretend party would be short-lived. Knowing we should be discussing our feelings, I'd try to bring up the subject, but it usually went nowhere. The resistance was exhausting and only created more friction, as if we needed any more. At that point, no one else was stepping up to implement helpful resources, either. Admitting that I was out of my league was tough; I didn't know how we would survive.

I thought it was brilliant when Beth recommended that my mom, dad, Andy, Kylie, and I see her together. To my surprise, they were open to the idea. I wondered if they were going out of obligation because I asked or thought they'd get something out of it. I loved that we could come together as a unit – strength in numbers, right? I quickly learned that the duality of that also meant revealing the depth of our group's dysfunction.

Our meeting with Beth "controlled" the pure insanity of trying on our own. A bare conference room with a giant formal table allowed a safe place for us to learn about our differences. First, we needed to understand we each brought our diverse upbringings into the situation. Meaning that from growing up when dinosaurs roamed the earth (just kidding to my folks) to Generation Z, the social awareness and intelligence we had were vastly different. Then, we needed to consider the distinct and individual experiences we'd had, too. All I can say is that the layers were thick. I wouldn't have minded if they were like a delicious chocolate cake, but these reminded me more of those nasty onions I don't like.

Beth reassured us that our story wasn't uncommon as she passed out materials on being a good listener and the fundamentals of a healthy dialogue. I didn't know if my family agreed with her approach, but I didn't care. I felt hope. We could finally navigate our differences. It wasn't fair to say our challenges had begun only because of our new trauma, although some of my family thought that. The truth was, they started long before Ally died.

One would think that knowing how to listen without preparing to be heard would be easy. Or how about how to validate one another without pushing our opinions. Guess again. Who knew there were steps to having a successful conversation about your day? This concept clearly wasn't taught in kindergarten. The fact we couldn't even fake it in front of a professional made it all that much worse.

There was no hiding from the truth; we needed to start from scratch. I hated not being able to talk to my family like I did Beth. If we can't get through that simple exercise, how in the hell are we really going to talk about Ally?

Of course, I expected everyone else would want to dive in as I had been for the past few months – but that wasn't the case. They saw it was working for me, so why not? Instead, my family looked at the materials, giving the impression they were already content with their comfortable rut.

Surprisingly, they played along, and after a few attempts, they appeared less self-conscious. Talking about our day was choppy at times, but we were trying.

As the meeting progressed, Beth asked if we wanted to try talking about Ally and how we were grieving. Right or wrong, I answered for my family and said, "Yes." With Beth looking at my dad, he went first.

"I'm over it," he said effortlessly as the words rolled out of his mouth.

How in the fuck could that be possible? I stared at him with an intensity that could pierce a metal plate. I then turned to my mom and watched her scoff at him, which told me she didn't believe him either. I'm glad I wasn't the only one. I tried my best not to take what he said personally. I did. But damn, it was hard. Fortunately, twisting back and forth in my chair distracted me long enough to find my calm.

Too bad it didn't last long. Next, Andy shared that he, also, was "done" grieving. My blood ran cold. How could he sit there so arrogantly and not blink an eye? It seemed like he and my dad were racing each other to some finish line, or maybe it's a guy thing? It even made me wonder if perhaps it was because Ally was a stepchild. I don't know. But Beth didn't seem startled by their comments. I questioned whether she'd heard this a million times with other clients. She validated their feelings and shared no opinion about them.

Beth turned to Kylie, who had little to say after rolling her eyes at what her dad had said. Her eye contact was minimal, and her usual animated hands lay in her lap. It was clear she was uncomfortable and focused on making jokes.

Kylie wasn't the only one. Beth was quick to point out that we all did it. It seemed "avoiding" was a typical response for us as a family. Huh, it never registered that humor could be a defense mechanism. It was a glass of cold water splashed in our faces. I didn't know about anyone else, but it got my attention.

When Beth moved to my mom, I could see she had something to say. I wasn't sure where it was going, but it couldn't be any worse than what the guys had said. She brought up the day of Ally's death.

Judgingly, she said to me, "I thought it was weird you were on the phone and not comforting the family."

Yep, that was worse. Thank God for the frosted glass surrounding the fishbowl of a room. I looked at everyone, hoping someone else would say something. Beth nodded to my mom, then turned to me, asking me to respond.

Talk about being put on the spot. My inner voice was blaring, "Why was it *my* job to comfort everyone else after hearing the possibility that it was Ally in the motel room? Wasn't Ally *my* flesh and blood?" I wanted to say something hurtful – what she said cut me like a knife. You thought it was weird *I* wasn't taking care of the family? What the fuck! Instead, I took the deepest breath ever and used every new tool I had. With my heart pounding through my chest, I started with how I had felt abandoned at the crime scene. I then shared my recollection that everybody went in a different direction, and *no one* comforted me. I corrected myself that, yes, Andy had given me a *brief* hug, so he'd acknowledged me for five seconds. And then, like everyone else, he was gone.

My mom didn't have a response; no one did. Their silence fueled my intense eye contact around the long rectangular table. I couldn't believe how pissed off I was! I wanted to cry, but my mama bear wanted nothing more than for them to hear my angry roar.

My confidence gained momentum as I continued why I justified my urge to tackle the giant policeman at the door. Hearing myself say it out loud sounded silly, but it was the truth at the time.

"I only knew one person I could trust to talk me down. It was Petra, and that's why I called *her*." I didn't think I was harsh, only honest.

My family's faces turned supportive, and yet the room still felt heavy and tense. All I knew was that if we'd been at home, someone would have stormed out of the room by then, or it would have turned into a knock-down, drag-out fight.

After wiping a single tear that ran down my cheek, I took a deep breath and slumped in my chair. I looked at Beth, and she was nodding in approval. I looked at everyone else, bracing for impact, but there was only silence. I didn't know why everyone was on their best behavior, but the fact we'd made it this far was impressive.

After what seemed like an eternity, my mom said with sincerity, "I now understand. We should have *all* been comforting each other."

Oh my God, she heard me! She heard my cry for compassion and understanding. Doing a double-take, I didn't expect that at all. The rest of my family nodded in agreeance. Their red noses and puffy eyes told me that, on some level, they knew I was hurting. Before I could comment, my mom openly expressed regret for not being there for me, which also surprised me. I wasn't looking for an apology, only an understanding.

As I looked at her, I felt a strong connection between us. It was beautiful. Beth then calmly and confidently chimed in, confirming that our feelings weren't right or wrong. "There is no training for what you've experienced," she said. Practicing acceptance for one another would be the key to our family's healing, but it wouldn't happen overnight. I cringed at the words she said, but they made perfect sense to me.

A heaviness lifted for me and, I think, for my mom, too. I never wanted a hug from her more badly. I only wished we had done this sooner. Nonetheless, a proud moment for sure – that was some heavy shit to work through, and we did it.

Thrilled, my family agreed to attend a few more meetings after that. I'm learning that accepting others feels more like maneuvering through rush-hour traffic. Ever heard the quote by George Carlin, "Have you ever noticed that anybody driving slower than you is an idiot, and anyone going faster than you is a maniac?" It takes a mountain to faze me after all that I have been through. It's a blessing and a curse, as they say. Human connections can be more difficult and sometimes suffer. I've had to relearn compassion for others and *their* experiences. I didn't always appreciate my family's pace for grieving. Not to mention understanding that their agendas didn't always align with mine was, and is, a chore sometimes. But it showed me that each of us had to find our path, and I could respect that.

CHAPTER 18

Déjà vu

FEBRUARY 5, 2019

PART I

This Monday seemed no different from any other Monday during the past several months. I was full of dread heading to work, and yet I looked forward to my eight hours of a pretend sanctuary from my *real* life.

After getting my delicious Starbucks nonfat vanilla chai tea latte, I said my typical "Cheers to a great day" to the team and switched hats into work mode. It was the start of our accounting period, and as usual, my focus was on nothing other than kicking ass. The harder I work at the beginning of the period, the more I can "play" at the end of the month. I don't know about you, but I think seeing a movie during the workday is a well-deserved treat.

Not needing a watch, my tummy grumbled, announcing it was lunchtime. As I devoured my weekend leftovers to keep on schedule, my cellphone rang, interrupting me. The number read "Unknown."

Adrenaline came out of nowhere. The last time I had seen that, it was the coroner. My heart dropped, and the world came to a screeching halt. After I hesitantly answered, a stranger introduced himself as part of the FBI Fugitive Task Force. His was a voice I would become very familiar with over the next month.

"Oh, my God! Why was he calling me?" I whispered. Frantic, I asked him to give me a second. Heading into my boss' empty office, I quietly shut the door, not wanting to create a scene. Huffing and puffing, I commanded self-control. My hands were shaking so badly, I could barely shuffle things around on her desk to set my laptop down. I rubbed my temples, thinking it would help. I told this stranger I was ready, even though I wasn't.

Using humor to introduce himself, this guy made me feel at ease. I couldn't help but envision him as Bruce Willis the way he spoke, and I even felt comfy enough to say that. And after I did, he jokingly told me he was more like Sean Connery as James Bond. I snickered, appreciating his wit because he most certainly didn't sound Scottish. So for my story purposes, 007 will be his name.

007 explained he'd received information from Detective Ferrell and would assist us with Arturo's capture. I was totally paralyzed, but the room started spinning. Holy shit! It's not like I didn't know this day would come; I did. But it wasn't on my radar, unless it was subconscious – but certainly not at the forefront.

Catching me off-guard, 007 asked me to identify Arturo via a public Facebook link. Are you kidding me? Did he seriously say a *public* Facebook page? The audacity! *What does Arturo think – he's invincible and above the law?* I couldn't take a breath deep enough to calm my nerves. I should've known that motherfucker was too conceited to stay off Facebook.

With my finger on the mouse, swallowing the massive lump in my throat was impossible to keep quiet. I wasn't ready for this. I didn't want things to change again. I'd worked so hard to reassemble my life, and for what? It wasn't fair! I'd already experienced the worst torture possible. What did I do to deserve it twice?

Not knowing what to expect, I still couldn't believe what I saw. On the screen was Arturo's supposed Facebook page. I shook my head again to the point of mild whiplash. Could we be this lucky? Yes, it had a different alias and a profile picture of only a face from the nose down, but it didn't matter – I knew it was him. I could never forget the outline of his features.

Scrolling with trepidation, I prayed for support. Of the handful of postings, there were three self-recorded videos. My body went numb. Aside from some longer hair, everything about Arturo was the same. I thought my eyes were playing tricks on me. Could he be this stupid? What was the point of his cryptic profile anyway? Did he really think people wouldn't recognize him? Or maybe *he* didn't think he did it? It made *no* sense.

My curiosity turned into a predatory glare. All three videos were of him playing the guitar, like a tutorial of some kind. He looked so happy and healthy – so full of life. I despised seeing him that way. Why did he get to do the one thing he loved so very much while Ally lay dead without a future?

Knowing that it would pain me in every way, I turned up the volume to hear him sing. The feeling was indescribable. Even though he sang in Spanish, every sound was so familiar. All I could imagine was him singing to Ally like that, which crushed my heart into a million pieces. Turning away, I couldn't look or listen to him anymore – I was disgusted and had had enough, slamming shut my laptop.

I knew 007 was patiently waiting for my response, but I didn't care. I'd never sat so still in pure anguish, unable to move or say anything. Did Arturo honestly think the world had forgotten he had murdered my baby? The very idea that he'd posted himself humiliated me in every way. It felt like a mockery of my pain as a grieving mother. And I didn't think the bitter truth of who he was could hurt any worse. I was so wrong.

I must have pulled words from the air, I don't know, but I confirmed to 007 it was Arturo. Hearing him agree gave me peace of mind. I had the same debate when I identified him at the police station initially. Did 007 really need my opinion, or was this again another pointless strategy, telling him what 007 already knew?

As we said our goodbyes, he offered to keep me in the loop every step he could. He preferred to keep it to only one contact and limit confusion. I struggled to say yes. In both directions, I saw only burning fires. Deciding on the lesser of two evils, I put my family first and went against my better judgment.

Hanging up the phone, I immediately called Andy. I needed him more than ever. I was a total wreck. I resorted to biting my nails as the phone rang; I had never done that before. Is that a deep-seated programmed response? I didn't get it. Thankfully, though, he answered within a few rings. And like an auctioneer, I rattled off how the authorities had called me.

Andy said so casually, "I know; I emailed Detective Ferrell. I copied you on it. Didn't you read it?"

I should have taken the call outside. Being in the office forced me to keep my voice down and not let out the raging bitch I wanted to be. I was furious with him. Couldn't he have given me a heads-up? Jesus! Didn't I deserve that? Can you imagine getting a call like that out of the blue? Do *you* check your personal email every five minutes at work? Come on! It was ridiculous.

I hatefully whispered, "What in the *fuck* do you mean you emailed Detective Ferrell? And you didn't tell me first?" The odd sensation of betrayal surged in my belly.

Andy didn't appreciate my questions, as though I had diminished his efforts somehow. He described how he and Alex had been contacted by a "good Samaritan" that morning with an over-the-top condescending tone.

Now I am going to keep these details vague. The last thing I want to do is compromise the good Samaritan's (aka Sam) identity in any way. So, here's the gist of it. Sam had come across the information about Ally's murder from Andy's and Alex's continued re-postings via various social-media outlets. Sickened and wanting justice for Ally, Sam chose to come forward, sharing the Facebook link.

Pacing the office, I was such a mess. One side of me was full of appreciation for Sam's noble efforts for Ally and us. I'd never been so humbled by the good deeds of a stranger before. I couldn't even fathom the decisions that had to be made to step forward like that. Whatever the reasoning, I hope Sam knows how grateful I am.

The other side of me hurt because I didn't understand how Andy could disrespect me the way he did. It sounded like he *used* Sam as an excuse. I made sure to correct Andy with my snarky tone that it wasn't Detective Ferrell who had called. It was 007. And how he wanted to talk to only *me* moving forward. I knew it would sting, but I wanted to knock him off his damn high horse because his actions hurt me.

The silence between us was deafening. Is this what we needed? Was it helping? Neither of us would admit to being a jerk.

Instead, Andy softly said, "I love you."

I took a deep breath and knew what that meant, and some of my armor came off. Andy was apologizing. I said it too, hoping he knew I was also.

After we said our goodbyes, I sat down and growled – literally. Clenching my hand in anger, I was surprised it didn't bleed from my nails. Suddenly, I felt intense heat over my neck and chest. My shirt hung, drenched from sweat. I thought I was having a heart attack or something. It scared the shit out of me. All I wanted to do was escape and go home.

Becoming hysterical, unsure of what to do next, I texted Beth and asked her to call me. I knew I wasn't her only client, but still. She *had* to know something was wrong. I had never done that before. But what if she didn't see my message for hours? What if it was her day off? I begged every higher power. The last thing I needed was another lesson in goddam patience.

To my surprise, Beth's name appeared on my cellphone. Holy shit! It already felt like an eternity, waiting for those few seconds. Slapping the green "accept" button had never felt so damn good. Huh, what were the odds she wasn't busy?

Beth asked as her usual self, "So, what's going on?"

I envied how calm she was. With all her training, I wondered if she'd ever felt like I did. Whom would she call? Or would she talk herself down in a mirror? An interesting question for sure. Someday, I'd have to ask her about it.

Trying to find my bearings, I anxiously said, "Beth, I need you to help talk me off the ledge. I just identified Arturo. He's been located."

Shaken, Beth replied, "Oh, dear God."

I'll never forget having that conversation with her. It felt all too familiar, calling someone I trusted to keep me sane when nothing felt right. I resented it. All I could see was the motel room in front of me when I was just as helpless as I was now. But Beth being Beth, she didn't falter in the slightest.

She assured me I was in a safe place. I told her the necessary details of what had happened. She was hanging on to every word I said. Asking where I was, she directed me to find the courage to ask for my accounting team's support.

"They are going to need to be your tribe, the one you need," Beth said.

I had no intention of putting up a fight. Whatever she said, I would do. I needed to trust her wisdom. Agreeing, she then confirmed we had scheduled an appointment the next day but offered that I could call again if need be.

At a total loss with my hand on the door, I gazed out the office window. It felt like an out-of-body experience, with only clear glass separating me from the people I knew. I watched the team smiling, going about their everyday business to meet those ever-so-critical corporate deadlines. I knew that I had stood among them only moments ago acting the same. And then, in the blink of an eye, I witnessed the reflection standing in front of me – the one who had just identified her daughter's murderer.

Staring at the bereaved mama I indeed was, I touched the glass, feeling the painful truth. Everything I knew, everything I'd worked so hard for all those years, no longer mattered. At that moment, something within me changed. I didn't know exactly what, but I was sure of one thing – I no longer belonged.

Emotionally overwhelmed, I slowly opened the door, wiping away the tears from my eyes as if it mattered. Who wouldn't notice my flushed face? As I peered around the group, everyone seemed none the wiser. But when my eyes met Rachel's, I lost it. As she darted my way with her arms open wide, I welcomed her hug. I gathered my tribe and headed to Starbucks, knowing they'd support me. And at the same time, I hated knowing work was no longer my sanctuary.

———————— ✥ ————————

PART II

THE NEXT FEW DAYS WERE CHALLENGING, TO SAY THE LEAST. I HADN'T talked about Arturo for almost a year, and now I couldn't run from it. All I can say is that making up for lost time is incredibly overrated, that's for sure.

The news spread like wildfire to make matters worse for those we told. So much for keeping it a secret. But I get it. It was the first time there was the hope of catching Ally's killer. Who could keep that to themselves? I'm sure I'd do the same thing. With that said, I still despised being the center of attention.

While at work, keeping up the charade of wearing my "I'm fine" mask became impossible. There must have been an imaginary ticket dispenser somewhere with a sign offering free therapy by my desk. One by one, co-workers approached from every corner.

I welcomed each "guest" as I usually did, assuming we'd talk work stuff, that is – but the conversations were rarely about that. Most wanted to share a supportive thought or two. As much as I dreaded talking about my story, I appreciated the kind words and apologetic gestures. I was witnessing this beautiful example of humanity at its best.

Nevertheless, leave it to a few bold co-workers to remind me of the worst. Stunned, I stood there as they spoke so freely and loudly about their desires to torture Arturo. Oh, my God! Didn't they care if their comments could be disruptive or offensive to anyone within earshot? What about *me*, for crying out loud? I wished for my own office to hide behind the door. It was embarrassing. In all reality, their rampages lasted about thirty seconds – but still. The emotional whiplash left me wondering whether I should be more appreciative or offended.

As if that wasn't bad enough, the twenty to thirty daily text messages could have made a tune of their own. Some had sentiments like a thoughtful greeting card. Others, not so much. The intensity of their insufferable cavemanlike mindsets against Arturo was upsetting. What the hell? Was the text for me or more for them to feel better? At least it wasn't another person saying it to my face, I guess.

Turning my phone to silent mode didn't help much. I kept seeing the bright screen flash in my peripheral vision. It's not like I could put my phone away. 007 could call at any given moment, and I didn't want to miss that. Well, that wasn't *always* true – you know what I mean.

No matter how hard I tried, I couldn't focus on my work and didn't give it the undivided attention it deserved – I shifted gears constantly from accounting to feelings. Not to mention finding my mistakes didn't help my state of mind either. Maybe I should have worked from home instead, although I doubt it would have helped. I already felt secluded on my island as it was.

Coming home, I was doomed – the news about Arturo was fresh on Andy's mind, too. It gave him a soapbox to repeatedly express his opinion, whether I had asked for it or not. Much like many others, he saw his untamed anger reignited, fueling his graphic and barbaric intentions of making Arturo suffer.

Can I ask? What is it with people and cruelty? My question isn't about *having* an opinion – I get that everyone is entitled to one. I am trying to understand why people have created such horrific fantasies that, in comparison, are probably a hundred times worse than what Ally had suffered (let's hope).

It seems I didn't know people I once thought I knew. I really didn't. Suddenly, they used one of the oldest and most well-known Bible stories as if it were their gospel. You know, the eye-for-an-eye tale. Here's my issue with it. It seems one-sided and used only out of convenience to justify a situation when someone is upset. If we truly lived with this mentality, wouldn't we all have been blind at a very young age? So the saying from Gandhi goes. There is no way humans haven't misinterpreted this concept somehow. Am I a follower of the Bible? No. But I have enough sense to question why a superior being would encourage personal revenge. I'm sorry, but that doesn't sound evolved or wise at all. It sounds more human-made and egotistical, if you ask me.

Most people didn't understand that hearing these monstrous ideas day-in, day-out was terrifying. To think their imaginations possessed the capability for such destruction made me question whether they were any better than Arturo. Yes, I just said that. It was even worse when they spoke about it with *such* conviction and overconfidence. Especially when they mentioned having the "right connections" to make their plans happen. And I am supposed to *feel* safe around you?

It's not that I disagreed with parts of what they said. In the beginning, my resentment consumed me, too. In my grief and anger toward Arturo (plus everyone else, including me), I struggled with mean thoughts, and some even scared me. Yet, once I decided to reassemble my life instead of feeding into the emotion, it was enough to remind me it wasn't who I was or who I wanted to become. I never mentioned choosing the redemption path with anyone, except with Beth and Karen. And for a good reason.

Humans have a tough time with the idea of forgiveness, the other "F-word." They often think that if they forgive the person who has wronged them, they somehow say the "bad thing" is OK. Or some hold the belief that carrying a grudge makes them *more* powerful. So one day, when the wrongdoer will (hopefully) beg for forgiveness, the act of granting such a wish would seem like waving a wand to release their painful spell, expecting loyalty after that. Forgiveness isn't about absolution, though people seem to forget that!

I have a different stance. Forgiving someone is about me, as the victim, not Arturo, as the murderer. It would be so easy to let the anger of loss sit on me, to crush my will to live through this. It would be easier to make Arturo the center of my new norm – spending every moment hating him and making sure I did everything I could to make him suffer for his sins.

Through my journey, I recognized the twisted relationship Arturo and I had. Every second I didn't forgive, I let him have my power. I found this adage that resonates in every way: "Holding on to a grudge is like drinking poison and expecting the other person to die." All things considered, the only way to *not* hurt me more was to make this choice every day. It was the only thing that made sense. Every day I decide to forgive him gives me the freedom to move forward and make something positive out of this tragic situation.

Don't get me wrong – it's fucking hard, and there are plenty of days I don't want to. But without it, I can't even fathom where I'd be. It's helping to free me from the depths of resentment, confusion and even guilt. Rather, I'm moving toward finding a reason for all of this. Not to say that Ally was a sacrifice, not at all. Her murder doesn't have a reason, but I needed a new purpose as her mom. That being becoming what I deem as a true survivor. One who can acknowledge she was victimized and not let her tragedy define her. Which then becomes the victor to thrive in life again and help others. And if I can do this, then Ally didn't die in vain, and I'd have my justice for her.

Because I didn't drink the Kool-Aid that sought hard-core revenge like those who stood behind the eye-for-an-eye mentality, trying to explain my position on forgiveness was downright grueling. And I thought talking politics was terrible; I stand corrected. It didn't matter if they were family, friends, or even a co-worker; they'd often rush me and arrogantly tell me how to feel. Was what I had to say that hard to hear? So much for my opinion mattering, assholes.

I'll admit that maybe it would have been better to share my redemption choice long ago so it wouldn't have been such a shock to everyone. The division between us was devastating, especially from Andy. Do you know what it's like to live with someone and have such differences? We'd argue for hours about it, and his love no longer felt unconditional. Arturo even took that from me.

Andy even once told me with such pride, "I wish you'd get hurt to burst this bubble about forgiveness. So you can see what it's like to want revenge."

If anything, I found more humor in his ignorant comment. While Andy's anger was understandable and familiar, I resented him forgetting that *my* daughter was murdered. Seriously – how could he *not* see the ridiculousness of this statement? But it showed me deep down he was a ticking time bomb. I'd really thought that our effort to work on our marriage and bridge the gap in our differences had narrowed for the past few months. And with one mention of Arturo's location, like an earthquake, we'd split apart. It was Day One happening all over again.

I had few trusted resources to speak freely about my ideas and how I chose what was right for me. I missed Kylie being home. Now in college, she lived on campus, which was almost two hours away. If she were back, she would have listened and entertained my ideas, not making it seem like I needed to defend them. Although Ally had been gone almost a year, Kylie gave the impression that Ally's death was more of an out-of-sight, out-of-mind kind of thing. However, her moving for school may have been a way to escape the hurt. I'd imagine she was striving for some sort of normalcy in her life again, where she could be in a world that she was building for herself. It was all understandable, but I'd be lying if I said it didn't hurt.

Something triggered for me. How could I forget? I wondered, not only for Andy but for family and others we had told, whether giving up the right to the death penalty was a factor in their behaviors. It had to be. It's time for a flashback.

Sometime in the third week of October 2017, I'd received a call from the legal team, inviting our family in for a meeting. Because the authorities still suspected Arturo was in another country (revealing it was Mexico) and a U.S. citizen, they wanted to discuss the terms of how extradition would work. *"Oh, dear God,"* I thought. "More lawyerese I'd have to work through." Before I finished my dreadful thought, they mentioned how tough this meeting could be. An interesting statement, I'd say. They then explained that we (as a family) would have to agree to give up on the pursuit of the death penalty for extradition to take place.

Huh. I had no idea this kind of process existed. Why would I? Admittedly, it was fascinating to learn why it's a hard-and-fast policy of the Mexican government, and it's a big reason why people flee when they might be subject to the death penalty. It's hard to deny the logic, but I didn't want to be considering any more of this legal crap. No offense.

I became speechless. Not for me; I didn't have one doubt about it. At the very least, it was music to my ears. It was everyone else I was worried about. For most, they had openly shared that the death penalty was the golden ticket they'd been looking for the entire time. And for those who wanted Arturo to suffer, I assumed they felt the same.

Telling the legal team my thoughts and concerns, they listened. They assured me, in their non-warm-and-fuzzy way, that I wasn't the first to be in this position. That's great and all, but it didn't change the fact we were about to face another hurdle – one where I yet again would get to stand alone. I mean, maybe they were just words of hatred, and I'd be wrong. Or perhaps someone else believed in what I did. For once, I'd love nothing more than to be surprised in a good way with something like this.

Scared shitless, I told my family about the upcoming meeting. It may have been an email or phone call; I don't recall. It didn't matter. My only intent was to give them some time to process before the meeting. I did nothing other than describe the basics of what the legal team had explained to me. Keeping my opinion to myself, I guarded it with my life. I didn't want my beliefs squashed again.

As predicted, the news sparked pure outrage. The majority wanted to grab their torches and pitchforks, ready to protest. It's not like I didn't get it. They'd already lost Ally, and now they had to surrender what seemed to be the only acceptable punishment. I'm sure that had to feel awful.

And it makes me wonder what Ally would want concerning the death penalty. Would she want Arturo to suffer as she did? And if she didn't, would that have changed my family's perspective?

I didn't envy what they had to work through between you and me, and honestly, I didn't want to be around when they did. It was time for them to hold up their own mirror. I avoided the topic after that at all costs. It was a rare occasion when I got to take a breather from being a support system or learning some great life lessons after Ally died. Its timing couldn't have been more perfect, like receiving a much-needed gift of self-preservation.

However, someone (I don't remember who) brought up how Karen had mentioned Mexico within all the chaos. I felt like a total dumbass for not remembering and completely in awe that they did. How cool to witness that even for a brief moment in our situation's muck, they could focus on her psychic vision's validity.

Now it was October 30, and I was sitting at the rectangular conference table's head, fearing what was about to happen. Not only was our legal team there, but so were Detective Ferrell and Detective Bullock. Were they crowd control or what? What purpose did it serve them being there other than making the mood more intense? Thank God for the bottle of water I could play with.

The legal team didn't waste any time and began the meeting as scheduled. I appreciated it in every way, mainly because I counted down every second for this to be over.

Opening the floor for discussion, the legal team invited everyone to share their thoughts and opinions on the subject at hand. Oh, my God! I wasn't ready for that. I began sweating like a pig. Why would they do such a thing? Were they prepared to get their asses handed to them? Although, I suppose this happens to them more often than not in their line of work. I have to say, I almost wanted some popcorn for the show.

Watching the faces of Andy, my folks, Amy, Kristin, Eric, and Barb was more nerve-wracking than anything. I still didn't know if they'd accepted the cold, hard truth about giving up the death penalty. Would we overcome this obstacle and become stronger or be ripped apart? What would happen if not everyone agreed? The thought made me sick to my stomach.

Oddly, no one said anything. It didn't make sense. I thought for sure Andy or Eric would have jumped at the chance to be vocal. They usually do. So why not now? Instead, the awkward silence loomed like never before.

I believe it was my mom who finally spoke up first. Frankly, the order of how it happened is insignificant. One by one, around the table they went. Each family member acknowledged how they supported the idea of the death penalty, even Amy. My heart dropped. I didn't see that coming. It's true that we'd never discussed it before, but never in a million years would I think she'd believe in that.

Now, with everyone staring at me, I was the last to say anything. I couldn't clench my jaw any harder. I had no idea how I'd say I didn't want Arturo to die. Nothing they could say or do would change my mind. What would it mean if I stood alone? They all became blurry as my eyes filled with tears. What about Ally? Is this what she'd want? Do I dare bring that up? At that point, I wanted to run far away.

Sighing, I opened my mouth to blurt out whatever it would be, and the legal team interrupted. Seriously? What was I supposed to think after all that buildup? I didn't know if I had missed the greatest moment of my life or if I was more relieved that I didn't have to say a peep.

Changing the direction from feelings to facts, the legal team explained further the hows and whys of the situation. Since Arturo was a U.S. citizen, Immigration and Customs Enforcement would need to arrest him with law-enforcement help because he would be extradited – probably to Dallas. Then, once he'd set foot in the U.S., he'd be arrested at the airport by local law enforcement. And after that, generally a day or so, they'd release him to 007.

Studying my family's squinted eyes, they raced back and forth. I assumed they were mentally drawing the checklist just as I was. Yes, there were a ton of steps and possibilities for hiccups every step of the way, but it sounded like the authorities had done it a ton with great success.

Switching gears again, they brought up local cases we may have heard of. Once they mentioned the Aurora movie-theater shooting in 2012, the room became still – it was a painful memory for many reasons. Not only was that theater our favorite place, but my mom had taken Ally and Kylie there in the morning on that very day. Thank you for reminding us how lucky we were, but what did this have to do with us? What kind of point were they trying to make?

I should have known this was an epic climax moment. What the legal team told us next was downright unbelievable. Even after the defendant killed twelve people and injured seventy others, the jury didn't have a unanimous verdict for the death penalty. You could hear a pin drop. They further explained that it takes two or three (-ish, I don't remember) unanimous juries after that, which the governor can then overturn.

The shades of red on my family's faces and their body language said it all. Each had the same epiphany. Not to discredit Ally's murder by any means, but if that guy from the movie theater couldn't get the death penalty, what would Arturo's chances be of getting it? Would it really be worth all the anguish to have it later overturned? Not to mention, what about what it would put *me* through?

I'm not sure who spoke up first, but I think it was Barb this time. She thanked the legal team for thoroughly explaining the process, and although she wasn't happy, she understood it was in our best interest to give up our right to the death penalty. My heart warmed, and within seconds it was like an echo from everyone else.

Talk about manipulation with a purpose. And if I was right, I'd just witnessed the power of our legal team. First, they let people feel empowered to express their feelings. Everyone had a voice. Well, almost. And once they felt heard, they were ready to listen. Then, the legal team could paint the real picture. In turn, they had a better chance of people using the facts instead of their personal opinions. If that were the case, it was impressive and absolutely brilliant. Is that how they'd handle the court situation? If so, I had more trust for them representing Ally than ever before.

Walking out of there having spoken fewer than twenty words, I felt validated in every way. But deep down, having been through it before – I speculated whether this was all necessary. Did they really need us to "give up" the pursuit of the death penalty, or was it another ploy in which, in the end, we'd answered what they already knew? Trying not to energize my idea, I focused on what I *did* know. Today was a victory – we came together as a unit. Yet, I also knew that some would hold a grudge and not want to let it go.

PART III

AFTER RECEIVING A TEXT FROM AMY THAT READ, "IT'S A TERRIFIC Tiffany Tuesday," I confirmed it on the calendar. It was indeed

February 12. Replying something cute and witty like I always do, I hoped it made her smile. When, in fact, seeing my sour reflection in my computer monitors made me feel like a shmuck for lying. I suppose there was some potential that the day could turn great, but really, nothing felt terrific at all.

Glad I got to the office early, I was by myself for a little while. For some reason, working in the dark creates the illusion that real-life is a little less real. The peace and quiet was a well-deserved treat from the past week. Truth be told, though, I probably surfed Amazon more than anything.

Sipping my delicious favorite latte, I decided that maybe some things weren't so terrible after all. Setting down my drink, I noticed my phone displaying 007's number. Well, perhaps my thought was a bit premature – talk about a crabby-Patty attitude. To his credit, he was a man of his word. He contacted me almost daily, so it's not like every communication held some critical detail I had to absorb. Sometimes he was just checking in on me, and he didn't have to do that. But the bottom line was that seeing his number held me hostage – every single time.

All right, Amy, you were right. The update from 007 turned my frown upside down for sure. Immigration had agreed to be a part of Arturo's capture! I was shocked at how easily the process seemed to be going. Now, all 007 had to do was prepare some paperwork, which shouldn't take more than a few days, and ICE could use the collected intelligence it had of Arturo's location and boom, done.

It'd been a while since I had done the happy dance at work. Noticeable to the arriving accounting team, I whispered the good news. I hated interrupting their morning routines, but it's not like everyone hadn't been interrupting mine. Turnabout is fair play. I thought my update was just as warranted as when someone once shouted, "Winning!" upon getting their first house contract.

My good news received awkwardly mixed reviews versus homeownership from my peers. For most, they were my cheering section. It was nice to feel like they had my back. Yet for a few, the sheer shock on their faces told me that my reality continued to make them feel uncomfortable.

I didn't know whether to apologize to ease the tension or cry because I felt like an outcast. But what was I supposed to do? I didn't want to pretend anymore. Trying to play both sides was tearing me up inside. How could I accept my reality if I had to keep it bottled up? Talking about it makes it real, doesn't it?

Unfortunately, that means for everyone. I knew it wasn't personal how some reacted. My story provides a harsh reality, one that no one wants to hear. I needed to understand I couldn't make the truth any easier than I already had been for those I told. It was up to everyone else to decide how to handle the situation, and I had to let it go. The nice thing was that those few eventually smiled and nodded, and I returned the polite gesture.

Much like the entire week, my update about Arturo sparked Andy on another rampage. He was a broken record of fury and disgust. Internally rolling my eyes, I sighed and listened. I hoped he couldn't tell how uninterested I was. Where was my teddy bear? I missed him so much! I feared the worst for our marriage if we didn't catch a break soon from all the ugliness surrounding us. There was *no* way I could continue this way.

I could not hold it in any longer, as I was about to lose my shit and unleash Holy Hell until he caught me off-guard.

Smiling, he said, "Thanks for sharing, babe. It *is* great news."

I had no words. It wasn't typical of Andy to act this way. He's never switched gears like that before. What the hell? Was it a trap, or did he have a change of heart? Although as I stared into his eyes, they said everything. He didn't want to fight. I immediately hugged him, and he hugged me back. Squeezing him tightly, I knew feeling close to him was long overdue. We kissed so passionately that we could have given even the cheesiest love story a run for its money. And since that's all I'll kiss and tell, you can guess what happened next (wink).

Now it was Friday, and driving home from work, I was looking forward to date night. Who doesn't love picking up takeout, a chocolate ice-cream Reese's Peanut Butter Cup Blizzard from Dairy Queen, and watching a movie all snuggled up with your partner?

The thought of a relaxing evening felt heavenly. This past week had taken quite a toll on Andy and me.

As I soared through traffic, hardly anyone was on the road – I must have just missed the horrible afternoon traffic, thank God. I turned up the music, feeling invincible as if the universe were paving the way for me to get home to my guy.

I was screaming at the top of my lungs to the radio – some call that singing – but then the song stopped playing. I was pissed. It was pretty rare for me to get my groove on like that lately. I knew what it was, though. It was that second of silence when you're about to receive an incoming call. Sure as shit, it was 007.

As usual, my adrenaline coursed through every cell of my body. Taking a deep breath, I answered the call as casually as I could.

"Hey, 007, happy Friday," I said. He usually returns my greeting in his goofy way, but not this time. Something was wrong – he was all business. To be fair, I didn't know him all that well, but it didn't matter. There wasn't a hint of emotion from his monotone reply.

Pulling over on the highway seemed like the logical thing to do. My heart was thumping so fast; I thought for sure it would jump out of my chest.

Psyching myself up for the worst, I no longer heard the whizzing cars going by. Silence surrounded me, forcing me to focus on nothing else except for this moment. I listened intently as he updated the collected intelligence about Arturo.

007 explained that Arturo was no longer at his presumed residence. *Oh, my God! Are you serious?* I was so confused. Why hadn't Immigration arrested him already? 007 sighed. I could tell he was biting his tongue. He reminded me there were only certain things he could share. My jaw hurt from grinding my teeth. He continued that somehow, Arturo must have been tipped off.

I was livid to the point that smoke must have been coming out of my ears. I wasn't so sure 007's assumption was correct. Arturo moved at least five times during his and Ally's relationship, unable to pay the rent. Regardless, it was another nightmare come true. How was I supposed to tell everyone this news? I would get blasted from every direction, even though I was only the messenger. Why was this happening? So much for everything running smoothly! It wasn't fair!

The mascara I wore didn't stand a chance of staying put as my eyes flooded with tears. I hated this! I kicked and silently screamed like a temper tantrum, hoping 007 didn't hear me. I could only imagine what people driving by thought, although I was probably just a blur as they passed. Besides, in this day and age, what are the odds they'd stop to see if I needed help anyway?

Through the noise in my head, I heard 007 begin talking again. It all sounded so jumbled, and I couldn't make sense of it. I was such a mess. Searching desperately for a napkin or a tissue, I asked him to hold on. He was easygoing and didn't rush me. I appreciated that. After blowing my nose a final time, I wiped my eyes as if it made a difference. Swallowing my pride, I sheepishly asked him to continue.

007's tone was different – there was a sense of optimism. He mentioned there was intelligence of Arturo working at a women's shelter. Holy shit! Seriously? I must have had ten scenarios run through my mind. They centered on the notion that he either was looking for his next prey or trying to right his wrong.

It didn't surprise me that Arturo had found a place to work. His charm was hard to deny. But at a shelter? Ally was always the one wanting to help others, not him. This choice seemed beneath him, from what I remembered. Maybe work was scarce? Or perhaps he was working there as atonement as a way of asking for forgiveness? Was he even capable of that? I didn't know. I suppose none of it mattered, really. The only thing that did was that Immigration knew his whereabouts and was about to arrest him so he couldn't hurt anyone else.

Every step I took walking up to the house, exhaustion consumed me. I didn't want to tell Andy the update, yet I knew I couldn't keep it to myself. When would this stupid fucking roller coaster ride end? All I wanted was to enjoy delicious ice cream on our date night. Was it too much to ask for a "normal evening"?

Andy was eagerly standing there when I walked inside. Dreading what was about to happen, I prayed he'd had a "good" day and would take the news well. Putting my head down, I whispered, "Do you have a minute?" Geez. Could I have made it any more obvious with the classic tell-all question?

I told Andy the update, bracing for impact with every word I said. Surprisingly, he wasn't upset, and his demeanor seemed more like a professor solving a complicated mathematical equation. It didn't make sense to me.

Pulling up Arturo's Facebook page, Andy scrolled to the bottom. There was a fourth video of him. How'd I miss that? The timeline 007 had put together, aligned perfectly with what he had said about the shelter. Holding each other's hands, we watched together, speechless.

Arturo stood before almost thirty people giving a presentation, dressed in a black jacket, dark T-shirt, blue jeans, and white tennis shoes. My first impression: He looked respectable.

The room was cramped. People sat between desks, bookshelves, and even a hanging projector screen. It didn't seem to be an issue for Arturo. He had no problem moving around with ease. His eye contact was impeccable, and he kept the audience engaged. It was impressive, to say the least, especially when they laughed at his jokes. Admittedly, I envied his skills. I had to take a damn class to learn how to be a presenter.

As the video continued, we did a loose translation of Arturo's Spanish. Basically, he told the audience he'd be using music to help them learn English. He was adamant that when you find something you enjoy doing, mixed with learning, it helps you focus more. Again, we were speechless.

Pulling out his guitar, he sang in English, proving his point. They applauded as if he were a rock star. Sighing, I couldn't deny that using the guitar was a brilliant idea. In a way, I almost felt sorry for the audience for not knowing who stood before them. Although I suppose it's fair to say if I didn't know any better, his poise and passion would have sold me in a heartbeat too.

I stared with disgust. What an absolute waste of pure talent. This kid could have had a real shot at a decent life. Instead, he wasted it when he murdered Ally – and over what? Something totally dumb, I'm sure. Would we ever know? Now, two lives were cut short from making a difference in this world. Ready to throw up, I couldn't watch it any longer.

Andy then curiously said, "Huh."

I should have known. He is famous for making a random remark so you'll ask him, "What?" I never understood why he couldn't just come right out and say, "Want to hear something interesting?" Groaning, like usual, I took the bait.

Andy brought up Karen, asking if I recalled our first meeting. Of course, I remembered it. How many psychic sessions had we been to, geez? I had no idea where he was going with his comments, and I wasn't in the mood to play games. Andy looked perplexed while reciting how she described Arturo in Mexico and in a school of some kind. Turning to me, he asked me if I had seen what he had. I gasped. Holy shit! Yes, I did.

At that moment, Andy and I connected on a spiritual level. We saw the same thing and agreed without words. We both understood that the women's shelter wasn't technically a school; however, Arturo was most certainly teaching in a classroom. Subjective or not, it was good enough for both of us.

I loved what Andy and I shared. It was such a relief not to go through the motions of another ugly fight. I didn't know what was happening with my man, but I'd take it. It gave me hope in so many ways. Not only for us as a couple but also for sharing the update with others. Maybe they'd be more focused on something cool versus the bad during this nightmare too. Fingers crossed.

I was enjoying a quiet weekend when 007 called on Sunday the 17th. It took me by surprise. I know that sounds silly, but I had forgotten that his schedule is very different than mine. Those guys work crazy hours.

Sounding upbeat, he stated he was cautiously optimistic – they'd collected intelligence of Arturo's new address. I was still confused why Immigration hadn't arrested him at the shelter, but everyone we shared with thought this was exciting news. At the same time, it scared me to death. Yes, I wanted him off the streets too. Then again, the second he's caught, my life would become bogged down in a new way.

Most people tried to offer the comfort that *when* he's convicted, I'd be able to "move on." It sounds nice, doesn't it? Sure, I get to check a box; however, I think they missed that Arturo could and probably would appeal until his last breath. It would then mean the legal crap would continue for years, and if Ally's ring was deemed hard evidence, I couldn't have it back until the entire process was over.

I wasn't sorry I didn't feel as thrilled as they were. The bottom line was that Arturo's capture or conviction still wouldn't change that I don't have an exit door to my living hell; I'm the one with the real life sentence.

It wasn't till February 25 that I received the second-most challenging call of my life; Arturo's extradition had begun. He had been apprehended in Gomez, Palacio, Durango, Mexico, at his current residence by Mexican Immigration. From there, he was transported to Dallas on the 27th, and the FBI Fugitive Task Force team then formally arrested him at the airport.

CHAPTER 19

Scattered Wisdom

APRIL 19, 2019

I know I've said it before: Every day since Ally's death is a new first without her. It's an endless growing tally I never asked for nor wanted. Getting sucked into the negative was now almost a daily occurrence. Not that it wasn't before, but this was the pit-of-despair kind. Having your kid murdered – I'm not sure it gets more awful than that. So, when something cool happens, I love to share it. Not only does talking about it make me feel happy, but I expect my listener to remind me of my story when I'm down in the dumps.

Since my first introduction with Karen, we'd had another family session, and then I had a handful of one-on-ones readings. They had all been rays of sunshine in one way or another. Even now, I'm smiling ear to ear, thinking about them. That kid of mine has blown me away with her pursuit to let us know she hasn't gone far and is still by our side.

Andy secretly set up another meeting with Karen days after my 41st birthday. Man, my guy is two-for-two with surprising me this way. But this time, we were going to use Skype, and he invited my folks to join us for an hour and a half.

Sitting in our front room was tight. Scrunched together so we'd all be on camera, my folks sat on our couch, Kylie and I took the floor, and Andy paced in the background. It was nice to see Karen again, although I couldn't help but giggle. Looking cute like she did in our first visit, she wore her readers this time.

After an already mind-blowing thirty-seven minutes of listening and interacting with Ally, Karen offered to answer any questions. We had a slight pause, and I asked her, "Um, how has she been trying to reach out?" Validating that I had asked a great question, Karen began describing how the differences would impact us individually based on our learning styles.

Explaining to Andy that Ally would connect with him by touch, Karen asked if he does things with his hands. As he answered, we heard the Xbox beep, and it turned on. Looking at each other in surprise, then turning back to the TV, we were all staring at a message that came across the screen: "Sorry Ally." I thought for sure someone would make a noise, even a gasp, but no one did. You could hear a pin drop.

Karen was none the wiser and had moved on to Kylie, explaining how Ally would come to her in her dreams. Was it weird that she couldn't hear the beep or didn't notice the bewildered look on our faces?

Karen excitedly asked, "Did you get a dream with her?"

Kylie impatiently replied, "Um, not yet. Sorry, so the Xbox, um, we all have profiles, and it just popped up and said, 'Sorry Ally.'"

With total amazement, Karen answered, "What?"

Kylie eagerly continued, "And it's done that a couple of times to her when she's been playing the Xbox, so that is what we were just pointing at."

As everyone stared at me, smirking, I said, "Yeah."

Karen exclaimed, "Oh, I have total chills! Is that just off the wall or what?"

Kylie and I both laughed and simultaneously slurred, "Yeah."

Karen provided different examples in her experience of spirits connecting with loved ones using electronics as energy sources. It felt like yesterday when I saw Ally's message for the first time after she died. I never once doubted it was a sign. Because of the Xbox camera's facial recognition with each of us, I knew the camera must have recognized Ally in the room with me. When I told Kylie after seeing it for the second time, she was giddy to share that she had too!

I intently watched my family's expressions as we told different stories. Andy and my dad looked like scientists calculating the probability that it was or wasn't a malfunction of the Xbox. It was interesting to watch them process similarly. On the other hand, my mom seemed uneasy and was on the verge of tears. I wondered if she'd remembered me telling her about the Xbox message after it first happened.

Looking back to the TV, you couldn't miss seeing Karen's giant smile, and her arm hair was standing straight up again, providing yet another validation. I closed my eyes, feeling the most profound appreciation for Ally's effort to connect with us. Not only did her message affect us individually, but we'd experienced it all together firsthand.

With fifteen minutes left, Karen asked if we had any more questions. I hoped someone else would speak up, but the room was silent. Not wanting to waste our time, I blurted out what came to mind.

"Is there anything else that we could be doing for her that maybe we're not doing that maybe she'd like?" I wished I could shrink and disappear into the couch after saying such a terrible sentence, but Karen was graceful, confirming it was a good question.

Asking for Ally's thoughts, Karen said, "She's showing checkers or a checkerboard."

I about shit my pants as my mom shot me the look of utter shock. I may have even smacked Kylie in the shoulder. My mom and Kylie looked like little kids on Christmas morning in pure anticipation of opening presents. I loved it. Meanwhile, Andy and my dad still oozed suspicion. Come on! There was no way Karen could know that.

Karen asked, "Is there any reference to playing checkers?"

Kylie said, "Mom got a checkerboard from her work once, and we got it out the other day."

I followed with, "We just played it on my birthday."

My mom proudly clarified, "Last Sunday."

I thought about my party, the first since Ally died. Every happy moment was paired with such sadness, and to be honest, it probably weighed more toward the sad. And now, I sat there, having an internal pity party. I was ashamed that Ally had to remind me she wasn't really gone. In my mind, I could accept the concept, but my heart was too full of grief. I appreciated that she hadn't given up on me.

I wasn't sure it could get any better with only minutes left. My spirit cup was already full. I should have known from our first meeting that ending with a bang is how this goes.

Karen said, "Let me just see if there is anything else from Ally." There was a pause. "She's *so* funny. She's like, be quiet everybody. Now I'm going to fart."

Without hesitation, everyone laughed and shook their heads. Geez, that kid of mine. If there was one thing she wasn't shy about, it was farting. That girl loved to rip one.

Finally, seeing the boys blush was a beautiful moment for me. I saw their expressions become less and less stern throughout the entire meeting. However, at this moment, something in their faces told me that what Ally said had clicked and truly sealed the deal for them. Of course, it had to be about a fart. I should've known. It was the absolute perfect ending to our meeting.

Can I tell you how much I love all those stories? They were awesome. I know that word gets overused, but for sure, they really were.

Shifting to my one-on-ones with Karen, they've been instrumental for many reasons. Given that Karen is a counselor herself, I've found her philosophies are pretty similar to Beth's. I don't know if it's their training or what, but sometimes it's downright scary how in sync they are. I've shared with them both how their guidance is often the same, just said differently. It's as if the universe had connected them and they unknowingly were backing each other up.

Now, does that mean I get the benefit of talking to Ally sometimes with Karen? Yes, but I don't make it a habit. We call Ally in when it feels right – I know she's busy too.

Throughout our meetings, I've jotted down many of Ally's quotes on Post-it notes. Some were random, and others were specific to the time of our call. I'd then stick them under the clear desk pad in my home office to see them when I worked from home. Not only was it comforting, but the perfectly placed colorful Post-it notes framed my keyboard, giving my desk a dash of style.

It was early March 2019, and I kept processing a blood-boiling conversation with a co-worker earlier that day about Arturo. I had instant regret after commenting that he *still* hadn't been extradited from Mexico. There's nothing I like more than listening to a biased lecture on how broken the criminal system is because of the dysfunctional bureaucracy.

It's not like I could even get a word in edgewise to express my opinion about Arturo, either. I mean, doesn't it say a lot about him? Innocent people can't wait to get into a courtroom and declare their innocence. And yet guilty people generally want every delay possible. Even though his ploy was sad and cruel and only prolonging the inevitable, it didn't matter to me which jail he was in – he wasn't hurting anyone anymore.

Sitting at my desk utterly irritated, I laid my head down as if it'd help calm me; I felt lost. I didn't care how disgustingly dirty my desk pad could be. Could it make me feel any worse than I already did? Well, actually, yes, because my cheek stuck to the plastic. Peeling my face from the no-longer-clear pad (from my makeup foundation) made me want to cry. Owe!

Shifting the pad back into its place, I realized something different about my desk. My notes surrounding the keyboard appeared brighter than usual, screaming at me to notice them.

From left to right, the neon Post-its said: "Mom, you have a territory problem – stop trying to fix things. You want to protect everyone from who you are. Your interpretations are your own. Stop negotiating your life."

Frazzled, I had to reread them in the same motion more than once. Holy shit! There were so many questions. How did I unknowingly place four separate quotes from Ally in perfect order? What was it about that moment when I *read* what they said? I didn't know how to feel. I shook my head in awe, sighing till I was blue. Was I more impressed that Ally's wisdom was so vast or upset that she knew how miserable I was?

Through the dark, I saw a flickering light – I knew what to do. Smiling, I said to Ally, "Thank you, kiddo. Better late than never, I suppose." Seeing how my everyday conversations about my story weren't going as I had hoped, I decided to take my part-time journaling to the next level and write this book. It would be my way of telling my story through my eyes. A virtual narrative where you could feel what I did. And no one could interrupt me, tell me how to feel or dismiss me anymore. Knowing it would happen on my terms would give me the confidence to be vulnerable.

Once I had told everyone my grand idea, I heard mixed reviews, which wasn't surprising. In many ways, I agreed. I could admit I'd never *written* this way before. And for others, I think their self-projection got the better of them. Addressing one's feelings can be super-scary, and it isn't for everyone.

When I told Beth, she voiced how it could challenge me but in the right way. Do you know what was also fun? I loved our debates about how silly it was that basic grammar had changed. It was entertaining to theorize why someone thought that spaces after sentences needed to become one and no longer two. Seriously? This new standard is how we choose to evolve? How sad.

Writing about my grief and healing became a necessary tool for reassembling my life. There was no escaping what I needed to address, and I didn't want to for the most part. So I promised myself I'd work through every hurdle, one after another.

Shaking in my boots, on April 19, 2019, I shared my first version of my introduction with Christine, a reacquainted friend from Ally's funeral. How could I not?

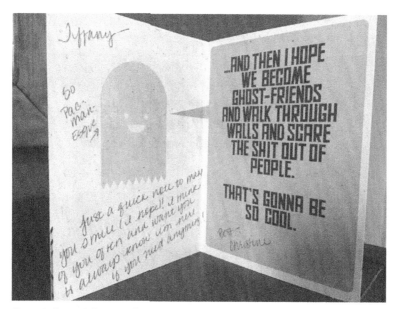

Receiving this random, most perfect card made me laugh for hours, even snort. I trusted Christine's input, not only as my sick-minded friend but also as a published author. Bless her heart for the editorial suggestions and encouraging words:

"It's very good! I am so happy you are finding an outlet for this – and I think you will be able to help people. You have an incredible story to tell people – a story of the obvious tragedy, loss, and sadness; but also a story of redemption, forgiveness, strength, and letting go and letting 'life' take over. Love it!"

I'd never thought in a million years I'd connect with writing and notice such restorative power. Christine's critique only inspired me more. Now addicted, I felt it was no longer a hobby like journaling; it became my mission.

CHAPTER 20

More Than I Bargained For

AUGUST 9, 2019

For the past thirty-two years, the Parents of Murdered Children have hosted numerous National Conferences around the United States. Who knew such a resource existed? When Phil announced during a POMC meeting that the thirty-third conference would be in Denver, Andy and I didn't hesitate to sign up for the two-day workshop. Kylie expressed little interest, which we found disappointing, but we also understood.

I was overwhelmed with over forty workshops to choose from, each lasting an hour and a half. How do you even decide which ones to attend? There could be two or three classes that overlapped that seemed interesting.

I peeked at what Andy had circled on his schedule. It was predictable: An Inside Look at the Criminal Justice System, Familial DNA Database & Genealogy Searches, and Ask the Forensic Expert.

Mine was, too: Mother's Grief, Getting to a New Normal, and Staying Healthy in Times of Crisis.

Undoubtedly, it made perfect sense. Arturo's extradition left us pretty scarred (for different reasons), so we again defaulted to being individuals. What? You didn't think my superhero story was going to be short of more drama, did you?

If you remember, on February 27, Mexican Immigration had extradited Arturo from Mexico to Texas. What I didn't tell you was what happened next. This guy challenged his extradition, claiming a wrongful arrest – I'm not kidding. Sharing this twist left me bewildered at those who were shocked beyond belief and professed their righteous disgust. Come on. How could you honestly expect anything less? It's easy to point the finger at someone who *should* take responsibility, isn't it? But what if the roles were reversed? Would *we* be the first to turn ourselves in? It's safe to say I didn't make a lot of friends with my comments.

However, by day ninety-two, even I'll admit it tested my patience. It was then that the Dallas court served Arturo with the governor's warrant – a document whose purpose I'm still unclear about. Anyway, our legal team was unsure why it took so long and assumed the Dallas court had already served him. Seriously? Oh, wait, there's more. Without flinching, Arturo denied it was him, claiming mistaken identity!

You'd think I was making this up because of the ridiculousness of his strategy, right? But if anything, yet again, it showed his desperation for prolonging the inevitable. And if there were any questions to his character, he left no stone unturned. Taking an additional thirteen days, Arturo was finally extradited from Texas to Colorado's Arapahoe County Jail on June 11.

Most believed that the trial would happen instantaneously once Arturo's transfer to Arapahoe was complete. Ugh – if only. Another reminder of how my beloved movies were misleading. Here's a crash course in how it really goes. First, there's a formal filing of charges, which is pretty self-explanatory. Also, bail is determined. Second, there's a preliminary proof-evident hearing, which basically means the judge will decide if there's enough evidence to have a trial and which evidence is allowable. Third, there's an arraignment for the defendant to plead guilty or not. And *then*, the trial date gets set, depending on the prosecution and defense schedules. Mind you, our legal team warned that the average period is about two years.

With that said, let me circle back to the conference. Andy was preparing for our proof-evident hearing scheduled for November 6. He was on a mission, but so was I. Neither was right or wrong. So I asked Andy to attend the How Traumatic Loss Affects Family Relationships workshop at the POMC conference the next day. He agreed to go. As happy as I was, I wondered when he'd step up and invite me to attend some kind of healing resource with him.

Once the opening ceremony began, they announced that more than 300 people had registered. My eyes closed in disbelief. It explained why so many were standing in the back with me. How can there be so many of us? Looking around the room, I saw it was clear that violence doesn't have favorites. I didn't know whether to feel comforted or cry. Great. Another slap in my face how real this was. By now, you'd think I wouldn't need another one, but I guess I did.

If hearing the attendance wasn't jaw-dropping enough, along the wall they had plaques called the "Murder Wall" listing the birth and death dates of over 3,800 loved ones who had died by murder/homicide. I gasped. It didn't even include Ally's name – I never sent in the form. How many more were there? Not able to hold it in any longer, I let my tears flow like a waterfall.

One of my favorite mama bears from the Front Range Chapter, Julie, stood next to me with her daughter Courtney. I adore them both. We are the epitome of opposites attract, complementing our differences since the first day we met. They teach me how to be louder like the roaring lionesses they are, I teach them how to whisper – more like a mouse.

It's for sure an entertaining dynamic for our POMC group. Especially since Julie and Andy had gone to Columbine High School together (yes, *that* Columbine... acts of violence surround us all in Colorado) – small world, eh? Julie was a senior when he was a sophomore, and she still treats him like a little brother. He retaliates just like one too – it's hilarious.

Taking a deep breath, Julie gave me her usual boobalicious hug, and I felt safe. But it didn't stop me from hating that we were there. I didn't want to do anything but cry and feel sorry for myself. How could this be happening? I stood there stunned, not hearing anything else the announcer said.

After a short while, it was time to head to the first workshop. Andy called me over to meet some police guy who had helped with our case. I didn't care. I felt like such an asshole, but I despise showing up late. It's not in my genetic makeup. I shook the police guy's hand and thanked him for his service. Robotically, I excused myself and headed straight to class.

Walking into the Grieving Mothers workshop, I thought it was eerily silent. Thankfully, Julie and I went together. Sitting in a small, dull conference room, ten heartbroken women stared straight ahead while spaced apart as if it were a typical presentation. Somewhere along the line, I assumed we'd be all huddled together, given the topic. Interesting that that wasn't the case, but I got it.

Standing before us was a mature, well-poised lady, almost like a guard at Buckingham Palace. She welcomed us to her workshop with a monotone voice, but I trusted she'd be a little livelier once she began. Maybe she needed some coffee to get going like I sometimes do.

After giving a quick overview, she introduced herself as a longtime member of the POMC and immediately shared her tragedy. Huh, it certainly did feel like one of our support meetings. Not opposing the usual routine, I wondered if each host would do the same and for how long. I understood the need to tell their story to seem relatable. On the other hand, I wanted to absorb as much material as possible.

Sitting there in one of those godawful banquet chairs, I couldn't help but get uncomfortable. Not only was my butt already sore, but there was also something else. I didn't realize how different listening to a horror story in the morning was versus our usual evening POMC meetings. It didn't sit well with me at all. I suppose it's like going to a haunted house – the scary seems appropriate only after dark.

Once she had completed her intro, she flipped over the first page of her easel pad. I appreciated her old-school approach to her presentation and giggled, too. It was pretty evident this gal didn't work in a fast-paced corporate-America job.

Listed were various topics to discuss, from the death day to the grieving process – the majority of the bullet points I'd already experienced in one way or another. I didn't look forward to the ones I hadn't yet met. Nonetheless, reassurance warmed my heart. Before my eyes were more validations, I wasn't alone, and I wasn't crazy. The room also seemed more at ease, as though the other mothers had the same epiphany.

Before I knew it, the group was no longer quiet. Each bereaved mama shared examples of dealing with their surviving loved ones throughout their journeys. I was in shock – their stories didn't differ that much from mine. I didn't know whether to be more pissed or find relief that I wasn't the only one.

One mother spoke about how a family member had tried to be helpful by setting the dinner table. They made a simple comment that they couldn't find the placemats. The mother was too overwhelmed in anguish to care about a proper setting. Not thinking straight, she snapped back with a nasty response. It turned into a mini-war, leaving them both angry and unapologetic for days. We all sighed in understanding. Why couldn't that family member toughen up their skin and not take her reaction personally? Seriously?

Collectively, we all agreed there are always good intentions somewhere. But when did the label of friend or family suggest there is automatic knowhow to be supportive? In some respects, we found them to be more harmful than helpful. I think Julie even shouted an "Amen!" Of course, we were grateful and knew their hearts meant well. None of us wanted to take away what felt right to them.

The energy in the room embraced me to the core. It became obvious many of these mothers were desperate to find a safe space to vent – it wasn't bashing, by any means. We merely didn't know how to be honest with our loved ones, anxious that we'd hurt their feelings. I felt so connected to each of them – I understood that feeling all too well.

Out of the blue, it hit me. Seeing how we can't have and would never want a do-over, I wrote down our wish-list items to share with others, so that maybe, just maybe, someone like us wouldn't experience another unnecessary heartbreak. Haven't we had enough already? It doesn't even have to be because of a violent crime either. On a larger scale, *any* hardship would be appropriate. Each time you do this, it's like an homage to Ally – you are helping people where she can't.

Finding the courage, I told how our house was a continually turning revolving door. It was reassuring to have friends and family nearby; other times, not so much. The noise they made was stressful, and their talking became too loud and their movements distracting. It seemed more like a typical Super Bowl party than anyone considering the *actual* tragedy I'd experienced.

Through the chaos, if anyone noticed me, the echoing question of what I needed became predictable. I appreciated that friends and family thought I'd be coherent enough to answer such an inquiry. But instead, it was more of an impossible demand. I was incapable of knowing what would help me, other than wanting the nightmare to end.

An idea? In my mind, this would have been the perfect situation for the assigned person to facilitate setting up a time to regroup and ask the guests to leave. It had to be clear how bogged down my family was with this and that. We needed someone from the outside to kindly help us focus on one another and self-care.

Like a broken record, I avoided by using the polite response, "I'm fine. Thank you." I even smiled when I didn't want to. Repeating myself only made me angrier and wasted what little energy I had. What did I do? Adamant about reversing the roles, I took care of others. It was easier to focus on making sure others were comfortable than to think of myself. The party needed a host, right? It also seemed nicer than lashing out and having a tantrum.

One after another, more topics flew around as the fellowship continued. I again found the courage to speak when another subject struck a chord with me.

The first week of Ally's death, random deliveries of yummy sentiments arrived by the truckload: Einstein Bagels, Village Inn, Edible Arrangements, Safeway, Whole Foods, Honey Baked Ham, and Famous Dave's BBQ. I love free stuff as much as the next person, but holy shit! It was way too much.

Among the food, a real treat received was a large toiletry basket, containing tissues to hand moisturizer. There wasn't a product I couldn't use. Who knew that a body wash could feel so spoiling because of a name brand? I mean, that was when I *actually* showered. I've discovered Febreze is quite the lifesaver. The thought was genius! Mainly because Kylie and I didn't bring anything home from that stupid Walmart trip where we were made to feel like freakish mutants.

Now, that doesn't mean I didn't welcome the food, especially the frozen meals. The thought of cooking was sickening, and I didn't have the strength. It's fair to say I was useless as a caretaker and felt insecure as a mother.

My friends and family came to me from both sides. If they weren't asking me what I needed, they scolded me for what I *should* be doing. Talk about feeling like a five-year-old.

Had I eaten or had anything to drink? Probably not. It didn't matter what I said – they just kept pushing food. If someone handed it to me, I'd give our dog scraps when no one was looking – Nikki wasn't complaining. Problem solved.

Yes, I got that I needed to keep up my strength, but come on. It only conjured the evil darkness within. Maybe I should have had some split-pea soup, and then I could vomit it all over them, just like in the *Exorcist* movie.

An idea? An example of lunch. The appointed contact could offer half of their premade peanut-butter (unless there's an allergy)-and-jelly sandwich to their bereaved loved one. A small piece won't feel as daunting as a complete meal. Then, offer them a glass of already-poured water. They'll need to hydrate, too.

Realizing how much food we had, I felt the burden of having it go uneaten become taxing. I swear that damn commercial about the hungry children kept playing on the TV, tugging at my heartstrings. Wasn't starvation a more immediate crisis than mine? I mean, I wasn't hungry, but others were. As a result, I'd invite as many guests as possible to stay for complete meals.

Admittedly, I debated if the perishable foods should go to waste versus having an intimate meal (nibble) with Andy, Alex, and Kylie. Unsure how to ask guests to give us uninterrupted time, I took advantage of what I had. If I saw my family, great; if not, I trusted that I'd see them later. I felt so rotten for bargaining. Although to be fair, my family wasn't fighting for my time, either. How could we not see how precious time together would be? So I used what I observed as neglect from family to rationalize my behavior.

An idea? In my mind, this would have been the perfect situation for the assigned person to facilitate setting up a time to regroup and ask the guests to leave. It had to be clear how bogged down my family was with this and that. We needed someone from the outside to kindly help us focus on one another and self-care.

Thank God that Andy eventually understood the torment I carried for the excess food. Talk about a shining moment for him. Regardless of what we sent home with guests, we still ran out of storage space. After about the eighth day of receiving more perishable food, he took it upon himself and discovered our local Ronald McDonald House. I was grateful he had stepped up, and we donated the surplus of food in Ally's name. So, for a moment, my moral compass balanced.

An idea? Appetites are scarce initially, so if you do send food, go frozen all the way. Or perhaps deliver a practical yet spoiling basket weeks, months, or even a year later. Contrary to popular belief that this could reopen a healing wound, it could actually let your bereaved loved one know you haven't forgotten about them or their grief. It's easy with today's technology – just set a future reminder.

It felt like another roar from the crowd. The bereaved mothers mutually agreed there is no defined timeline of how long healing can take. But how are our support systems helping us when the newness wears off?

Taking a deep breath, I let my posture relax into the chair. As if I'd received a standing ovation, I wanted to take a bow from all the support I received. Saying my truth out loud in a POMC meeting was already empowering. With this group of gals, it was downright intoxicating.

After we heard the last of the stories, the room silently echoed what only we could understand. The empathy felt effortless among us. How could we have such an unspoken bond even though we'd never met? Or was it bigger than that? Maybe the universe humbly brought us together for a reason.

The fire alarm unexpectedly sounded. The panicked hotel staff entered our workshop and demanded that we leave and head outdoors. I wondered how many in our class would get triggered by that kind of behavior.

Gathering my things, I wasn't in a hurry at all, nor was Julie. We found more amusement in watching the staff than anything, sharing a couple of eye rolls. It didn't feel like a real threat after what I'd been through, and I knew Julie agreed.

Lollygagging toward the lobby, a few hundred fellow POMC members surrounded me. They, too, took their sweet-ass time to get outside. My mommy ears didn't let me down. I overheard them discussing how they didn't feel the need to rush after their tragedies, either. Unknown to them, I felt another meaningful validation. At the same time, I also worried about us. Were we all now desensitized to any new crisis? Eh, maybe that's not a bad thing.

Finding Andy outside, I asked him how his first workshop had gone. Surprisingly, he said he had attended the Father's Grief workshop instead of An Inside Look at the Criminal Justice System. Can I tell you how speechless I was? I didn't see that coming in a million years. It wasn't like anyone had influenced him – not that I knew of, anyway. I gave him the biggest hug and couldn't wait to hear more about it. He smiled and played it off like it wasn't a big deal – I should have known. Nevertheless, it was for me.

After the fire drill was over, the schedule resumed as though nothing had happened. Time for lunch. The assigned tables had Andy and me with most of our Front Range Chapter group, with the rest directly across from us. I enjoyed discussing the day thus far, although I couldn't quote any of it.

Thankfully, therapy dogs were casually walking around – it was nice to have the option to rub a fluffy belly now and then. While giving those at the table most of my full attention, the rest became more focused on the two remaining workshops. Could I handle any more information? I wondered if Beth would approve. There must be a justifiable reason why therapy sessions are only an hour.

Just like in school, the bell rang and lunch was over. Racing to the Getting to a New Normal class, I tried rebooting my attention span to allow for new information. I desperately wanted to learn how to fit in with society in whatever way that meant. Maybe I'd been doing an OK job, but what if I had missed something that could ease my feeling of aloneness?

Walking into this workshop, I didn't see any presentation tools. Huh, interesting. All I saw were two instructors who made me smile from ear to ear. The spunky duo reminded me of what I hoped Petra and I would look like when we got older.

Also, like the Mother's Grief class, the pair did a brief overview of the material and spoke about their tragedies. They, too, were members of the POMC. As horrified as I was by their experiences, I appreciated the predictable outline. Tuning out for a few minutes gave me some much-needed rest until the topic began.

After the duo wrapped up their introduction, it seemed that there wasn't much time left for the curriculum. I grumbled. While I wanted to learn, I also loved the break. My sponge was already full. Wondering how many other people in the class felt this way, I debated how I would fill out the comment card they handed me.

I did my best to take notes through their question-and-answer approach, but my arms became heavy with exhaustion. However, it was easy to hear the main takeaway they wanted us to have: life is never the same, and what I thought was normal will never be the same. I bit my quivering lip to keep from crying.

One of the mistakes we, as bereaved, make is not recognizing how changed our life *actually* is, they explained. I sighed in disappointment. All I heard was them speaking directly to me – as if they knew how much I downplayed my grief.

I appreciated their advice for getting through the rough patches for myself and my loved ones. They used a flight attendant as a metaphor. The instruction to place the mask on yourself before assisting others is predictable, yet how many listen? It should be a rule applied in everyday life, they coached. Before we can help anyone, we need to make sure we are first taking care of ourselves. I'll never forget that visual.

The duo also mentioned that we, as bereaved, would need to have extra patience with others. My muscles tensed. Are you serious? Another thing I'd have to do to ease someone *else*? It didn't seem quite fair, honestly. The air was getting thin from rising above all the time.

Hearing hurtful and stupid things is unfortunately inevitable, they explained. And quite possibly, we have already. "Have faith. Time heals. Get over it," or any sentence that starts with "At least" named a few. Heads nodded in unison, and grunts rumbled throughout the room. Were they agreeing or admitting they had said one of them too?

I can't imagine someone saying, "Get over it," to one of us. What kind of careless asshole would dare say something so insensitive? I would punch that jerk in the face if they said that to me. And on the flip side, I had to admit I was guilty of using "At least" a time or two. Shit. I guess I need to make a better effort too.

It's true. None those phrases would make the pain more bearable or offer support in any way. Instead, they only belittle the most unimaginable hurt someone can experience.

I added my helpful tip to the group, seeing as someone *had* said these things to me. While I wasn't witty enough to have this response I saw somewhere, I'll be ready if there came a time for a do-over.

"Before you tell a grieving parent to be grateful for the children they have – think about which one of yours that you could live without."

Sitting slumped in my chair for the remainder of the class, I didn't know what was more uncomfortable now, my ass or my ego. As much as I wanted to hear the rest, processing any more data was impossible. Too busy beating myself up, I was a poster child for what not to do. I was glad for the reality check, and of course, I wasn't. All I knew was that petting a therapy dog wouldn't cut it after this.

This time, I dreaded heading to the next workshop, Staying Healthy in a Time of Crisis. The title alone sounded overwhelming. My head was already in a vise, and it was only getting tighter. Was I going to hear more of the same thing? Or would there be something new that I would take away? I debated whether I could honestly handle another hour and a half of the information.

I sensed a very different vibe from the other two peering into the room. Our host was a guy. Not only was he preparing an easel, but he also had a giant screen with a slide show ready to begin.

He introduced himself as a full-time teacher, respected author, and speaker; I giggled. Of course he was. He screamed it from a mile away with his neatly trimmed beard, wire-framed glasses, and khakis. All he was missing was a sweater with elbow patches. Not to mention, it explained all the visual aids.

Just like the other two workshops, he began with his tragedy. Except this POMC member kept his story short and to the point, as in about five minutes. Thank God. No offense to the other presenters, but this guy truly understood the value of teaching us his assigned material.

Slide after slide, it was like drinking from a fire hose. At this rate, I'd be qualified to become a therapist by the day's end, I joked to myself. Luckily, much of his material overlapped with the other two workshops. The consistency of hearing the same message said in different ways only ensured that it would sink in.

His scientific teaching approach about the brain and how trauma affects it was fascinating. Someone asked him to describe how PTSD worked. Within seconds, he jumped to the easel and drew a diagram like a game of Pictionary. Man, this guy knew his stuff.

I instantly thought of Beth — everything she'd been coaching about PTSD rang true. The drawing couldn't have said it better: Getting stuck in the past meant reliving the experience, and the unknown future only fuels constant concern, so being in the present moment lets us take control of our lives to feel safe. I loved feeling like I understood the concept.

As he ended, he reiterated that there is no magic solution for us. Bullet point after bullet point, he offered healing suggestions that made sense: Make the unsafe safe, eat meals together, build a support team, and learn to laugh and play again. It was beautiful.

It was almost dinnertime, and we all gathered where we had first met that morning. In the back corner, photos hung, honoring our loved ones. Witnessing the pain of my other favorite mama bear from our local chapter, yes, another Juli, crippled me. It's not like I hadn't experienced it during our meetings or even when I attended the trial of her child's killer. There was something different in this setting. Perhaps it was the sheer magnitude of seeing our photos together or just the day itself. I don't know.

As we waited for our food, Julie and Courtney introduced a new friend they'd made: Kasia, from Chicago. She'd come to the conference by herself, leaving her surviving older teenagers at home. I wasn't surprised they had found a "stray." Naturally, the Front Range group adopted her as our own because, without a doubt, she fit right in.

All I can say is that it felt *so* good to act silly – look at us! Finding a group of misfits (me, Julie, Courtney, Andy, and Kasia) to have such fun at an event like this told me everything I needed to know. The awful truth about my tragedy no longer outweighed why I was there; I felt purpose.

CHAPTER 21

Out With The Old

I think it's fair to say we've come a long way together and developed a close relationship, don't you? So I'm going to be blunt. Sometimes I hate telling my story.

Believe me – it's not personal. To you, it may feel like the flip of a page, but for me, it's finding my way on this yellow brick road. It has been nothing short of needing one Band-Aid after another. I wasn't kidding when I said that initially, and perhaps you'd agree I should have bought stock, too.

After the National Conference, I decided to read my book from the beginning. Of course, rereading the earlier chapters sucked because of the content. I can't imagine a day I won't cry thinking about Ally's funeral. What I found interesting is my tone, though. It's numb and robotic, more like a humdrum storyteller sharing a play-by-play., Both Beth and Karen have stated in their professional opinions that my behavior was normal. I have to say, even though it's exactly how I felt and what happened in real life, I wouldn't say I liked it. I missed the "old" me.

As I continued to read, I could start witnessing how I changed. With my numbness lifting, my vulnerabilities allowed my character to come through. I hadn't looked at my growth that way before. In some ways, I judged myself. Come on. We all have the should have, could have, would haves. But at the same time, it wasn't all bad.

Things started making sense when I got to the chapter about seeing myself as a monster. I wasn't just writing about what I'd experienced; I was also unconsciously leaving myself clues for a later a-ha moment.

I touched the words on the screen as if I could feel them. Through my blurry tears, I knew that the monster I once saw was only my fear of letting Ally's murder define me. And once I reread my last words – "I felt purpose," from the previous chapter – my energy soared through me like a warm sunrise. Before me was every undeniable validation I'd ever needed. I left myself permission to accept that I was ready to become the survivor I wanted to be: the "new" me.

I want to start with how I've reconnected for the most part with my beloved pastime, movie-watching. Exciting start, right? I'd say so, because watching movies has always been an event filled with anticipation for me. I'd get my drink and candy and make a mad dash to the theater (or couch). I'd then wrap myself like a burrito in my soft, fuzzy blanket, and once the lights dimmed, I was more than ready to surrender my imagination for a few hours of amazement.

From Chapter 6: This Only Happens on TV, do you recall when Andy and I celebrated our tenth wedding anniversary in 2016 with friends and family? And we gave Ally and Kylie each an identical diamond band from my wedding ring? Boy, I hope so. I'm pretty sure I've made it clear how crucial getting Ally's ring back is to me. But anyway, that's so not the point, back to my anniversary tale.

What I failed to mention earlier is the best part. Our event had a *Zombieland* theme, just like the movie! Can I tell you how much fun it was to watch Ally and Kylie put together the favors? They had a ball making tons of survival kits, including hand sanitizer, ChapStick, and Twinkies.

After our hilarious zombie vow renewal, we all sat around and watched the film while eating the essential popcorn and candy. I knew my parents had never seen it, and hearing their grossed-out reactions was actually better than the movie itself. Totally epic!

I missed moments like that. I missed enjoying Family Movie Night on the couch. I missed going to the theater and bitching about my sticky shoes from all the spilled soda. I missed dreaming about becoming a makeup artist because it's my favorite part. But I especially missed subjecting my parents to all my beloved sci-fi movies such as *Resident Evil, The Final Chapter* for my 40th birthday. Is anyone noticing a trend? LOL!

So one night in late fall 2019, I approached Andy, asking if he had a minute. Knowing he thinks this is the "something's coming" question, I grasped my fingers so hard that my knuckles were white. It was silly. It's only Andy. But as we all know, sharing a vulnerability isn't easy, no matter who the recipient is. Of course, he agreed with a look of suspicion.

I told Andy how finding my way through this colossal disaster has put new meaning to the phrase "The struggle is real." I emphasized that that's why I repeatedly watched the same movies and how my Rolodex of them had become minimal because I needed to feel safe. Frankly, I was saying the same thing in ten different ways, but really it was only a long-winded way of referring to my continued battle with PTSD.

"Babe, strangulation scenes are a trigger for me," I told him.

"They are?" he replied.

"Are they *not* for you?" I asked, confused.

Andy said, "No. Movies are forms of entertainment, and I'm not emotionally invested like that. Sure, I'll yell for Godzilla, but that's like rooting for a favorite team. So I separate movies from reality unless it's like a documentary based on real-life or something like that."

Nodding, all I could do was smile, hoping my eyes weren't as wide as the millions of questions I had as to whether Andy's perspective was more of a blessing or a curse. I had to remind myself to stay on topic, and some things just weren't worth dissecting, at least not then. So instead, I responded, "Huh. Alrighty."

We chatted a little more, and I must have made it clear I wanted to watch new movies again but that I needed his support. Andy was so sweet and offered to hold my hand from now on. So that if I needed to squeeze the shit out of something if I'm triggered, I could. I had no idea if it would work, but it didn't matter – it told me he heard me. In that moment, I realized we'd turned a pivotal point in our marriage since Ally's death. I only wished I would have spoken up about it sooner than later.

Feeling empowered, I also decided to talk with my folks and Kylie. If we were going to continue Family Movie Night, they also needed to be in the know.

Long story short, all three of them were oblivious that strangulation scenes could be a trigger. Are you kidding me? Guess not, because they each said, "Oh, that makes sense." Ugh. Aside from the gut-punch, they offered me different ideas of supporting me. But deep down, after a score of four-for-four and none of them had seen what I deemed obvious already, I threw up my hands in defeat. I'm all for having a teaching moment, but I was also *so* tired of having to explain myself all the time.

Since then, movie-watching has definitely tested me, but it's getting better. I'm using a coping technique Beth taught me during our "Prolonged Exposure" work, and that's to "name the trigger as is." It's to "ground" me so I can focus on what's happening now instead of the past. Meaning the scene in the movie is not a recurrence of Ally's murder; "… only a memory – albeit a life-changing one."

You know, before all this happened, if someone were to tell me that I would need to understand the difference between the present and what a memory is, I would've probably mocked the statement. I just don't get how our brains can rewire themselves after experiencing a traumatic event, undoing years of basic foundational concepts without our permission. It blows my mind.

I've found that when a strangulation scene is predictable, it's not so bad to manage the trigger. However, when it slaps me in the face, a surge of panic showers over me, and I feel like Dorothy in *The Wizard of Oz* chanting, "There's no place like home" over and over. It's awful.

Having said that, though, I've made Andy squeal a time or two from squeezing his hand so hard. And between you and me, it's been pretty damn satisfying and does help me find my grounding.

But am I in a hurry to try meditation again? At this point, I'd have to give that a big fat hard pass.

So for now, I'll stick with movies. Besides, how could I pass up the opportunity to share the much-anticipated movie sequel *Zombieland: Double Tap* with my folks?

CHAPTER 22

Wicked Whiplash

MARCH 19, 2020

You're probably wondering what happened at the trial at this point in my story, right? Sigh. In a perfect world, I'd get to tell you how everything went according to plan, but what in my story has so far?

Last I told you, we were waiting on the proof-evident hearing on November 6, 2019, and the purpose was for the judge to decide whether there was enough evidence and which evidence was allowable. Sound about right? Good.

As you can guess, waiting for the hearing was pure torture. The lingering torment of an internal debate shadowed my every move – should I or shouldn't I see and hear the evidence about Ally's murder?

Everyone I talked to had similar opinions, which didn't help push me in any direction. Yes, I could know the truth of those fucking marks on Ally's ears and whose blood was on the pillow thrown into the dumpster. Sure, there's a chance she didn't suffer like the girl in *Atomic Blonde*. But ... what *if* she did, and it's worse? Was that really a risk I was willing to take? It all came down to one thought: Did I want to see the crime-scene photo of Ally lying in the bathroom all alone, dead?

"Fuck no!" Besides further pain and agony, what value would any more details have? Do I need the validation that Ally might have defended herself for at least a short time just because that's how I made up my own story? Indeed, I could have one last proud-mama moment, but it's not like I can high-five her or anything. No. It seemed to me that the truth I had was enough. And for the first time, probably in my entire life, I felt at peace with letting go of the need to know everything. Some say ignorance is bliss, and although the last thing I felt was blissful, I wholeheartedly got what they meant.

Here's the thing, though. Some also say, "You are only given as much as you can handle." Remember how I wanted to give this statement the middle finger because *if* I'd been "weaker," would Ally still be alive? Now, it was going to get two! One would think having to carry on a debate over the evidence about my murdered kid would be enough. Guess again. Someone or something thought I had room for some more. Let me explain.

You see, our attorneys finally let me in on a bit of a secret. If you recall, Arturo went to jail on domestic-violence charges after punching Ally in the face a few months before she died. And our attorneys wanted to use that in our case. Which meant they wanted me to act as a witness at our hearing! If you guessed I about lost my shit, you'd be right.

They were quick to explain that I'd be testifying only about the events leading up to Arturo's domestic-violence conviction and nothing more. I wasn't sure if that was supposed to make me feel better, but it didn't. The last thing I wanted to do was sit in front of the judge, the jury and my friends and family spilling my guts publicly. Talk about adding insult to injury.

I talked to Donna, my victim's advocate, about it. Throughout this process, I had felt she'd had my back since Day One. No matter my questions or concerns, she had never dropped the ball and always followed through, getting me answers. It's safe to say that working with the attorneys and court gave her the ability to provide a trustworthy level of sympathy for my suffering during it all. She was, for sure, a bright light in this dark tunnel of Hell.

Donna talked to me as if we were old friends, so casual and confident.

"You'd make a great witness because you don't vilify Arturo," she said.

At first, I didn't know what to think, and I didn't respond. Donna must have noticed my silence and further explained what she meant. She went on to tell me how she thought the compassionate nature she'd witnessed in me was admirable and influential. Yes, I might be angry and everything else, but I don't push an agenda of vengeance as many people do. And because of that, jurors can seek the truth without added harmful distraction. She also said that it's not just jurors; it's all people, too. Boy, talk about a validation I never expected in a million years.

I mean, she was right. I've had strong morals all my life regarding retaliation. If I had to define it, I'd say people who crave vengeance are just hurt egos looking to return the favor – the old eye-for-an-eye thing again.

When Eric and I divorced, it was a difficult time for sure. We didn't necessarily end on the best terms, but they weren't awful, either. Still, I was hurt. Badmouthing him to Ally seemed like the natural thing to do. And it would have been so easy to get her on my side because she was young and impressionable. But was that a good thing? And what would that have taught her?

Instead, I wanted Ally to have a fair chance to draw her conclusions about her father. Maybe their relationship would be amazing, or perhaps it wouldn't. Regardless, it was so important to me that she'd have that kind of real-life experience, and I'd be there to support her through it. Isn't that my job as a parent? So I chose the path of forgiveness. Yes, one of my favorite F-words.

I'm pretty sure that I wasn't fully conscious of why I chose to let my anger toward Eric go back then. All I knew was that when I looked into Ally's baby blue eyes or played with her blonde curls, it didn't make sense to hold on to the bitter feelings. So, without his asking or apologizing, I let them go.

I know I made that sound easy, but believe me, we'd be here all day if I explained what I had to go through to get there. Let's save that for another book, OK?

My point is that I made my choice to move forward, and I didn't want my past to hold me hostage. And honestly, I wish that for everyone else. We all deserve to be happy, and we can do that only if we let our love and tolerances make the world a better place.

When I say all that out loud, it makes me feel like I'm a reincarnated hippie of some kind. And I'm cool with that; however, let's get one thing straight: there isn't enough peace and love in the world for you to ever find me without a bra.

As Donna and I wrapped up the conversation, I was more at ease about things. Little did I know that she was saving a doozy for the end. Because the attorneys would present me as a witness, by law, I wouldn't be allowed to sit in the courtroom for the hearing. I didn't know whether to jump for joy or cry instead. On the one hand, it sealed the deal that I couldn't change my mind about seeing the evidence, but on the other, I'd have to testify in the trial instead. Fuck me.

The day of the hearing came as fast as it went – it's pretty much a blur. The few things I remember were telling everyone who attended not to share a single detail with me unless I asked and how I sat in the most dismal waiting room with Maddie.

She looked so grown up with her hair pinned-up and dressed in a grey suit. I couldn't help but smile. We started with the typical small talk, but it didn't take long before she began twiddling her thumbs and looking down at the ground, tear after tear falling. My heart broke into a million pieces as she expressed her guilt for dropping Ally off at the motel. Every blubbery word she said turned my compassion into pure rage. I hated it! I kept screaming that someone needed to release her from this misery on the inside. Seriously, what kind of teenager, or anyone for that matter, could handle such a burden?

There was no way I was going to let this continue. Using the same mommy tone as before in the police station on Day One, I looked at Maddie, and I'm sure I interrupted, and I told her I wasn't mad and how much I loved her. That poor girl stared at me in disbelief as her lips quivered and her nose reddened even more.

"Maddie, listen to me. I'm not mad, and I never will be. I love you, and you did nothing wrong!" I prayed for strength as I took her hand into mine. Then, I repeated myself one more time, word for word.

I couldn't tell you how long we sat in silence until she smiled. All I hoped was that she believed me and would give herself a break.

It was about that time that my entire immediate family and some of Andy's friends filled the waiting room one by one, so I knew the hearing was over. The room was full of deep-felt energy. Kind of like we won a game, but no one was cheering or bouncing up or down.

It was interesting. Perhaps later, I'd inquire about what it all meant. Instead, I asked only one question: "Did anyone show up for Arturo?" Unanimously, everyone shook their heads side to side. My heart hurt for him. What an awful thing to sit through by yourself, even if you committed murder.

The attorneys began recapping a few necessary details and answered some questions. Most sounded like Charlie Brown's teacher to me. But I heard two things that meant the most to me. First, the attorneys were pleased with the judge's decision to schedule the arraignment hearing on December 9, 2019, and that's when Arturo would plead guilty or not guilty. And secondly, I would, in fact, be testifying in the trial.

As much as I was happy for our "winning team," deep inside, I struggled with self-pity. It's not that I didn't get their self-motivating need for justice, but I didn't want to go to trial, let alone participate as a witness in it! But it seemed that no one had considered what it would mean for me to go through this. And it was moments like this that only emphasized why I felt like I was on an island.

December 9 also came as fast as it went. Arturo pleaded not guilty to first-degree murder, and the trial was set for April 7, 2020.

Most were appalled that he didn't take responsibility and pled that way. For me, it wasn't surprising by any means. I mean, who in their right mind would agree to life without parole right off the bat? After all, his first defense was to claim that it was mistaken identity!

Did you know that as a defendant in a murder case, you have the right to offer a plea deal for a lesser charge before the scheduled trial? I didn't. To be fair, aside from my divorce and a few traffic tickets, I hadn't been exposed to the legal system enough to understand why so many have such deep-rooted opinions about it. I'd only thought they were conspiracy theories more than anything. But now, my eyes have been opened to a complicated world with layers like an onion.

After a quick Google search, I discovered a ridiculous ratio between plea deals and trials. Recent studies vary, of course, but for the most part, plea deals are accepted about 95% of the time versus the 5% that go to trial. With those odds, it's enough to say why wouldn't someone use a system to their advantage – it's the law, right? It's not their fault that the design of our legal system is beyond dysfunctional. So why not play the game for a possibility of a lesser sentence?

As you might have guessed, my opinion ruffled some feathers, but I was getting pretty used to it. It just blows my mind how people can be so righteous when pointing the finger, but put the mirror up to them, and let's see how quickly they look for a way out. I digress…

Aside from many eye rolls, I took from that day that there was a legitimate chance for a plea deal. It would spare me from the cruelty of trial, and his ability to appeal would be minimal, preventing this bullshit from being dragged out any longer. And that's what I wanted more than anything.

It was nearly impossible to keep my apprehension at bay as time passed. Using all my recent coping techniques became too much to handle. I had two little angels on my shoulders, constantly bickering back and forth. Don't shove my growing concerns under the rug because facing them can lessen their power. Yet don't talk about them too much because the constant need for reassurance only reinforces an unhealthy mindset. But make sure to have hope without creating expectations to dodge disappointment while planning to be proactive and respond to challenges. For the love of God!

Somehow, though, I made it through all the milestones: Christmas 2019, New Year's, my dad's birthday, Dan's birthday (Barb's husband), Eric's birthday, my birthday, Kristin's birthday, Valentine's Day (also Amy's birthday), and finally Andy's and my wedding anniversary in late February 2020.

I couldn't tell you how I hung in there through what felt like slogging through molasses, honestly. All I know is I couldn't wait for this exhausting cha-cha to end. I thought grieving for Ally was tough enough all by itself, but adding an upcoming trial ... for the love of God! I'm not Superwoman.

Although that darn someone or something again thought I must be kidding myself. The world as we knew it was facing an unprecedented pandemic. As the buzz about COVID was ramping up, things were shutting down. Come to find out that the courts weren't immune, and my dance was about to change tunes in a way I never expected. On March 19, I received the email from Donna that our trial, initially scheduled for April 7, would be postponed without a future date.

CHAPTER 23

Divine Intervention

OCTOBER 17, 2020

All right. It's time to roll up our sleeves and dive right in to the latest controversy in our world's history: COVID. I don't know how your experience has been, but mine overall – it's been a blessing in disguise.

Like most, when our governor issued the Stay-at-Home Order, I worked from home. The concept wasn't new because I had worked from home on Fridays for quite some time; however, an entire five days in a row seemed a little scary.

It didn't help my mental state when we received word from Donna on April 3 that our trial was postponed due to the virus. I still didn't want to go, but it didn't lessen the blow. All that time preparing emotionally was for nothing! What a waste! Although, I'll give it to them for trying to keep the ball moving. They rescheduled our go/no-go status conference to June 1 for a June 16 trial date.

However, our case was facing something unusual now. Because of COVID, the court would need to re-evaluate the speedy-trial timing. I'd forgotten there was a six-month limit from the arraignment date (when Arturo pleaded not guilty to Murder One on December 9, 2019) to be tried. It was quite a hot topic at the courthouse and on the news, not only for our case but because *no* defense team wanted the timing to start over, essentially forcing their clients to lose their constitutional rights. I didn't blame them one bit. However, our attorneys felt confident that it was out of our hands because of the circumstances with the virus.

On April 7, I received another call from Donna, who said we didn't need to worry about the speedy-trial issue. It was concluded (by someone important) that the virus was an extraordinary circumstance, so the deadline was extended. I didn't understand how this happened or who had the power to determine this, but it didn't matter. I just was glad the defense couldn't declare that Arturo's rights were being violated and call for a mistrial. And by the way: not sure if you saw, but this topic was all over the news. Not just for us but for all cases in Colorado (at least) where the defendants opted for speedy trials. Another one for the history books.

All this drama didn't help during the first couple of weeks working from home. The house was eerily quiet despite having the television on for background noise. Well, except for Zoey, our newest dog (Nikki passed away in 2018).

She didn't know what to do without being in her kennel during the day. That girl was bugging me every five minutes! Ugh. Being at home made me realize what I'd missed. Like escaping my desk for some lunchroom chitchat or walking Denver's downtown 16th Street Mall to grab a bite to eat or listen to street performers. Not to mention the people-watching! I'm not sure if other downtowns have random people in costume, but seeing Gandalf almost daily was always a real treat.

Aside from these petty distractions, or lack thereof, after another few weeks, I was in heaven. No longer having a two-hour commute each day was proving to be in my favor, and an eight-hour workday was just that. Now, I could exercise in the morning before work for about 45-60 minutes, take Zoey on two short walks during the day, and then after work, that hour was mine to do whatever before considering dinner. I'd never felt so relaxed. I noticed my attitude was more positive, and I got work done faster with fewer mistakes than before. It's like my work/life balance was coming together without making time for it.

Everything was going swimmingly until one morning, I tossed Zoey's ball and it happened to bounce upstairs, rolling into Ally's room. I didn't think anything of it until I found myself paralyzed standing in front of the doorway. I realized that Monday through Thursday, during my work hours, I hadn't been in her room since she died.

My ritual was highly predictable and comforting. Repetition was good for me now. Each morning, I'd pop in looking for anything out of place and wish Ally a good day. In the evening, I'd invite her to watch a movie with me in bed, and Fridays I added an extra trip to water her plant. It makes you wonder if I was subconsciously or consciously keeping just a little piece of Ally alive by doing this. But now, my reality surrounded me without fail. Do you know what I mean? I guess I was so busy figuring out working from home, I hadn't connected the dots just yet.

I didn't know what to do. My heart raced, and my legs felt like concrete. Right before me was Zoey's ball, yet I couldn't take a step forward to reach it. As I focused on how the dust settled on Ally's black ladder shelf and desk, Zoey stood by my side. She must have sensed it was off-limits. I then felt the room start to spin, and my emotions hit me like a tidal wave. I burst into tears and fell to the floor.

With my head tucked into my legs, I rocked back and forth for what felt like forever. I have yet to wail when I cry, but this was a close second. I hated everything I felt – the sadness, the pain and how incredibly alone I was. Between my gasps for air, I kept whispering, "Why did this have to happen?" I missed Ally so much! I couldn't stand the thought of another minute without her. And yet, what else could I do about it?

Poor Zoey stared at me, unsure what to do. She began to whine, and I could hear the whoosh of her tail beginning to wag. Within a second, she nestled her nose under my arms and started licking my face. At first, I was pissed. How dare she! I was perfectly content in my place of misery, feeling sorry for myself. Wasn't that my right? Although, try explaining that concept to a dog. I wanted to yell at her to go away, but I didn't. Instead, I began to laugh from her licking all the snot under my nose. Sometimes her tongue even got into my nostril, making me laugh even harder. I'm pretty sure I sounded like Elmo at that point. But I have to tell you: It felt so good to laugh. Man, did it ever! It seemed like all my worries no longer were my priority and I was free – even if it would last only a short time.

Over the next few weeks, there wasn't enough laughter in the world to get me out of my funk. With work now in a good place, I became shockingly aware of my surrounding reality. Everywhere I looked, constant reminders of Ally's death stuck out like a sore thumb, and home felt more like being in a damn prison than anything.

Any chance I could, I sat on the couch sucking up the boob tube, enjoying the mindless retreat. Except, flipping through the channels, COVID was on every local station as though nothing else were happening in the world. The negativity and controversy were toxic to my psyche, not to mention Andy's endless opinions. Can you guess how he felt when government and medical officials suggested wearing a mask and social distancing? I didn't mind doing my part – it was the rule-follower in me. But that guy, ugh.

I didn't feel like talking about what I was internalizing. Everyone's lives were already so upside down from COVID – it seemed like that was enough. So instead, I just sat with it every day, riding each wave as it came. Isn't that what Beth was coaching me to do all along?

Come early May, Andy joined me at home, but thankfully he made an office in the basement. I say that lovingly, of course!

The first two days, I was worse than Zoey, going downstairs to see how he was doing. I even made him lunch as an excuse. But by the third day, I was over it. LOL. Knowing he needed to focus on work, I made sure to bug him when something important happened. Here's an example of a worthy trip downstairs.

On May 20, I received an email from Donna stating that because of COVID and the courts' current closures, our judge would be resetting our trial for a new date during the upcoming June 1 go/no-go meeting.

Admittedly, I had mixed feelings again. On the one hand, I was frustrated by my built-up anticipation because it was deflating like a sad, squeaky balloon. But on the other, I felt complete relief. June could be one of the most brutal months for me at work, and I didn't want that burden to go to my team. And in a way, it fueled my desire for a plea deal even more. I wholeheartedly believed the realism of going to trial was setting in for Arturo and that he'd come around to making a deal.

My hope didn't always outweigh my exhaustion, though. When I logged into the Webex call on June 1, my fingers felt like a thousand pounds as I tapped my desk, waiting in suspense like everyone else. Seeing the judge and attorneys on camera, I thought they looked so tired. It was a sad observation, and yet it made sense. This COVID thing was really creating unnecessary havoc on an already-complicated system.

Bracing for the inevitable, I watched Arturo sitting in a brownish, thrown-together cubicle. I didn't have my camera on, so I knew he couldn't see me. However, Andy was sitting at his desk downstairs with his camera on. I could see him scrutinizing his screen, so I assumed Arturo was looking at him, too.

Aside from the unflattering jumpsuit, Arturo still looked like the cute kid I knew. While he sat there motionless, I didn't see any visible signs he'd been in a scuffle or anything. Still, when I heard the chains rattle when he bounced his knee up and down, it was a little unsettling. It was interesting to see him from my desk this way. As if the Webex call provided a level of safety. Yet I didn't need it. I had no feelings for him whatsoever. It reminded me of when I saw him in person the first time in court. He held no power over me and wasn't going to get a lick of my energy.

What did get my attention was when the judge threw out some options for open dates in July and August to reschedule. As I watched the attorneys scramble as they whispered to their counterparts, there was no denying their frustrations. Both sides commented on needing to shift things around to make any of the dates work. It was clear that our case would bump someone else. The judge then said our case would prioritize all others except for any trial involving a minor.

Ouch! Yes, I got that we were one of four high-profile Murder One cases and all, but at the same time, I didn't particularly appreciate knowing we were pushing others to wait either. I knew what they felt like, and it seemed like this was only the beginning.

After a few minutes, the attorneys agreed to August 4. My jaw hurt from my tightened teeth grinding their little hearts out. Even though I didn't mind the trial getting pushed out so far, it meant "closure" was getting further from reach. The judge also determined that for the August 4 date to work, she'd need to declare our case a mistrial. It was a standard procedure, and all it did was reset the clock for the speedy trial (again).

Dear God! Keeping track of all the dates was becoming tiring, and it was getting way over my head even though I'm a deadline kind of person. At that moment, I felt my heart and feelings become entirely numb to this trial bullshit. I don't mean to call it that, but you'd be stupid to think it was going to conclude anytime soon. All it did was get in the way of my healing and my family's, and I hated that. As if we hadn't been through enough already. Jesus!

I wouldn't say I liked carrying such a pessimistic attitude. It was heavy and didn't look good on me. Yet, *what* could I do about it? I tried my best to make each day great and meaningful, but I'd be lying if I didn't admit there was a constant shadow I fought with.

As the weeks turned into months, I began calling the court "the dangling carrot." The August 4 trial date was postponed to September 22 because of the virus. I was so over it! But like I said before, *what* could I do about it?

On the morning of Friday, October 16, I saw my feet in front of Ally's doorway. Oh, great, here we go again, another freaking meltdown. But as I was standing there, something was different. I was fixated on the gray box sitting on Ally's desk – the one that contained her ashes.

I never got around to making the urn to hold her ashes. And the thought didn't intrigue me then, either. I tinkered with the notion that perhaps I should spread her ashes somewhere beautiful, which instantly turned me green. Instead, I felt inspired by the idea of creating an art piece from Ally's ashes. It sounded crazy, and it didn't.

I sat on Ally's bed, and suddenly my mind played a mini-movie as if it were already prerecorded, waiting for this very moment. I saw every piece of art I had ever created and realized that I had been using art as a creative outlet my entire life.

Opening the square gray box, I saw a Ziploc "dime bag" and a much larger bag of ashes twist-tied with a metal tag. I gasped. I didn't remember the smaller bag being in there when Alice gave it to me after Ally's cremation. It felt like a gift from her and the mortuary team because the thought of opening the main bag made me downright nauseated. After our nineteen years together, this was all I had left of my precious daughter.

I searched the internet furiously to find an artistic medium, and I didn't want to duplicate any of my past pieces. Thank God for YouTube once again. It took only a few videos to discover that using resin to infuse ashes was quite popular. This was it! Faster than I could say, "supercalifragilisticexpialidocious," I'd ordered a beginner's set of molds and resin from Amazon.

I told Beth and my family about my latest and greatest idea. Surprisingly, they all supported me. I thought for sure I'd get pushback for such a strange idea, but then I figured they are probably pretty used to my unique sense of design. Let's be honest: My parents drank frozen orange juice for an entire year so I could have the lids to paint and hang. So why did I think this would be any different? I don't know.

When the package arrived *one* day later (thank goodness for Amazon Prime), I went straight into "artistic mode." So what does that mean? Mostly laughter from those observing.

I'll have my favorite movies playing with no sound: *Aliens*, all the *Resident Evil*s, and the same with *The Lord of the Rings*, to name a few. I have them all memorized, so it's not like I need to hear them anyway. And at the same time, I'll be listening to an array of music, Metallica to Cher, just like in high school. As I channel my energy into my work, my process may also come with some lousy singing and dancing, but you know, it is what it is. Moving on.

Jumping right in, working with the resin wasn't too hard. Sure, I got it everywhere, but I anticipated that. But when it was time to add Ally's ashes, I stopped in my tracks.

Staring at the "dime bag" of my precious daughter made my emotions flow like a raging tornado. At first, I saw my pain and anguish from the dull, grayish dust in the bag. It sucked. I cried, staring at the undeniable truth that this is all we are in the end – ashes to ashes and dust to dust. I cried even harder, thinking about how Ally deserved to live so much longer and end up in the hands of her kids, not her mama's.

The song "Club Can't Handle Me" by Flo Rida came on from my shuffle without warning. It's one of Ally's favorites, and since her death, I've deemed this song as her will – wishing me to listen. As the thumps played, I didn't think it was a coincidence at all. Oh, no. My energy shifted, and still holding the bag, I saw it differently. I now witnessed the beauty of the soft, delicate ash and the strength from the tiny bone fragments amid them. She wanted me to see, feel, and understand the symbolism of love. And no matter her form, I could still make beautiful memories, always bringing her with me.

There wasn't a word I could murmur to describe my feelings about my vision coming to life. As I hung the resin sphere on the stand, my hands trembled in pure excitement. It exceeded every expectation I had for it. I stepped back and stood there in awe, looking at my finished piece.

I hugged myself, realizing I'd never loved making art like this before. I studied it intimately, noting how each fragment of ash and bone lay where it should. The shimmer from the resin colors complemented one another as if dressed for the Met Gala. There was nothing to pick apart or wish I'd done differently. It was absolutely perfect.

There was no denying it. The way I felt creating this piece filled my spirit cup beyond the stars, and the way I felt receiving it made me want to deliver that experience to everyone. I knew everything that had happened led me to this very moment – I'd found my calling. On October 17, Everlasting Echoes was born.

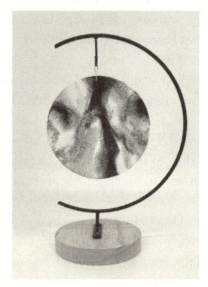

After telling Beth about starting my own business, she said, "No mud, no lotus?" I loved the idea because how could I deny it? The support to create memorial keepsakes, with or without ashes, was overwhelming but in the best way. I would have never thought in a million years I'd become an entrepreneur. Nor that it would stem from my most trusted hobby since I was little. There was no hiding behind the curtain anymore; I now believed I was meant to be in front of it.

And it wasn't just me. Andy started a nonprofit, The Ally Remembered Foundation, supporting domestic-violence awareness. It's like the universe whispered, "Go get 'em," or something. I don't know, but we both were on a mission to turn tragedy into triumph. And thank goodness the discovery of our new passions came when they did because COVID postponed our September 22 trial date till 2021! And then this stubborn virus didn't stop there. It also delayed the trial date of February 9 to April 13. Ugh.

Now, I know I've thrown a shit ton of dates at you. So what I want to do is provide a timeline of the critical dates to make sure we are on the same page.

July 2, 2017: Ally was murdered.
February 25, 2019: Arturo was apprehended in Mexico.
February 27, 2019: Arturo was extradited to Dallas.
June 11, 2019: Arturo was transported from Texas to Arapahoe County, Colorado.
November 6, 2019: The preliminary proof-evident hearing (if there was enough evidence and what would be allowed) was concluded, and we were a go.
December 9, 2019: Arturo pleaded not guilty to first-degree murder.
April 7, 2020: Original trial date.
June 16, 2020: New trial date.
August 4, 2020: New trial date.
September 22, 2020: New trial date.
February 9, 2021: New trial date.
April 13, 2021: New trial date.

Huh, as I look at this, I can't even find words right now – shocking, I know. Since Ally died, my OCD that everything should be organized and tidy has been torn to shreds. I don't know how to live in such a scattered awful mess. It's like one minute I'm begging any higher power to tell me what I did to deserve this torture, and the next, I'm cheerleading what I've made it through. I'm just so scared I won't find my pulse in these extremes, you know. How I *ever* downplayed the gravity of this most horrible fucked-up rollercoaster ride is beyond me.

Wow. I feel like I should brush myself off after that revelation. If I haven't said it before, thanks for letting me vent. It's an absolute comfort to share all this in a safe place.

CHAPTER 24

Could It Be True

APRIL 2, 2021

What was so special about this Friday? At first, it seemed that nothing would be out of the ordinary. We'd have our typical go/no-go meeting and walk away like the entire last year, checking the necessary box to appease a process.

All these status conferences really did was give us an excuse to "see" each other, and sure, it was nice. But we were done within a few minutes and on to the next agenda item within our day. Having said that, the constant meetings didn't change my ever-growing hope for a plea bargain, not at all. I just tried to look at it this way: All this time was watering the seed I had planted with the universe.

But as I logged on, the vibe seemed different. Our judge looked more serious than usual, which I thought was impossible. She kept shuffling her papers as if she had a lot to go over, which made sense to me. There would have to come a time when trials would come to fruition. Seriously. How could they not?

As the judge and legal teams started their typical commentary, everyone was on pins and needles. This wasn't a routine reschedule like before, because the courts were pushing to get things going again. But the conversation did present more questions than answers.

If we were a go on April 13, depending on which courtroom they'd have us in, only six or seven public seats (total) would be available in the courtroom due to social distancing. Meaning that family members would have no choice but to draw straws for the few open seats from both sides (if anyone came for Arturo, that is). And if you weren't one of the lucky ones and had to sit outside, the trial would be on Zoom, but no one knew if it would be audio, video, or both.

Abruptly, the meeting ended with a notice that we'd have another the following Friday unless we heard from Donna beforehand as to whether we'd be a go or not.

My heart went out to the judge and legal teams. What a mess! It wasn't their fault the guidelines were changing every five minutes. And I'm sure they were doing their best to accommodate in whatever way they could, but this meeting no doubt ruffled feathers like never before. Within seconds of the call ending, Andy's phone and mine were blowing up.

Even though there was a debate about getting the trial over with, everyone agreed it made better sense to postpone. The what-ifs were just too great. Could the legal team articulate the facts as they usually would while wearing masks? Would the jurors hear testimony effectively, being sprinkled all over the room because they also had to social distance? How would the evidence be displayed clearly for jurors to see from great distances? Not to mention family members' biggest concern: Each one felt they *deserved* to be in there.

I could empathize with their concerns for sure – well, except one. As you know, because I was declared a witness, I couldn't be in the courtroom anyway, which gave me some relief that I didn't need to take on my family's egotistical struggles. I mean, I totally got where they were coming from – after defining immediate family, there were

13 of them. That didn't include Maddie, either. And if it came down to it, I was prepared to go tooth-and-nail for her to have a chance to be in there.

With all that said, I held a secret that I hated sharing, but not really. You see, I was No. 17 on the witness list (out of 35, I think). Crazy, right? Anyway, once I finished my testimony, I *could* be in the courtroom, essentially kicking one of my family members out! Ugh.

Everyone knew I was still on the fence about sitting in, but they understood if I chose to. Which I think made my family even more high-strung about the five or six remaining seats in the courtroom. Some thought I should decide who went in, and I was like, "No, thank you!" Instead, I told everyone they'd have to work it out, perhaps take turns, and I'd support whatever happened. Can you imagine what that would be like, having to pick? Total yuck! It was the best feeling not to take that on and such a proud moment to share with Beth! Obviously, it seemed like extra drama our family didn't need right then.

Going into the weekend felt weird. Not knowing whether we were going to trial was worse than a reschedule. Everything felt so up in the air. Typically, I'm pretty good at going with the flow, but this tested my patience to no end. What I'd forgotten was that it's not about whether you like an answer but the power of having one itself. I think I was so worn down that I didn't know how to deal.

Trying to find solace, I started an art piece in the basement (excuse me, my studio with washer and dryer). Right as my hands couldn't be more covered in resin, my phone rang. It was Donna. Holy shit! Why would an advocate be working on a Sunday?

"Hey, Donna," I nervously said. Jumping right in, she was frank and didn't go through the usual niceties. She explained that Arturo's defense attorneys had received a call Saturday, and he wanted to talk plea deal! And as a result, they'd be visiting him in person the next day to confirm this development.

I'm sure you can guess, but I was dancing around like a football player who'd just scored a touchdown. And I'm sure Donna did, too, because she reminded me to keep calm and that nothing was official yet. "Understood," I replied while still smiling from ear to ear. After we agreed to chat Monday, I darted upstairs to tell Andy.

"Guess what," I shouted, interrupting whatever Andy was doing.

"What?" he replied, playing along.

"Arturo called his attorneys yesterday and wants to make a plea deal! They will see him tomorrow to make sure he hasn't changed his mind. Isn't that the most exciting news ever?"

Andy didn't say a word. He stared at me with his poker face, trying to find his bearings. I knew he'd never be as excited as me because Arturo could offer another shitty and pathetic plea deal. Yes, I did just say "another." Let me explain.

A few months after Arturo was apprehended, I had a call with our attorneys when all this court stuff was beginning to take off. One of them made what felt like an out-of-the-blue statement referencing how they had turned down a plea deal from Arturo. I don't recall my response, whether it was "Pardon me?" or "What the fuck?" but it doesn't matter; it was news to me.

They explained that a panel of selected attorneys meet regularly and approve or deny any received plea deals, and ours was rejected. Talk about testing my mama-bear patience. This would have been a terrible time to ask my opinion about our justice system, that's for sure. It's not that I don't understand how our attorneys represent the state and all, and their case is against Arturo, but seriously, doesn't the family get a say? Aren't we the ones who have to live with their choice? Come on!

After taking probably the deepest breath of my life before speaking, I said to them just that. I couldn't tell you if it came out harsh or not, but it didn't matter to me. They immediately took the position that they didn't know that I'd be interested in a plea deal. Thank goodness we weren't in person – there was *no* way I could've controlled my facial expressions. Candidly, I fired back that they were right – they wouldn't have known my stance. *However*, no one asked me, either.

Once the awkward silence passed, they shared why the panel rejected the plea deal. Arturo offered Heat of Passion (I believe that's right) and something like 20 years. Trust me when I say I screamed as you just did, asking how in the hell they came up with that charge? From what I understand, once someone pleas, it isn't about the "what" you did; it's about the "how" long. But at the time, I didn't think to ask. So there's a chance I could be wrong.

Regardless, I agreed it was a total joke, but more importantly, they should have notified me that an offer had come in and given me a chance to express my opinion first. Our attorneys quickly acknowledged my point, and I felt like I had advocated for myself as best I could.

I was so exhausted by the end of that call. I didn't want to tell anyone about it. I knew how furious I was – I could just imagine how the rest of the family would act. However, the lawyers advised that we should have a family talk about it. If we agreed with the idea of a plea deal, they said they would let us know if another one came in so we could be a part of the process.

And so we did. Can I tell you how awful our conference call was? It was just as intense as talking about letting go of the death penalty to extradite Arturo. I had never seen the same group of people so stretched beyond their comfort zones – not only once but now twice.

It seems like another add-insult-to-injury detail to my story, and it is. I watched and listened to each family member struggle with the idea of a plea deal. I mean, I get it. Here it is, we lost Ally to murder. And yet Arturo gets to play "Let's Make a Deal," which would mean lessening their perception of his punishment more and more.

I hated being on my island again. It makes me cry even now thinking about it – I had never had to speak up for myself like this before, aside from when I was with Beth. I felt so selfish for my feelings. But I needed my family to understand what this was doing *to me*.

Now, did I go into every detail? No. Instead, I focused on a higher level of my mental well-being. I explained the daily anxiety I was experiencing about the trial, specifically having to testify and, more so, the possible exposure to any evidence I couldn't unsee and unhear.

I also threw out the idea that if Arturo got a plea deal, his release could be way more challenging for him to reacclimate with society. Meaning if he were *way* older, what kind of job could he get? Especially given his record. Not to mention how old his friends and family would be. To me, that sounded like more punishment than having a roof and food provided daily. But because I believe in rehabilitation, it would also give him the chance to do some good still.

No one interrupted and raced to share their opinion. Instead, it felt like the silence, except for my heart beating louder than ever before, told me that my family was taking the time to consider my thoughts.

Barb and her hubby, Dan, asked how old I thought Arturo should be at his release. I tossed out, "No younger than his early 50s." I think it was then that my mom said she supported me and whatever I wanted, and no matter if he served 10 or 50 years, it won't bring Ally back. I instantly felt her warm hug through the call. Then, I heard support from everyone else. Well, almost everyone. Andy had to make it a point to say he still believed in the death penalty and how much he wanted to beat Arturo to a bloody pulp. He went on and on for what seemed more overkill, but everyone let him air his feelings. After that, he said if everyone else supported the plea idea, he would too for the best of the group. I didn't love his response at all, but regardless, I felt we were unified enough for me to tell our attorneys.

So circling back to telling Andy the news about Arturo's latest plea, I truly hoped he remembered what he said all those many months ago, reluctant or not, about agreeing to the plea deal idea. Surprisingly, he didn't say anything other than, "OK. Let's see what it is." I didn't know if it was his counseling or late-night Enneagram studying he'd been doing (I may have spied a time or two); it was good enough for me.

Donna called Monday, and sure as shit, Arturo wanted to move forward with his plea! Can you believe it!

Arturo offered our attorneys a guilty plea to second-degree murder and a 50-year sentence. Before you get excited, assuming he'd be around 70, there is a ton of legal math that is just ridiculous to calculate. Basically, this offer boiled down to Arturo's being released in his early 50s (assuming good behavior). So with that, our attorneys called me, and we had an emergency family meeting to discuss whether this was acceptable, seeing how it was spot-on from our discussion. As a whole, we agreed it was. On Tuesday, our attorneys took it one step further by rebutting with 50 to 60 years (which could add two to four-ish servable years) and having the judge decide those additional years. Arturo, along with the defense, accepted. On Wednesday, April 7, 2021 (one week before our scheduled trial), Arturo officially pleaded guilty to Murder 2 and a parole violation from his earlier domestic-violence case involving Ally. I know I didn't mention anything about that charge earlier – shamefully, I had forgotten about it. But really, it doesn't matter because the deal would consolidate it with Murder 2 anyway. With that said, the sentencing was then scheduled for June 17, 2021, at 1:30 p.m.

CHAPTER 25

You Get What You Give

JUNE 17, 2021

After almost four years since Ally's murder, my anticipation for that afternoon exceeded all those eagerly awaited Christmas mornings as a kid. I'd finally be rid of a judicial nightmare that only twisted the knife in my broken heart. Sure, I've shared the crucial details, but I'd easily have a book over a few thousand pages expressing every bloodied knee over how genuinely crippling the ebb and flow of the process had been.

I'm just so grateful for trusting myself to start therapy very early on because without it, I can't tell you where I'd be. Well, if I made assumptions, they'd all end in a for-real straitjacket or death. No, thank you. So I know this may sound messed up, but I welcomed the thought of being able to just grieve for the loss of my daughter.

Every slow and meaningful step I made walking into the courtroom represented making my final appearance. Although there wasn't a roaring crowd, I felt like I should have had a theme song, kind of like a professional wrestler. Because before me stood our attorneys wearing some form of purple (Ally's favorite color), and behind me followed my family. One by one, my mom, dad, Barb, Dan, Kristin and her daughter Emily, Eric, Becca and her girlfriend Dee, Amy, Kylie, and Andy shuffled into the left side of the courtroom.

Since April 2021, the courts had lessened restrictions on how many people could sit inside, thank goodness. But did you notice someone missing? Sadly, Maddie decided not to come (as in an hour before). Like I used to with Ally, I tried every mommy trick I knew to try to persuade her otherwise, but my opinion didn't matter – Maddie had made up her mind. And all I could do was shake my head in disappointment while supporting her choice. It sucked.

It didn't make me feel any better when I looked at the defense team on the right side of the room. Aside from this having a lousy wedding vibe, there was no one present for Arturo, just like before. I suppose, in a way, I'm glad his parents didn't come – I could only imagine what drama it would bring. Nevertheless, someday I'd like to talk with them and express my hurt for them.

As I continued looking around, nothing seemed different from before. It smelled just as stale, and the furniture and technology were still severely outdated. OK, there was one new thing. Someone had added a shower-cap-looking bag over the podium microphone because of COVID. Good grief, it was tacky-looking.

After a few minutes, three bailiffs brought in Arturo. He was still recognizable, but he no longer looked like the cute kid I once knew. He was a man, almost six feet tall! He must have had one of those late growth spurts boys can have. I couldn't believe it. He wasn't muscular as though he'd been lifting weights, nor fat, but he was evenly thicker. Sorry, I don't know how else to explain that one. He didn't have any visible marks, but his skin was unflatteringly pale. Perhaps his short dark hair and red jumpsuit made it only more obvious. He wore different glasses, which fit his face; that was nice to see. Talk about a transformation. It made me wonder if Ally would've found him as good-looking as when they met.

Studying our judge, I couldn't help but snicker. It was probably just my nerves, but still. She was sporting the same blonde bun and looked identical to what I remembered. I whispered to Andy how impressive it was that she hadn't aged a day and how I wished I could've said the same.

At 1:30 p.m. on the dot, she started the proceedings. Thankfully, her "Judge Judy" all-business attitude hadn't changed either.

The defense attorney explained why Arturo should receive 50 years and not 60. I have to say we should have made bets beforehand what their strategy would be. A real missed opportunity there. Because once he said something to the tune of how a teen's brain isn't fully developed and wouldn't be until their mid-20s, I closed my eyes, remembering all the times my mother used that to justify Ally's behavior to me. I wanted to turn around so badly to see how she reacted, wondering if she rolled her eyes or nodded in agreement.

He didn't have much else to say after that. It's not like he was trying to convince the judge that Arturo wasn't guilty. This was all for a measly few years of servable time.

Turning to our attorneys, the judge invited them to speak. It was then that I realized I hadn't seen them "in action" before.

Our lead attorney jumped up like he was ready for a fight without hesitation. Even though I believed this was all for a few measly years, it mattered to him. When he spoke about Arturo fleeing to Mexico, his intensity and objective seriousness made my heart rate go through the roof. He was impressive, and I could even feel Andy mentally high-fiving him with approval.

Man, it was one rip after another. Wishing I had popcorn; I'm glad I didn't. I would've choked and probably died. Why? Because our attorney was almost too good and saved his best zinger for last. He used scientific evidence that strangulation can take up to *eight* minutes for the victim to die.

I closed my eyes as hard and fast as I could, trying to stop the sheer panic that ravaged through my veins. Oh, my God! Was it true? Is that how long it took for Ally to die? Or was he using this data from a worst-case scenario to demonstrate the severity to the judge?

I scrambled, trying to remember what the coroner had said. No! He explicitly said strangulation could take *only seconds*. Right? Wasn't that what he'd said, or did I misunderstand? Jesus! I didn't know what to think! Because, technically, what the coroner said wasn't wrong then. Perhaps he left out the possibility that it took up to 480 seconds on purpose to shield a bereaved mother from an ugly truth. I don't know.

I hated that I could never *unhear* what our attorney had said! That was the exact reason I didn't want to be at the trial, for Christ's sake!

I squeezed Andy's hand, hoping it would stop me from making myself more nauseated. It didn't. But thankfully, our attorney announced he was finished and sat down.

The judge nodded and turned to the defense. She asked if they had anyone who had a statement they'd like to share on Arturo's behalf. My heart stopped when they said, "Yes."

Here is the transcript of that statement.

(This statement is done through Webex.)

THE COURT: Thank you. Did you wish to make a statement to the Court?

MR. GARZA: Yes.

THE COURT: All right. Can I get a name, please?

MR. GARZA: Mario Garza.

THE COURT: And what is it that you would like for me to know?

MR. GARZA: Thank you, Your Honor, for the opportunity to allow me to address these few words. My name is Mario Garza. I am the Senior Pastor at La Vid Internacional Ministries. I wish to express my deepest condolences and respects towards the victim's family's great pain. As a father, I can only imagine the magnitude of this great loss. I am praying for quick consolation and strength to the family during this time.

I saw Arturo born as my wife's nephew. I watched him grow alongside my children, and he was treated as such. We, as his family, especially his mother, are devastated by this event and wish for this to never happen. From his childhood up to his adolescence, he never displayed any signs of violence, despite the absence of his father. He was always a hard-working, obedient son.

As a Pastor and father, Arturo will always have my prayers. Adolescents grow and make their own decisions as young adults. According to counseling, bad decisions such as this one are made due to the influence of bad company and drug influences. Your Honor, today justice will determine judgment and sentence over Arturo's life. Arturo and the late young woman are two destroyed lives. We can see the faces of many young people that due to the lack of attention and care, they see themselves involved in great tragedies such as this one. In other words, we take this tragic example of two young people to re-evaluate our roles as parents and counselors towards our current generations. We do not only see a victim and a perpetrator but a devastated society due to the loss of family values at a center of its core. We all, as parents for both parties, have failed on both ends. For my part, that will be all, Your Honor. Thank you.

THE COURT: *Thank you.*

Wow, I didn't see that kind of end coming, getting blamed and all, and neither did my family. Like wildfire, I heard all the whispers behind me asking one another if he really just said what he did. I mumbled to Kylie, "Oh, he's one of *those*," while rubbing her leg. Even though I mocked his opinion, I started a new tally in the back of my mind. As sad as it is, he won't be the last that believes *I'm* responsible somehow. Kyle and I smiled at each other and rolled our eyes. Andy, on the other hand … I'm not sure he shrugged it off as quickly.

After a few seconds of awkward silence, the judge turned to our attorney, asking if we'd like to read our prepared Victim Impact statements aloud. Let me start by saying that I struggled to write mine. I'd have to guess that sounds ironic since I'm writing a book and all, but it was.

Over the years, I'd heard how empowering and therapeutic it can be to write a statement from my Parents of Murdered Children family. Some said it helped start their healing process, and others said facing their offender gave them a sense of peace. And some truly believed it swayed their judge's sentencing – all great reasons to write one if you ask me.

However, little do people know that Victim Impact statements are sent in beforehand for approval (at least ours were). No, you're not reading that wrong. One would think you can say anything, right? I mean, that's what you see in the movies, isn't it? Unfortunately, this "opportunity to tell your story in your own words" has limitations. Best said, it's another disappointment in the legal process for many people.

So what are the boundaries? Basically, the statement can contain details about one's suffering (physical or emotional), financial impact, and necessary medical or psychological treatments for recovery. Seems fair. But it can't have any accusations against the offender. And there's the total gut punch! That sucks for a suffering loved one, doesn't it? But to the court's point, the blame has already been determined. Hence this statement is solely about expressing your hurt related to the trauma.

Maybe I was overthinking it. Lord knows I do that more often than I'd like to admit, but I couldn't shake the idea that the "ask" of this process was more like a step backward than forward from where I was in my healing. Still, I compromised with my resistance and prepared what I thought was a summary of my journey.

As I stood in front of the podium and looked eye-to-eye with our judge, I froze. I didn't know whether I was intimidated, overwhelmed or what, but I couldn't help it. Every millisecond that passed, my eyes became blurrier and my hands tightened, holding on to my paper for dear life. Why am I reading this aloud? The judge and both legal teams already had a copy of my victim's impact statement, and so did Arturo. So what was the point? So my family that hadn't read it could hear me be a broken record telling the same story? I broke into tears and began shaking from my anger. Thankfully, my mask muffled my uncontrollable noises and the snot running down my face. Although not enough to go unnoticed. The judge saw, if not heard, what I was going through, and she softly advised me to take my time.

"For fuck's sake, Tiffany, pull it together," I thought. It was the one time I didn't mind my bitch of an inner critic speaking up. Because she was right, the last thing I wanted to do was take my sweet time up there. Hell no!

I glared at my statement until the words finally became legible and cleared my throat. Unsure of my tone, I read each word as intended.

> **"Thank you for taking the time to hear my account of Ally's murder and its impact on my life. Let me begin by saying that Ally didn't deserve any of this, and this senseless act has been nothing short of excruciating. No parent should outlive their child, period.**
>
> **Living in a world I once knew and trusted, my grief for Ally can be debilitating and lonely, often leaving me feeling like I'm on a distant, secluded island. I've found that most people will never understand my earth-shattering tragedy. And few can comprehend what it takes for me to get out of bed or what it's like to remain a wife and mother.**
>
> **It doesn't matter what day it is; I have a permanent appointment on my calendar that haunts me. I can never reschedule or take a vacation from it, and each flip of the page counts as a forever-growing tally of my emptiness without my most beautiful daughter.**
>
> **It's nearly impossible not to let my sadness for Ally overshadow birthdays, holidays, and family events. I love all my family, especially my other kids, with all my heart. Still, Ally being my only biological**

daughter, the bond we share is irreplaceable, and now she's no longer here to celebrate anything with me – including her future.

It's sickening to think how Arturo stole her dreams of joining the Navy, helping others, and someday having a family of her own. So it's not only me that's missing proud-mama moments; the world is also suffering a great injustice by her death.

While anxiously awaiting trial, COVID appeared and introduced an ugly twist to the already-painful saga. It caused several continuances, only adding insult to injury. I was stuck floating in what seemed like limbo, and the emotional black hole was exhausting. Not knowing what else to do, I focused my energy on Ally's legacy.

Through this, I came to understand my definition of justice for Ally. And for me, it means only one thing, and that's how I will survive this tragedy. This conclusion has been instrumental to my survival. It's teaching me the meaning that every day will only be bittersweet at its best and what it's like to have a healthy balance between grief and my future. And because of that, I've come to understand the importance of my voice and sharing my beliefs. Not only about the awful chaos but also the silver linings.

I've built a tribe of some of the most amazing people, providing me unconditional support in whatever way they can. New doors have opened, showing me an unexpected career path I love. And most recently, I'm grateful for receiving Arturo's latest plea deal.

Whatever his motivation, his decision was a gift to me. In my mind, his choice released me from being subjected to further torture during the trial process, and I can now begin rebuilding in its entirety.

As of this month, it's now been four years without Ally. And the truth is, today's outcome means very little to me – it's only a consequence of action, not justice. And although I will never understand why

Arturo murdered my sweet Ally and my life has been turned upside down in unimaginable ways, my belief in reform hasn't changed. I do hope Arturo will find his way for whatever the future holds for him.

To sum up, as I've said, justice for Ally is MY survival. However, despite any positive efforts towards Ally's legacy and my future I make, nothing will ever change the reality that I'm still a parent of a murdered child, and I'm the one with the life sentence. Thank you.

Tiffany Starrett, Mother of Alexandrea Raber"

As I sat down after delivering my statement, my head throbbed from every direction. I was drained. I swear I felt better after running my five-hour marathon compared with that. Kylie smiled in support as she handed me a tissue, and Andy took my hand, helping me sit down. Before I could say "Thank you" to him, he'd already headed up for his turn.

I cringed, bracing for impact. That not only would Andy read his statement, but he'd also share his hateful opinion about having to write it twice – his first submission was rejected.

He indeed had some serious accusations against Arturo and the court, along with some colorful language that even made me squirm, but I totally got it. He told his story and fulfilled the assignment – that is, without reading the fine print. So when he got word that he needed to make some edits, boy, he wasn't happy. But what I loved was that he didn't let his anger discourage him from "playing by the rules." And I have to say, as I witnessed him reading his second version, it was even more powerful than his first.

"Today, I stand here surrounded by family and friends, and the cold, hard truth is, I shouldn't be, but I must. That decision was made by Arturo, not by me, when he chose to be selfish and self-centered for his own accord. The action he took that day in July when he murdered Ally has forever altered the lives of so many, including my own, in ways that no one here will ever comprehend. The hatred I have towards him and his recklessness will never fade

out. It's permanently burned into my memory, a lifetime scar.

As a result, myself and our entire family and circle of friends have endured years of pain and suffering that will never truly end. There are times I wonder if he will have any remorse or a single fiber of his being that feels guilty and wishes he'd made a better decision that day. To me, Arturo took Ally from this world and the ones who loved her with no concern for them, only himself. He's nothing more than a selfish coward and a predator who never deserved the love Ally gave him and the passion she exhibited, believing she could help him become a better person.

I know this because we talked about it, and Ally knew he had many issues. Many conversations were me repeatedly stating the evil I was witnessing, hoping she'd begin to see the writing on the wall. The last words she spoke to me were "You're right, Dad, he's not a great guy, and I see what you're saying." I was delighted, believing she now had some understanding of the real truth about the relationship and was happy she was moving past it. However, I overlooked her passion for helping others and missed the signs about the fear and control he had instilled in her.

These are two factors that I feel played into her coming back after his release. She truly believed she could help him, yet I feel the fear instilled by Arturo gave Ally a false sense of reality at the same time. HE took advantage of that innocence, corrupted it and, when he could no longer control her, ended her life.

I do not feel that today brings any moral sense of justice. Life sentence, death sentence, or however many years he receives for murder will never justify the emptiness we have with Ally being forever removed from our lives. For us, his actions made it a life sentence. We only have memories, pictures, and her ashes, placed in her room, left untouched as a somber reminder of her. There will forever be no more birthday parties, graduations, family vacations, maybe grandkids one day, and the rest of what life offers us as family. Gone is Ally's laughter, silly demeanor, smile, and future that held so much promise.

Arturo's actions created chaos, heartbreak, sadness, depression, loneliness, anger, jealousy, and resentment that we've spent years trying to undo. A daily part of our lives now that myself, my wife, Ally's brother and sister, and our family and friends never asked for. Ally's murder has been a curse, yet it's revealed a few glimmers of hope in some respects. Each of us will say there were gifts received, born from Ally's ashes, that we are thankful for. But I would gladfully return them to have her back.

Arturo and I had a conversation once where he told me Ally was in good hands, and he explained all the things he was going to do to take care of her. Two jobs if necessary and making sacrifices with so much more. Those were merely more lies and deceit and speak volumes of his character here today and forevermore. I hope Arturo understands the magnitude of his actions someday. There is simply no way for him or anyone on the outside to physically feel the pain we have had over the last four years. Maybe one day he'll have my forgiveness, but it's not going to be today!

We can only continue to move on and forward, picking up one sliver of the broken pieces at a time while we struggle to comprehend what our new "normal" lives are without Ally. For myself, I must stifle anger, ego, and so many other feelings daily, knowing it's the right path for me so I can be a better father and husband and support mechanism to those around me. I will leave these proceedings today no better than when I arrived, still knowing Ally won't be outside the courtroom door waiting on us with open arms and hugs."

As Andy sat down, I wanted to hug him so badly. I was so proud of him. We'd come such a long way separately yet also together, and I knew our marriage was in the best place it could be.

The judge turned to the defense like clockwork, asking if Arturo would read his statement aloud. Thankfully, our attorneys gave me the heads-up beforehand that he'd written one, although they didn't seem impressed. They said it's pretty typical that the defense attorneys coach the offender to write one.

Is that supposed to make it less meaningful? I don't know about you, but throughout my life, I can't even count how many times I had to nudge my kids, or even Andy for that matter, to "do the right thing." In my mind, it doesn't matter how you get there, and what's important is the action itself.

I took Kylie's and Andy's hands as Arturo began shuffling the few feet toward the podium. Even with his hunched posture, it didn't help the unsettling sound of his chains constantly clinking. Seems almost barbaric somehow. Sigh, it was awful.

He took out a paper from his pocket as he reached the podium. He adjusted the microphone without hesitation and began to read his statement.

THIS TRANSCRIPT CONTAINS DEFENDANT'S STATEMENT ONLY.

THE DEFENDANT: *I want to apologize to Ally's family and friends for taking Ally away from them, especially Ms. Starrett who was always kind to me and gave me good advice and support. I know I have caused her incredible pain and that she will always carry this pain. I wish I could go back in time and fix this. Every day, I wake up and think about what I did. It is such a nightmare realizing that I took Ally away from her family. She was a great and beautiful person. I know that her family and friends will always have a hole in their hearts. I took away Ally's future and took her family's happiness away. I can't imagine the pain that I caused. I'm sorry for running away and not facing the consequences of my actions. I believe there is a God of love and justice and justice should be served. I believe I should be* *punished for what I did, and hopefully me being in prison will help to bring healing to Ally's family. I pray every day that they find peace in their hearts.*

Did he cry? No. Even a sniffle? No. Could he have said or done anything different to make his "remorse" seem more believable? Sure, he could have offered to trade places with Ally maybe. And I'm sure my family was hoping to hear something just like that. So it made me wonder for those who said they'd forgive him if he apologized *if* they'd follow through.

The thing is, I didn't *need* his apology, because I'd already forgiven him from Chapter 12: Behind the Curtain.

I know people have a tough time with the idea of forgiveness, and I totally get that. I've heard it a million times they can't believe I've chosen this. And their tone, ugh, it always sounded as if I'd done something wrong. But like I said before, the only way to *not* hurt me more was to make this choice every day. Why give him any more attention, time or thought? It was the only thing that made sense. Every day I decide to forgive him gives me the freedom to move forward and make something positive out of this tragic situation, my justice for Ally.

I saw Arturo's statement more like a good ending to a bad day because I knew what I saw. While facing the judge, when Arturo addressed me directly and recited his gratitude for my support, he turned his head ever so slightly in my direction. I took that as if he wanted to have eye contact, one of the most respectful gestures since the beginning of time. And that wasn't all. No one would know this (except Ally), but he said that exact phrase – "You're always kind to me and give me good advice and support" – when I took them both to lunch a few days before he was arrested on his domestic-violence charges, which told me what he said to me in court was authentic.

After he sat down, all eyes were on the judge. I don't even remember if Andy, Kylie and I held hands or not. But I'll never forget my animosity brewing inside. Our lives were about to change again without my permission.

In one fell swoop, the judge explained the court's position that Arturo was of sound mind knowing he violated his parole and how he had that paperwork in the motel room. And therefore, he would be sentenced to the full sixty years. There wasn't even time to react because she then concluded the hearing, and poof – just like that, it was all over.

CHAPTER 26

Life's A Sequel

THE PRESENT

Can you hear the swells of music playing in the background? This is the part of my story where our time together is finally coming to an end. It means the world to me that you stuck with me this far – thank you. So with that, I wanted to give you a parting gift, a feel-good ending. And no, I'm not referencing a massage here. (wink)

First and foremost, I'm thrilled to say that everything came full circle. After sentencing, Detective Ferrell and 007 personally delivered Ally's white diamond ring to me eleven days later! Can you believe it? It was an epic gesture that still leaves me speechless. The funny part was meeting 007 in person for the first time; I couldn't help but give him shit that I'd thought he'd be much taller and tattooed. LOL

Secondly, if you recall from Chapter 9: A Bit of Sunshine, Kylie's "lost" matching white diamond ring also made its way home! Her friend mistakenly put it in her jewelry box after Kylie took it off to go swimming. Hallelujah! Small things sure make up big miracles!

Since then, Kylie and I have created custom rings that are just gorgeous. She got the idea that our relationship is like yin and yang. So she gave her lost ring back to me, and we went shopping for two larger black sapphire bands (I taught her well). Now, our sets hug a matching silver cosmic-looking ring containing Ally's ashes. Kylie wears hers while wrapping up her senior year in college with a Criminology and Criminal Justice degree. So proud of that girl!

Remember Alex – the girl's big brother? He's working on moving from Florida to Colorado to "close the gap in our relationship living so far away." I can't wait to see him more frequently, to pick on each other and admire the beautiful keepsakes we picked out together. He wears a stunning silver compass cremation necklace that suits him perfectly since he and Ally shared a loved for the military – he's an honorably discharged army veteran. Thank you for your service, son!

I'm not a necklace kind of gal, so I chose another ring. This one is different because Ally's ashes look more moon-like than my other one. Needing some buddies, I paired it with two dainty stardust bands. My two sets of rings paint a complete story of the universe. I love them!

And last but certainly not least – my relationship with Andy is doing great. He still drives me crazy, as I'm sure I do him, but we're thriving in a way I'd never imagined from when we first married. It's like we have two new lives, and I couldn't be happier.

Tonight is actually date night, and he just brought home some takeout and delicious Dairy Queen blizzards, so I need to wrap this up.

So what can I say from all of this? Would I give anything to go back to how it used to be? In a fucking heartbeat! But that's not the reality I live in. Believing in my definition of justice for Ally, I know things will be OK. How can I say that? Because writing this book has taught me that even though it's hard to be naked and vulnerable in my new normal, all I need to do is look at the rings on my hand: They remind me that I choose to be the superhero of my story.

So, for now, I'm ready to put my pen down and, with my cape on, step forward into the next phase of my journey, making Ally proud.

ACKNOWLEDGMENTS

To my team: Sharon, Marcus, Christine, Bruce, Kasia, Beth, Karen, Laura, Andy, and Kylie, thank you for your loyalty and seeing my vision through. You *literally* held my life in your hands, treated it with the most exceptional care, and didn't take it for granted. Without that, I'm not sure I would have ever made it this far. Xoxo

And to my reader. Some content from my story may be uncomfortable to read, possibly triggering. From my experience as a trauma survivor, I feel it's my compassionate responsibility to share that for your discretion.

RESOURCES

THE FUNERAL HOME: HORAN & McCONATY

www.horancares.com

THE MEDIUM: KAREN STORSTEEN

www.karensinsight.com, karenstorsteen@comcast.net

THE THERAPIST: BETH PARKS

www.bethparkscounseling.com, bethparks@
bethparkscounseling.com

THE POMC: PARENTS OF MURDERED CHILDREN

https://www.pomc.com/

THE POST-SENTENCING SUPPORT: VOICES OF VICTIMS

http://voicesofvictims.org/

THE DOMESTIC VIOLENCE PREVENTION FOR TEENS:
ALLY REMEMBERED FOUNDATION

www.allyremembered.org

THE NEW BUSINESS: EVERLASTING ECHOES

www.everlastingechoes.com